REASONED
ARGUMENT
IN
SOCIAL
SCIENCE

REASONED ARGUMENT IN SOCIAL SCIENCE

Linking Research to Policy

EUGENE J. MEEHAN

CONTRIBUTIONS IN POLITICAL SCIENCE, NUMBER 53

GREENWOOD PRESS
Westport, Connecticut • London, England

Library of Congress Cataloging in Publication Data

Meehan, Eugene J
   Reasoned argument in social science.

   (Contributions in political science ; no. 53
ISSN 0147-1066)
   Bibliography: p.
   Includes index.
     1. Social sciences—Methodology. 2. Social
science research. 3. Policy sciences. I. Title.
II. Series.
H61.M484   300.1   80-1198
ISBN 0-313-22481-1 (lib. bdg.)

Library of Congress Catalog Card Number: 80-1198
ISBN: 0-313-22481-1
ISSN: 0147-1066

First published in 1981

Greenwood Press
A division of Congressional Information Service, Inc.
88 Post Road West, Westport, Connecticut 06881

Printed in the United States of America

10 9 8 7 6 5 4 3 2 1

Dedication

As this volume developed over the years, often slowly and painfully, it has been my good fortune to be able to rely consistently on the support and criticism of my long-time friend and colleague, Norton E. Long. It is appropriate, I think, that the work be dedicated to him, with all of the affection, gratitude, and respect that association has generated.

Contents

Introduction

Very succinctly, my purpose here is to provide a reasoned and defensible foundation for systematic criticism of intellectual claims, whether empirical or normative in substance. Although the structure is developed and illustrated primarily by reference to the social sciences, it is intended for general application and is not limited to academic inquiry. The development of the apparatus is carried out in two stages: first, a framework is generated in which systematic inquiry and its products can be linked to individual and social needs or purposes, suitably generalized; second, the structures and processes needed for systematic criticism of the conduct of inquiry, the knowledge claims arising out of inquiry, and the use of knowledge to achieve human purposes are elaborated and justified. The heart of the critical apparatus is the set of human purposes accepted as boundaries for the intellectual enterprise. The meaning of "knowledge" is identified or specified by reference to those purposes; *any* structure that can satisfy them reliably is accepted as part of the knowledge system. The focus of criticism is the argument that is provided, or can be provided, to justify an inquiry, support a knowledge claim, or defend a particular application of knowledge to purpose.

Two major types of benefits can reasonably be expected from acceptance and use of the critical structure. First, it should improve the overall quality of intellectual consumership, particularly within government and in social science. Second, it should also underscore the intellectual necessity as well as the social desirability of relating inquiry to purpose, knowledge to action. Without reference to human purposes, reasoned criticism of knowledge claims is literally impossible. Once knowledge is identified with the means used to achieve purposes, there is no viable alternative to the pragmatic criterion for evaluating and improving the knowledge supply. Taken seriously, the critical apparatus would reduce the extent to which desperate intellectual needs are ignored or remain unfulfilled while dubious or even pointless inquiries are supported from public resources. Persons suffering from extreme thirst quite properly concentrate their resources and energy on the search for water. In the desert that is social science, reliable water holes are exceedingly scarce. Other salutary effects that could reasonably be expected to follow from improved critical capacity could be of even greater value to social science. Most obviously, such improvements could reduce reliance on untenable assumptions or beliefs as a base for criticism or action, whether by governments, the private sector, the general public or academic persons. Equally important, competent criticism should produce the kind of positive support that sound knowledge claims deserve but seldom receive, removing the element of "guilt by association" which the inability to discriminate qualitatively tends to breed. Indirectly at least, that should assist the cumulation of knowledge in social sciences in fields where the available foundations are solid and dependable.

Development of the critical apparatus begins with human needs or purposes and works backwards to find the means of achieving them. Though it may sound innocuous, that procedure is extremely important. To begin with a conception of inquiry, which is implicit in all assertions that there is some activity called "doing science" that is valid independent of purposes served, is to return to Baconian dependence upon method under another guise. The worse consequence of that approach to inquiry is that anyone engaged in "doing science" is then immune to criticism based on the results of inquiry—and the criteria for "doing science" are self-proclaimed. In effect, that position incorporates an "essentialist," or "left-to-right" definition of "science," to use Karl Popper's felicitious term,[1] rather than treating "science" as a label for activities whose validity is established independently. Moreover, if that conception of inquiry is accepted, human purposes are left to be satisfied by accident, a costly and uncertain process at best.

If the essential human needs or purposes can be identified precisely and parsimoniously, and means can be found for achieving them within the limits of human capacity, then those means have enormous human significance, however they may be labeled. On the instrumentalist conception of knowledge, which is accepted here with respect to basics, knowledge is identified with the means used to achieve human needs or purposes. The central concern is the means and not the label. The goal is a system of means or instruments, a knowledge system, that is reliable, accurate, cumulable, corrigible, and useful. Reasoned argument must provide a justification for accepting and using claims of that order. How that can be done will occupy much of the space in this volume. Knowledge is construed as a human creation and not as a characteristic of the world. It arises out of human needs or purposes and is measured against them. And knowledge is power, in the simplest and most meaningful sense of the term, capacity to do.

Put in slightly different form, the substance of human knowledge is a body of assumptions, stated in propositional form, that can be used to achieve specified purposes in the environment. Some of those assumptions can be justified by deriving them from other assumptions that have already been established and tested. But the ultimate justification for any proposition is found in the correspondence between its logical implications and the results of real-world actions. At the foundation of the knowledge structure there will appear a set of fundamental premises or assumptions relating to the nature of perception, the meaning of logic or calculation, and so on, that cannot be derived from other premises. These basic assumptions make up the theory of knowledge on which the superstructure depends. They are testable in the same manner as any other theory, by reference to their consequences in use.

Indeed, a theory of knowledge will imply a theory of education that can be tested just as adequately as the basic propositions in some theories of physical science.

Knowledge comprises sets of assumptions or propositions about human experience in the environment; an argument is a set of reasons for accepting or rejecting a proposition or knowledge claim. The reasons may be general and methodological or detailed and specific; both the reasons for accepting and the reasons for rejecting the proposition must be included in the argument if it is to be considered "reasoned." The form of an argument is simple: "Proposition p should be accepted/rejected because. . . ." The definition is very weak and easy to satisfy. However, the quality of arguments will vary greatly, and evaluative criteria will therefore be needed. For example, "proposition p should be accepted because the astrological signs are correct," and "proposition p should be accepted because it accords with well-established scientific principles," are both arguments, though they obviously differ in quality. Arguments that include all of the reasons available to the "best knowledge" of the times, both positive and negative, are the best that can be produced. The focus of concern in evaluating arguments is not the likelihood that people will actually be convinced by them; that is an empirical/psychological matter. The goal here is an answer to the epistemological/methodological question, "*should* people be convinced by the argument?" The related question, "What are the implications of accepting a particular proposition," though used in argument, is actually a matter of logic and calculation, of formal reasoning, and is not a question to be argued.

In general, the quality of an argument is a function of two basic factors: the content or meaning of the proposition(s) being argued; and the sets of reasons offered as justification for accepting them. A generalized treatment of the quality of arguments must therefore include both a typology of propositions that can be used to classify knowledge claims in ways that facilitate criticism and a discussion of the conditions under which each type of knowledge claim should be accepted or rejected. The problem can be made more manageable by accepting two restrictions on the discussion. First, instead of seeking a classification that can be applied to every type of proposition in the human repertoire, which may be a hopeless task, criticism can be limited to the types of propositions needed for coping effectively with the environment—for maintaining and improving the human condition. Second, the criteria applied to each type of proposition must lie within the limits of human capacity. It would be pointless to impose criteria of acceptance that humans could not meet. Of course, it remains possible that future human needs simply cannot be fulfilled within the limits of the human capacity, but the survival of the species suggests that the limit has not yet been reached.

Given the conception of knowledge accepted here, the ultimate justification for accepting or rejecting propositions is pragmatic. The purposes for which knowledge is required, and in terms of which knowledge is defined, are a function of human needs in the environment. Those needs are established independently of the theory of knowledge. Argument based on a theory of knowledge provides a means of linking knowledge to use. And the use of knowledge for purposes that are themselves objects of knowledge, made possible by the ongoing character of the human situation, serves to integrate normative inquiry to empirical inquiry. That relation can be explored by a systematic examination of reasoned choice, and of the special form of individual and collective choice known as policymaking—development of rules of action that apply or make use of a priority system created out of human experience with choice.

There is no serious alternative to using pragmatic criteria to judge the quality of knowledge claims. None of its competitors can perform the required functions; pragmatism does provide a defensible base on which the structures needed to satisfy human needs can be developed. The clearest illustration is found in such fields as medicine and agriculture. Improvements in agriculture, and indeed the very practices that give rise to the concept of agriculture, arise out of endless cycles of tilling, planting, harvesting, and *consuming*. Most accounts of scientific development ignore or treat lightly the role that human consumption (or more precisely, the human reaction to consumption) plays in the process. Yet, without human consumption and evaluative reaction, the notion of agricultural improvement is meaningless. Similarly, advances in medical practice are established as advances by reference to their consequences for the health and well-being of specific patients. An approach to knowledge that concentrates on agricultural or medical research and ignores the consumers of their respective products would be seriously misleading. Of course, excess concentration on the consumer can be equally faulty, for example, if it leads the critic to ignore the limits of research and knowledge. The physician cannot be criticized for failing to cure what is presently uncurable. An adequate theory of inquiry will make reference to both aspects of the use of knowledge. At the very least, enforced attention to the effects of use would be an effective counterbalance to excessive methodologizing in social science. The spider who becomes so entranced in webspinning that it forgets the essential purpose of the web, to catch insects, soon perishes. Academic webspinners seem not to be bound by such limits.

This book is not intended as a contribution to logic or even to the "logic of inquiry." Since most books that deal with argument are produced in philosophy by philosophers, usually logicians, there is a tendency to equate argument with logic. Of course, logic is an essential element in any argument. But the questions under consideration here are not open to formal or logical solution. The distinction can perhaps be clarified by separating the two kinds of reasoning involved in argument, whether in social science or elsewhere. In one mode of reasoning, a general statement is taken as given, and its implications are explored formally and rigorously. Such activities are purely logical. In the second mode, the general statement itself is questioned. Such questions cannot be resolved by formal reasoning alone, although they may involve inferences. They require an appeal to evidence and to something that is perhaps best labeled "judgment." The question "Is this a case of that?" (Is that a cow?), for example, involves a judgment and cannot be resolved formally. A somewhat longer example will illustrate the difference more precisely. Assume a map on which an individual can locate himself precisely. If the map is accurate and the individual's movements are fully specified, his position can be calculated exactly. Such calculations are an exercise in logic or mathematics. If, however, the accuracy or adequacy of the map is questioned, the situation is different. Calculations may still be required, but other considerations will enter into the judgment—what has been included, what could have been included, the purposes for which the map was intended, and so on. Formal calculation decides any issue relating to the implication of accepting specified postulates or propositions. In effect, the logician is authoritative only so long as his premises are unchallenged. With respect to the validity of premises that refer to the real world, logical training confers no special status or competence and could conceivably be a handicap.

The kind of argument and reasoning developed in the material that follows may not apply to every question that systematic inquiry undertakes, and systematic inquiries may not produce evidence that can be used in such arguments. The claims made for the critical apparatus are limited strictly to the kinds of propositions needed for coping with the environment. Propositions relating to aesthetic matters or to religious beliefs, for example, may not be amenable to such criticism. There is no implication that such questions cannot be argued; they simply lie outside the scope of the present effort. In general, modes of argument that lead to contradictory conclusions cannot both be correct, but even that assumption is not essential in this context.

Finally, the approach to criticism employed here imposes one occasionally awkward limitation on the critic or user. *No* interpretation of meaning is allowed the critic; everything must be taken literally and exactly. Additions needed to "make sense" of material being criticized or to flesh out what an author "clearly" intended are not permitted. Ambiguities and inconsistencies, however minor, must be left unresolved. A good analogy is found in the way in which a computer treats incoming information. If the data are inconsistent, or the instructions cannot cover the case, the machine either ceases to function or produces nonsense. Until an argument is clear and complete, it cannot be criticized systematically. Of course, refusing to interpret or clarify meaning opens the door for the dogmatic skeptic. But such skepticism is in any case unproductive. If the meaning of every term is questioned, and the meaning of each term used to clarify the initial meaning is questioned in turn, the result is self-defeating. The goal here is production, criticism, and improvement of useful knowledge. Extreme skepticism contributes nothing to that end. However, the corollary requirement that all relevant assumptions and presumptions must be articulated and agreed before it can be said that genuine agreement has been reached must be honored, however difficult it may prove to be. As in arithmetic, the "correct" answer is only part of the solution to a problem. If the reasoning is ignored, agreement may be spurious. Here, too, critical standards must be tempered by common sense and everyday experience. It would be merely silly to demand a reexamination of every assumption in a field of study on the occasion of each use. It would be disastrous if the assumptions in a field were closed to criticism once adopted. Both extremes must be avoided, and what that means in practice depends on circumstances and judgment.

NOTE

1. Karl R. Popper, *The Open Society and Its Enemies*, Vol. II, (Princeton University Press, 1963), esp. Chapter 11, pp. 13-15.

REASONED
ARGUMENT
IN
SOCIAL
SCIENCE

Knowledge: Problems and Prospects

_____ 1 _____

The central focus in any argument is a claim to knowledge stated in propositional form. The kinds of propositions that must be argued, and the kinds of reasons that can be offered for or against those propositions, are a function of their content. The content of a proposition depends on the human purpose that proposition is intended to fulfill. The conditions that must be satisfied before a proposition can reasonably be expected to fulfill its intended purpose depends on the human capacity available for the task. In order to explore that set of contingent relations more fully, an account of the human situation must be provided in which the human needs or purposes that knowledge must satisfy can be identified along with the relevant conditions that influence successful completion of the task—particularly the limits inherent in human capacity. If that conception of the "problem of knowledge" can be agreed, a generalized solution to the problem will incorporate a theory of knowledge linked to significant human affairs, lying within human capacity, and able to account for the quality of past human performance.

THE PROBLEM OF KNOWLEDGE

Two basic features of the human situation account for most of the impediments to the development of an adequate body of knowledge. First, the individual is totally dependent upon the perceptive apparatus for information about the environment; second, the human observer lives in a flow of time at the juncture of past and present, *facing backward*. The raw material from which knowledge must be forged is comprised in the sum of human perceptions; what is perceived is already part of the past. The future is opaque; it will remain opaque. Only the past is available for inspection. Yet, human life is lived "in" the future, for that is where hopes and fears are realized, where the consequences of present decisions and actions are felt. Knowledge cannot be used to change or improve the past; it is needed to deal with the future. The "problem of knowledge" is therefore clear: somehow, the individual must learn how to use past experience to deal with the future, to satisfy human needs and aspirations with increasing efficiency and effectiveness. In its most general form, that is the heart of the classic "induction" problem.

There is nothing to study beyond the record of human experiences. There is no reason for study beyond the contribution that can be made to the human future, leaving aside simple enjoyment of the present. For humans, there is no alternative to egocentrism with respect to the human species. It is therefore both reasonable and appropriate to identify "knowledge" with the various structures and processes required for coping with the human situation. Theories of knowledge identify the conditions under which human needs or purposes (stated in terms of maintenance and improvement of the human condition, measured using human judgment in the light of human potential) can be satisfied. To carry out that program, a justification is needed for accepting and acting upon propositions that reference the future. The justification must be available *before* the decision to act to be useful. The only body of evidence that is accessible to the individual relates to past experience; experience is always singular and particular, related to a specific time and place. Future references require general propositions, statements not restricted as to time and place. Therefore, the justification for accepting or rejecting a knowledge claim cannot consist in a simple logical relation between past experience, as determined by observation, and the substance of the claim. Formal logic does not permit such operations. And if the ultimate potential of logic or mathematics is the self-recreating system or Turing machine, the dilemma is beyond resolution. That disturbs some philosophers very much indeed. But if the limit is valid, it must be respected, and some other means must be found for supporting general statements by referring to past experience and particular cases.

The acceptability of any proposed alternative means for justifying knowledge claims will depend in some degree on the substance of those claims, on the purposes the knowledge is expected to fulfill. Identification of those purposes is therefore prerequisite to developing a justification for accepting them. For that reason, it is useful to return to the basic human condition, to the perception-limited individual riding a metaphoric river of time, facing backward. Under those conditions, what primary needs or purposes must be fulfilled to produce continued survival and prosperity? Three purposes are preeminent, sufficiently so to be considered exhaustive. First, events that have not yet occurred or have not been observed must be *anticipated* reliably on the basis of past experience. If future events can be anticipated, the individual can adapt to the anticipated future in an appropriate way, within the limits of available capacity. Second, to maintain and improve the human condition, some capacity to *control* future states is essential. Third, the capacity to control future states generates an absolute need to *choose* from among the alternative conditions that can be brought about by deliberate human action. From this perspective, the "problem of knowledge" is to find ways of anticipating, controlling, and choosing, using past experience as justification for accepting the instrument in advance of the application.

Beyond anticipating, controlling, and choosing, a number of second-order requirements, for language, calculation, and so on, must also be satisfied before reasoned improvement in the human condition is possible. But a theory of knowledge that provides a solution to these three types of problems will suffice for coping with the environment. Of course, the intellectual or cognitive dimension of human interaction with the environment does not exhaust human capacity or human needs, but other problems are left to other hands. The primary task here is to identify the assumptions and procedures that make possible the satisfaction of those three intellectual needs within the limits of human capacity. That permits accurate identification of the kinds of propositions that have to be argued or justified and suggests the kinds of reasons that can be offered for or against them.

SOLVING THE "PROBLEM OF KNOWLEDGE"

The procedure by which the induction trap is avoided and human purposes in the environment are satisfied with increasing reliability and efficiency within the limitations imposed by the human situation is deceptively simple. A pattern of relations, which may refer to observables or to normative preferences, is *assumed* to hold for a particular situation in the environment. Once that assumption is made, the implications of the pattern (which is a formal or logical structure) can be transferred to the environment to produce the needed anticipation, control, or choice. Experience gained by using the pattern provides grounds for retaining, rejecting, or modifying the pattern before future use. Experience justifies the knowledge claim contained in the pattern. Knowledge can evolve and be justified in the endless cycles of trial and error, application and observation of consequences, that the ongoing human situation makes possible. There is nothing mysterious or arcane about the process. Norton E. Long provides a splendid and utterly commonplace illustration of the process at work:

We are not bemused by the fact that a hammer is an instrument devised in action for the purposes of action and improved in action for purposes of action that themselves improve with the improved possibilities the hammer's improvement opens up. Sextus Empiricus' arguments on the criterion against the dogmatists hold no terrors of an infinite regress for the improver of hammers. Like Sextus the skeptic, the improver of hammers, quite undogmatically unconcerned with metaphysical impossibilities, goes on in a humanly meaningful way to improve his hammer. Unwittingly agreeing with Marx that "heretofore the philosophers have only interpreted the world, the important thing is to change it," he goes about changing it. And men by their practice agree that he has made an improvement.[1]

The key to both creating improvements and judging that an improvement has been made is human experience with the result. If "men by their practice" is the ultimate court of appeal, there is no guarantee of concurrence in judgment on all occasions. So be it. If informed usage leads to disagreement, then the problem is simply beyond solution on reasoned grounds at that time.

Simple though it may be, the process of creating patterns, assuming their applicability, and testing them in use depends on a variety of preconditions. The individual must be able to organize perceptions, discriminate accurately, store and recall patterns more or less at will, and communicate them in some fashion to others. Further, the individual must be capable of some form of qualitative or affective reaction, and of conditioning that reaction on cognitive grounds. Otherwise, there could be no basis for preference and no grounds for reasoned choice. Language is essential, together with some capacity for formal calculation. All of these activities lie within human potential. Even learning, which is a creative action of astonishing complexity, is not really surprising given the enormous size of the neural system and the opportunities for individual and vicarious experience over vast stretches of time that living provides.

Beyond such fundamental human abilities, the procedure requires various capacities and conditions to function effectively. It is unlikely they can all be identified and articulated, but systematic criticism depends on some more than others, and two are preeminent. First, human capacity must extend to the creation of large numbers of patterns for organizing perceptions to fulfill different purposes. The patterns are not discovered; they cannot be borrowed from outside sources. The human ability to create such patterns is, of course, well established. How the patterns are generated is a mystery, and no procedure can be devised that will guarantee production. But it seems safe to assume that needed patterns will be forthcoming, particularly since assuming the opposite is both contrary to past experience and self-defeating. The second requirement is for an ongoing human enterprise, a dynamic system sustained over time and able to produce information relating to the results of action—what is called feedback. The ongoing character of the enterprise provides an escape from circularity by allowing for sequential testing of patterns over time. Moreover, it implies a world already supplied with patterns that have been used successfully to fulfill human purposes. Otherwise, there would be no human population. The quest for knowledge, in other words, begins *in medias res* and does not begin with a *tabula rasa*. There is no need, and no possibility, of beginning at the beginning. Adaptation and an occasional act of invention suffice to transform the human situation over time.

THEORY OF KNOWLEDGE

The development of reliable and corrigible knowledge that can be used to fulfill human purposes requires a number of fundamental assumptions about the relations between the individual and the environment. Taken together, they make up what is usually called a theory of knowledge. The assumptions have to do with (1) the relation between human perception and external "reality," (2) the nature of words and concepts, (3) the character of the patterns that make up the substance of human knowledge, and (4) the ways in which claims to knowledge can be tested. As used here, those assumptions are limited to what is needed to satisfy the purposes set for the book. They approximate, however, what philosophers would label empiricism, naturalism, instrumentalism, nominalism, and pragmatism. Within philosophy, each of these doctrines, suitably elaborated, is treated as an independent epistemology. In the approach to knowledge employed here, they are only limited elements in an integrated structure, not equivalent to their philosophic counterparts. Since the substance of the assumptions has been touched upon earlier, the treatment is brief and perfunctory.

Empiricism/Naturalism. The prime assumption in empiricism is that man acquires information about the world *only* through the sensory apparatus. The doctrine of naturalism, which is a close corollary to empiricism, asserts that there are good reasons for assuming there is something "out there" that is independent of the perceiving human, and therefore an external limit on such perceptions. From empiricism, it follows that the sensory apparatus is an immutable limit on the knowledge-generating capacity of the human species. More important still, human perceptions of the environment combine characteristics of the sensory apparatus with characteristics of the external world into an inseparable whole. Propositions justified by reference to observation therefore refer to perceptions of the environment and not to "reality." Once the two assumptions are made, both the idealist's claim to know absolute truth and the mystic's claim to have knowledge obtained from extrasensory channels must be rejected. Moreover, the assumptions imply a limited approach to testing knowledge claims: if propositions refer ultimately to human perceptions, their acceptability cannot be established by comparing them to reality or external truth. Some other base for criticism and evaluation must be developed.

Instrumentalism/Nominalism. Instrumentalism is identified mainly with the conception of human knowledge as a set of instruments or tools that can be used for achieving human purposes. The tools are actually patterns of organized human experience. The test of such intellectual tools, as with any other tool, is found in their use to achieve a specified purpose. The principal assumption taken from nominalism is that the meaning of words lies in the set of human conventions that define their use. Words have no "real" or "essential" meanings that can be discovered in nature; they must be created. Nominalism, in that limited sense, circumvents endless arguments about the "real" meaning of terms and the propositions that employ them. It also reinforces the view that inquiry is a creative process, and not an expedition seeking to discover knowledge or truth.

Pragmatism. Taken together, these four assumptions force humanity to deal with the world out of its own resources, generating goals and purposes as well as the means of achieving them. The search for knowledge is a search for working assumptions that are acceptable in the light of experience and that enable the achievement of purposes. The pragmatic test of knowledge claims is unavoidable once the correspondence theory of truth is abandoned. Of course, pragmatism does not solve all of the problems involved in testing knowledge, but it can provide an acceptable working principle in a human enterprise that is ongoing and cumulative. The very language learned in childhood contains large and complex sets of goals and purposes, tools, and assumptions. Merely being socialized to a language places the individual on the shoulders of countless generations of predecessors. Here the pejorative implications of cultural differentiation and differential socialization within a culture are distressingly apparent. The quality of the intellectual inheritance varies enormously; the criteria of quality applied to the structure by custodians of particular traditions do not always discriminate well. Uncritical absorption of tradition is poor policy, intellectually speaking, tending to lead to successive debilitations in the quality of the content.

Pragmatism, the practice of testing in use against purpose, provides the needed base for qualitative judgments about knowledge claims. And vigorous enforcement of quality control is essential to improvement. There is no alternative mode of evaluation that will demonstrate the differences between science and religion, magic and mathematics, ritual and research. Damning grasshoppers with bell, book, and candle is one way to deal with them; applying a good dose of DDT or a similar insecticide is another. Is one technique superior to the other? In absolute terms, the answer must be no! The intellectual apparatus available to man provides no capacity for making such distinctions. But if a purpose can be stated with reference to the grasshoppers, a qualitative distinction is readily made. If the purpose is to eliminate the grasshopers, DDT is much more efficacious than prayer; if the aim is to demonstrate piety by the treatment afforded the grasshoppers, the converse is true. The quality of the tool can be assessed by reference to the purpose that is stipulated; tools without purposes are a contradiction in terms. Even if purposes are stated, there are no absolute standards of excellence. It is said that Roman emperor, asked to judge a singing contest, heard the first contestant and promptly awarded the prize to the second. The judgment was mistaken, however, for it implied an absolute standard not available with respect to singing. Tools can only be compared to one another within the context supplied by some specific purpose or task. Texts based on the intrinsic properties of the tool, the pedigree of the inventor, the place where the tool is produced, or even the logical properties of the tool, are inadequate. Intellectual tools are evaluated by reference to their ability to generate reliable expectations, provide accurate control over the course of events, or produce the preferred choice in an appropriate situation. Given a human purpose, the various instruments available for attaining it can be compared in action. The purpose itself, construed as an instrument for improving the human situation, can be compared to other purposes that might be pursued in the same situation. Such comparisons, as Norton Long points out, open the way for the development of new purposes and new means for achieving them. Each modification creates yet another launching pad for a further set of experiments with the existing knowledge system. Not every launch will prove fertile and productive, leading to improvements in knowledge, but every launch has that potential.

What has been described thus far is but one way of approaching the problem of knowledge. There are many competitors; none is equally effective. A simple process of creating, assuming, and testing in use to achieve purpose can both account for and explain the success of the physical sciences, of the other academic disciplines where they have been successful, and even of athletic programs in basketball or golf. The process can also justify the judgment that there has been success and not merely change. Knowledge so conceived is necessary for man and possible to man. The capacity required is available; the conditions are suitable. The apparatus can serve both empirical and normative needs without major modifications in procedure. Most important of all, an epistemology founded on these assumptions is open to the same kind of testing in practice that can be applied to any theoretical structure. The theory of knowledge becomes the basic set of assumptions in a knowledge system, and it implies a theory of education, not of the physical or psychological sort but one relating to the character of performance. That is, the structure identifies the essential features of an individual (or collectivity) able to learn from experience, to adapt behavior to conditions and purposes to possibilities—in brief, a self-correcting structure. The performance of those educated to adjust their actions through self-conscious assessment of the patterns on which action is based and the results obtained in their use can provide evidence for the viability of the theory of knowledge. Preliminary efforts along these lines, though far from conclusive, have been uniformly favorable and supportive.[2] Theories of knowledge need not be treated democratically.

INSTRUMENTS AND PROCESSES

Accepting the proposed theory of knowledge allows reasoned criticism of claims to knowledge to be organized around the structures and processes required for the three fundamental human purposes: generating reliable expectations, exercising control over the flow of events, and making corrigible and defensible choices. It remains to determine the kinds of instruments and processes involved in the performance of each function and to develop appropriate critical procedures for each of them. Happily, the intellectual instruments, though very complex taken as a whole, are relatively simple in principle and construction, in the same sense that a large digital computer is a very complex structure made up of simple two-position switches.

The various auxiliary tools—particularly language, methodology, and logic or mathematics—must be taken as given. Language is an enormous topic, far beyond the scope of this discussion. Methodology, the study of study, seeks to make explicit and thus improve the instruments and procedures needed for the organization and use of experience. Although methodology is a valuable adjunct to a theory of knowledge, its uses are negative rather than positive; it serves to rule out rather than justify. Logic or mathematics comprises sets of techniques and procedures for organizing and manipulating abstract symbols in ways that allow precise calculation of the effects of change on patterns of symbolic relations. It cannot be too strongly stressed that the *application* of logic to observations is not a logical problem. Logic provides the engine for the human intellectual train, but the connection between engine and train must be forged by processes that are not formal and logical. The justification for using a particular logic will always refer to past experience in combination with formal logic, and not to logic alone.

DESCRIPTIONS

Each of the intellectual tools is a device for organizing experience. In use, the instrument is assumed, and a justification for the assumption is sought in the consequences of use observed over time in a dynamic environment. The basic building block in the structure is a *concept*, usually defined as a way of organizing perceptions. Concepts bound and identify the "things" that are thought about or observed, the elements from which knowledge begins. Concepts refer to classes of observables and not to singular events. One member does not suffice to identify a species; it remains particular. Only when a second specimen appears can the species be identified, even if only as "another one of *them*." Systematic organization of perceptions also depends on relational or logical terms, for example, such notions as above and below and faster and slower. No good classification of concepts is available, and concepts are very diverse in both characteristics and quality. Each concept has a set of one or more indicators, observables that are either part of the defining terms of the class or linked theoretically to it. Indicators inform the observer that it is appropriate to make use of the concept and they provide a way of measuring its value—that is, of determining the actual length of a board or the viscosity of a liquid. Metaphorically, concepts are the spectacles through which the world is seen or observed. They are the organizing principles that give meaning to the perceptions flowing into the neural system. In practice, concepts tend to become linked into conceptual frameworks, that is, sets of related conceptions that are useful for particular purposes or modes of action. Dentists, for example, share a conceptual framework when they are working, as do hunters or welders or farmers.

A description is a record of an observation, a snapshot of the world taken through a specific set of concepts or spectacles. Descriptions are stated in the form "*X* was the case," and, like any other proposition, they must be assumed and then justified—in the case of descriptions, by reference to observations. In effect, descriptions are problematic and uncertain in the same sense as any other proposition. The immutable "hard facts" sometimes presumed to arise out of observation are merely myth. Descriptions contain the summary record of human experience, the body of raw material from which knowledge is built and against which knowledge is tested. Some of their characteristics are particularly important: they are always stated in the past tense, they are always static, and they always refer to a specific time and place. Nothing can be inferred from them, though a description may not be compatible with certain inferences. They play a central role in every form of argument. A change is an assumption that is justified by reference to two or more descriptions of "the same" situation at different points in time. An expectation asserts that a particular description can be made at a time and place where observations have not yet been made. Control over the environment requires a capacity to produce a situation contained in a description. Choices lie between two or more descriptive statements of anticipated future events.

Three basic types of instruments can be used to generate justified expectations about the environment and to provide reasoned control over events: They are labeled *classifications*, *forecasts*, and *theories* (or explanations). These instruments perform their functions because of the way in which they are created and tested; there is no magic in the process. The names or labels are employed because the structures correspond reasonably well to technical usage in methodology and philosophy of inquiry.

CLASSIFICATIONS

A classification is a concept, produced by organizing observations in terms of their commonalities. Structurally, each class of things is defined by some finite set of factors or observables (referred to hereafter as *variables* and written as a capital V) whose values fall within specified limits. The class is defined by the selection of variables and the range of values that each variable can take. The class "robins," for example, will include all birds of a given size, color, eating and migrating habits, nesting practices, and so on. In effect, a classification is a generalized summary of past experience with a particular observable. If the analogy is not stretched too far, it is useful to think of a classification as a body of stored energy that can be tapped at future dates. A very simple procedure allows the use of a classification to produce a justified expectation. Basically, if a member of the class can be identified on the basis of a partial enumeration of class attributes, if class membership can be assumed, the remaining attributes of the class can also be assumed for the case in hand. That is, an entity (X) is observed; it is assumed that X is a member of class C because it has characteristics A and B; if all members of class C have attribute W as well, then X can be assumed, in advanced of observation, to share that attribute. For example, a bird is observed; on the basis of its markings, the bird is assumed to be a mallard duck; and on the basis of the known properties of mallard ducks, the bird is assumed to be tasty and nourishing when properly cooked. If the classification is adequate and has been applied properly, the expectation should be satisfied quite reliably.

The process of classification is at times taken to be paradigmatic of all scientific inquiry, particularly in approaches to science that do not differentiate the purposes that scientific knowledge can fulfill. That tends to produce an exaggerated emphasis on static analysis. The famous "white swan" explanation used in philosophy of science (*That* swan is white because *all* swans are white) or the voting studies carried out in political science illustrate the bias well. While it is sometimes useful to know that a particular attribute is widely shared by a specific class of things, that persons with large incomes tend to support members of a particular political party, for example, such classifications cannot be used to deal with the dynamics of social action, and they play a very limited role in the improvement of the human situation. Only theories provide a base for reasoned action. A classification is useful for purposes of action only when ancillary theories are available.

FORECASTS AND THEORIES

Change, which is an assumption justified by reference to the differences in observed values of some set of variables at two points in time, is the central concern in every knowledge system. To generate expectations of change or to provide a means for controlling change, patterns must be created that can link a change in the values of one or more of the variables in a set with a change in the value of some other variable(s) under specified limiting conditions. Such patterns will comprise sets of variables and rules of interaction that link their values over time. Some of the attributes of classes may be stated as forecasts—particular birds migrate when the seasons change, for example—but forecasts are established differently and have their own cognitive status. Two types of patterns, identical in structure but embodying different operating assumptions, can be used to deal with change. Both can serve to generate expectations about the future, but only one provides a means for controlling the course of events.

The weaker of the two instruments, here labeled a *forecast*, links the values of two or more variables by rule and includes a statement of limiting conditions. A *theory* has precisely the same structure and set of limits but includes an assumed causal connection between the variables. The result of the causal assumption is an enormous increase in the power of the instrument. Without a causal assumption, there is no reason to expect that a deliberate change in the value of one variable in the set will produce changes in the other variables predictable by rule. Indeed, the forecast may not function properly if the user intervenes in the relationship. It follows that forecasts cannot be tested in use or experimentally; other methods of justification must be employed. For practical purposes, a forecast is created using covariants observed in the past. While a forecast may include factors that are causally linked, as in weather forecasting, the association is not necessary for the forecast to function. As long as the instrument will generate accurate and reliable predictions, it can serve useful purposes. How to be sure the forecast will work on the next occasion? There can be no guarantee. The justification for the instrument lies in history. It can be strengthened by extending the time frame examined, by incorporating more than one set of relations into a single forecast, or by examining the situation to which the forecast applies for known causal factors that might inhibit or alter the change being forecast. In the absence of a causal assumption, forecasts cannot be tested experimentally.

Scientific theories (to distinguish them from most of the so-called theories in the social sciences) are structurally identical to forecasts. They consist of a set of two or more variables whose values are related by rule plus a statement of limiting conditions. However, a theory has been identified with the instrument that enables the individual to control events in the environment and that requires an assumed causal relation between the variables. This means simply that a deliberate change in one of the variables is expected to produce other changes predictable by rule. The causal assumption, even in limited form, makes for a much harder justification problem than in forecasting. Forecasters must find reasons for accepting a proposition in the form "If X occurs under condition C, Y can be expected to accompany or follow it." A theory requires justification for a much stronger proposition in the form "If X can be made to occur under condition C, Y can be expected to accompany or follow it." Because of the causal assumption included in a theory, it always implies an intervention strategy, in principle at least; therefore, it can be tested deliberately or experimentally.

In everyday argument, forecasts and theories tend to be intermingled and are often difficult to distinguish because they are similar in form. In many cases, the application of the instrument, the claim that is being made, actually determines the justification offered. The justification need be no stronger than the purpose requires. An instrument that is being used solely for prediction may actually be a valid theory that could be acted upon in the situation, but its theoretical status need not be established for that purpose. On the other hand, a knowledge claim that implies the use of a particular kind of intervention to produce specific results requires full justification as a theory, whatever the claim made by the user. Theories need to be testable but only in principle. Requiring test in practice would be too strong. For example, there are convincing reasons to believe that if the tilt of the earth with respect to the sun could be altered by a few degrees, the climate of the earth would be altered significantly and permanently. The theory cannot, for the present at least, be tested in practice, but the high degree of fit with other powerful theories makes the assumption acceptable and, indeed, unavoidable. There is perhaps more danger of overestimating the role of testing in science than the converse, given the tenor of popular discussions of the subject. Ultimately, theories must relate to and accord with observations or be abandoned, and there must be *some* observations that would, if made, refute it. But if a good fit can be established with several layers of accepted theory, that may be quite an acceptable working test, even though direct application is impossible.

Theories are acceptably construed in a number of different ways, each illuminating a different aspect of performance. First, a theory is a set of interacting variables that is isolated or cut off from the rest of the observed world and treated as a complete set. Internal changes can then be accounted for completely by the rules that govern interactions. In effect, a logic or calculus is imposed on the variables. No set of variables, however large or small, can in fact be isolated completely from the rest of the world; total separation is an assumption that is known to be false but is required to make the set calculable. Empirically, external factors will continue to influence the elements inside the set, even in the most fully isolated experimental situation possible. Some of the change occurring within the set will be due to such external factors. For convenience, those influences can be lumped together into an adjustment factor or "Fudge Factor" that can be assumed to lie between the theory and the environment. The sum of those influences is then a measure of the theory's reliability.

The Fudge Factor makes it practicable to use weak relations as theories, for the structure is fully calculable even though reliability may be low. That is particularly important in social science, where most known relations are likely to be weak. In a simple two-element theory, for example, reliability might be much less than 50 percent without destroying the usefulness of the structure—some forms of cancer treatment function at or below that level of reliability. To improve reliability, some of the influences lumped together in the Fudge Factor must be identified and their influence determined. They can then be incorporated into the theory or the set of limiting conditions established for the theory.

Another useful conceptualization is to regard a theory as a device that states either the necessary or the sufficient conditions for an event to take place. Either is a basis for action, although sufficient conditions are much stronger. If the necessary conditions for an event are known, propositions in the form "No X unless Y" (No freezing without temperatures below 32° F., for example) can be justified. Such theories can be used to inhibit change, as firemen inhibit fires by spraying materials on the combustion point that exclude oxygen. If the sufficient conditions for an event are known, the theory is more powerful and the event can be brought about. Both forms of theory suggest intervention strategies; therefore, both can be tested experimentally.

Finally, a theory can be construed as an unbroken chain of related changes at least one link long. As long as at least two changes can be linked by rule, an adequate basis for action is available, and the requirements for theory have been satisfied. The conceptualization calls attention to the usefulness of breaking one large link into several smaller steps or stages. Such elaborations may suggest more efficient or effective ways of achieving desired purposes. A classic example is found in malaria control. Knowing that the disease was carried by a mosquito already suggested that avoidance was an effective means of escaping the disease. Once the full chain of germ development was uncovered, it was possible to intervene at an earlier stage, killing the larvae by spraying stagnant water with oil, shutting off the oxygen supply. In principle, every effort to trace out a chain of causal relations ends in either indeterminacy or the infinite regress. Logic provides no basis for terminating the chain. A stipulated purpose in the environment, however, serves as a very effective stopping mechanism. When human purposes can be satisfied within acceptable levels of accuracy and reliability, the chain is long enough. If conditions change, it can be reexamined and perhaps extended another link or two in order to deal with the new situation. Pragmatic closure avoids the regress rather than solving it, but the end result is acceptable if the goal of inquiry is taken as fulfillment of human needs.

Production of the patterns or structures needed to control events in the environment requires an irreducible creative act that is known to occur but is beyond formalization. Lacking a procedure for creating patterns, a method of testing them will suffice for human purposes.[3] When actions based on known assumptions are taken under appropriate circumstances, the consequences of action are evidence for or against the assumptions. These are the minimum conditions for test as well as for learning. When all of the means available for testing theories have been exhausted, the structure remains uncertain and problematic in some degree, however small. That is no cause for concern, if only because it cannot be avoided. Bertrand Russell said that philosophy should teach men to live with uncertainty. Considering how much human misery has been generated by efforts to impose certainty for which there was no warrant, one could only wish Russell had been more influential.

CHOICE—THE NORMATIVE DOMAIN

The ability to anticipate and control events in the environment, which makes up the domain usually assigned to the sciences, is a necessary but not a sufficient condition for systematic improvement of the human situation. Science is not enough, and "it works" is not adequate as the sole criterion for evaluating inquiry. Indeed, science actually forces man to become a moral agent by providing him with the capacity to produce change deliberately, thereby forcing him to choose, to select one of a number of possible and foreseeable options. The crucial normative problem is to determine how that capacity should be used, how its use can be criticized, and how to determine the best choice possible in given circumstances. The central focus of normative inquiry is therefore an action or choice; they are analytically identical. The central problem in ethics is to justify and improve choices. In effect, the problem of choice exhausts the normative domain. Even if it turns out that the restriction is too severe, that there is much more to ethics than what is needed for choice (and I have found no reason to question the assumption thus far), systematization and improvement of choice-making will remain a basic intellectual problem for mankind. Moreover, that problem will have to be solved within the same limits that apply to empirical knowledge—the human intellectual apparatus is singular and not plural. A major virtue of the epistemological position adopted here is that it forces common treatment of empirical and normative argument, with due regard for differences in substance. The dualism that has characterized science and ethics for so very long can be abandoned if the theory proves tenable.[4]

Choices and actions are analytically indistinguishable; reasoned choices and reasoned criticism of choices can also be treated together. An action or choice occurs with any change, or potential change not realized, that can be attributed to a human actor. The effects of action need not be intended; the actor may not be aware of the action. But any human with the capacity to alter or change the environment has an effect on that environment whether or not the capacity is exercised positively. Failure to act is as much an action as any other. The effects of action are what they are and can be determined objectively; there is no need to inquire into motive or intent unless the purpose is to judge the actor. Even then, judgment of actor is contingent upon judgment of action. As long as the world is either different than it would otherwise have been or different than it could have been had some actor performed differently, an action has taken place. The consequences of action or choice are always stated in the form "This situation *rather than* that situation," for there must be at least two options. The minimum conditions for choice are an actor with some capacity to modify the environment and a situation where that capacity can be exercised. The content of the choice can be calculated from capacity and situation. Choices may affect the environment by altering the value of some set of observables or by holding conditions stable that otherwise would change.

The generalized solution to the problem of knowledge developed for use with efforts to anticipate or control events can be applied without change to normative matters. A pattern of relations that will solve the choice problem at hand is assumed; the results of acting on the pattern are used to support, modify, or reject the pattern. The justification for assuming the pattern is found in experience, including both direct affective responses and cognized or intellectualized reactions. Reasoned criticism depends on a systematic comparison of the available options, seeking reasons for preferring one to the others. No absolute scale is required. As with forecasts or theories, the ultimate basis for criticism is the informed judgment of individuals who must live with the resulting decision.

In principle, the quality of a choice could be criticized by reference to the characteristics of the actor, the nature of the action, or the consequences of the action. All of them have been tried at one time or another, but only the consequences of action seem to provide an adequate base for systematic criticism and improvement. Basing criticism on the attributes of the actor opens the way to gross inconsistency; the same action and consequences would have to be evaluated differently depending on the identity of the actor. Similarly, the actor's intentions or purposes cannot serve as a critical base, although they may be useful for criticizing the actor. Men act with different purposes in mind but produce the same results. They seek identical results by highly divergent means. Efforts to produce an evaluative typology of actions founder on a logical reef. Constant rules applied to changing circumstances produce results that differ depending on time and circumstances. There seems no way to construct a defensible evaluative base on so fluid a base without generating unacceptable anomalies.

A solution can be found, however, if the actor is ignored and the focus of criticism is the action or choice. For the consequences of choice provide a base for criticizing the choice. Indeed, nothing else will serve. The content of a choice (this, this, or this) is a set of alternatives and the consequences of choice is *this rather than those others*. The experience of living with these situations, directly and personally or historically and vicariously, may generate reasons for preferring one to another. Those reasons can be argued. Any reason is better than no reason, for the latter indicates that the choice is a matter of normative indifference. What constitutes the best reason, ultimately, is decided by the actions of informed persons who actually make the choice. The process is slow and will not solve all of the choice problems of mankind, individual or collective. But it provides a way of clarifying the content or substance of normative questions and suggests a way of resolving them. The resolution will not be absolute and may not be universally accepted, but that does not affect its potential value measured against current practice. Moreover, the procedure is feasible. Only a judgment of relative preference is needed; only the problems that actually appear in the real world need be dealt with; there is no need to bind future populations to outmoded universals or specifics, for priorities can be altered to reflect both current needs and current potentialities. Two generations, at two different points in time, may assign quite different priorities to what seems "the same" set of options without contradiction, or, more precisely, different priorities may both be justifiable at different points in time, even though both apply to the same situation.

Choices are reasoned and corrigible if they involve a systematic comparison of the outcomes available to an actor at a given time and place. The quality of the reasoning may, of course, be poor. Two instruments are needed to make reasoned choices, and the processes involved are much more complex than those required by theories or forecasts. The first requirement is a priority system—a structured ordering of the various alternatives actually available to the actor. While it is not immediately obvious, action also requires a rule of choice that will apply the priority system to the situation at hand, forcing the preferred outcome. The rules are needed because the priority structure has been generalized and its implications for the specific case must be calculated. An example may clarify the relationship. The physician whose priority structure ranks good health ahead of poor health for all patients does not solve the action problem until a rule of treatment is produced that will lead to better health for a specific patient under actual circumstances. In practice, the priority system and rule of action are usually collapsed but improvement of performance requires that the analytic separation be maintained. In any particular situation, either the priority structure, the rule of choice, or both may have to be modified as a result of experience gained from their use. The physician may find that different treatment is needed to produce good health or that good health accompanied by serious disfigurement is less desirable than somewhat poorer health unmarred by physical unattractiveness. As in theorizing, priority systems and rules of action are developed from the specific case, aggregated from below and generalized as experience allows. The justification for asserting that improvement has been made is found, as with hammers, in the actions of those who use them with full knowledge of the available alternatives. Priorities are the instruments through which individuals define the best life available to them; policies are the instruments used to pursue it.

Reasoned choice requires an identifiable actor (needed to determine the range of choices available) able to produce at least two specifiable alternatives. The content of the alternatives is determined by ordinary theories; no other instrument can project the effects of action on the future. Since the choice to be made depends on a comparison of outcomes, the projections must be structured to show the normatively critical dimensions of the sets of situations from which a choice is made. However, since any single alternative can in principle be conceptualized in endless different ways, some set of common denominators or normative variables is needed to identify significant aspects of choice. Otherwise, comparisons would not intersect, and there could be no reasoned argument. In principle, any variable can be normative in its implications. Hence, the crucial question is the value that the variable takes and the relative significance of different variables taking different values. In practice, the established ethic supplies a selection of variables considered important, and that serves as a point of departure for the normative enterprise. Without some such base, however limited, systematic development would be nearly impossible. However, every choice remains open in principle to criticism based on *any* legitimate conceptualization of the outcomes from which a choice is made. Obviously, one major factor in normative improvement is the introduction of new normative variables—as the effect of factory conditions on worker health was introduced in the nineteenth century as a basis for criticizing entrepreneurial behavior. Finally, actions are judged in terms of *all* of their consequences and not just a selection of them. Otherwise, it would be reasonable to eliminate cancer by killing the patient. The effects of action are what they are, and that is empirically determined. To the extent they can be foreseen using the available tools, all such effects must be taken into account when a reasoned choice is made.

At present, the variables needed for reasoned choice are not readily available. The focus of attention in traditional moral discourse has been the general practice, the broad features of individual and social life. Little of the philosophic product can be applied to genuine choices. How weak this area of intellectual development has been is easily demonstrated: the reader need only ask how the quality of life of an ignorant and poverty-stricken peasant can be compared to the quality of life of a wealthy and educated aristocrat. What terms are available for conveying the differences adequately to a third party? The apparatus is clearly inadequate. Yet, without it, there can be no adequate basis for either individual or social choice.

Two major points can perhaps be made about the variables and assumptions required for justifying choices. First, they will refer to individual, human attributes: choices will be based on the impact of man on man. *Homo Mensura*, man is the measure of things, is unavoidable. For without human life, the whole enterprise is absurd and without meaning; there would be nothing to value and nothing to do the valuing. Human actions that produce no impact on the life of any person, that generate no change in the human condition, are normatively indifferent. More important, actions that produce change in social structures and other institutional arrangements are of uncertain normative significance until their effects have been translated into specific consequences for specific populations. Natural disasters such as hurricanes and earthquakes have very unfortunate consequences for human populations, of course, and the concepts used to judge those effects unfortunate will appear in reasoned choice, but there is no human choice involved in an earthquake. Hence, there is no action to criticize. The person who knows of the hurricane and fails to warn his neighbor, thus bringing about the neighbor's death, simply employs the hurricane as an instrument. The person's actions are subject to criticism; the hurricane is not.

The second point that can be made about reasoned choice, a corollary to the first, is that in the very limited sense of life *qua* life, one human life can be assumed to be equal to any other. Obviously, the consequences of changing specific lives can vary enormously. But in the rockbottom sense of a life, in a choice between two lives where nothing else is known, no good or noninvidious basis for distinguishing between them has been discovered and none seems likely. Radical individualism in ethics and the equality of human life *qua* life may not take the normative enterprise very far, but they do serve to delimit the area of normative concerns. They are thin. They are not trivial.

Considered as process, normative inquiry may begin with either a situation or an actor. A situation (deplorable human conditions) may attract attention on normative grounds, leading to a search for improvement; an actor, particularly an actor who occupies public office, may have to choose among a number of very significant and far-reaching outcomes. In either case, the situation must be real, the actor must have a genuine (as against a legal or formal) capacity to alter it, and the range of options must be determinable. The disabilities placed on society by the very low level of social theory are most apparent in this context. For the choice made to be testable and improvable, the priority structure must be known and the rule of choice must be sufficiently precise to *force* selection of one option rather than the others. Otherwise, the action is indeterminate and beyond test. Even if all those conditions are satisfied, it may be very difficult to decide whether the results of action call for changes in priorities, or in rules of action, or even in the theoretical structure employed to project the alternatives.

Two minor clarifications in the normative apparatus may be useful at this point. The consequences of action are stated in the general form "This outcome or situation rather than those alternatives." Priorities are assigned to complete outcomes, specified in terms of some set of normative variables. Within each set of outcomes, the ordering must be transitive. But there is no need for an integrated or overarching set of priorities from which all others are derived. Each subset is ordered uniquely—a consequence of development from below or from the specific case. And the ordering that applies to individual elements in the structure does not apply to combinations. That is, even though A is preferred to B (tea to coffee, say), it is possible without contradiction to prefer coffee with cream $(B + X)$. That is the basis on which compromise occurs. When priorities are disputed, settlement on reasoned grounds is contingent on each side giving reasons to support its position. If the disagreement remains, reasons are requested in support of the first set of reasons. This process of "pushing back" the argument to the prior assumptions from which it derives continues until agreement or impasse is reached. There is no guarantee of success. As long as the Caligula syndrome—the effort to design rules and priorities that will deal with monstrous and excessive cases—is avoided, there are fairly good empirical reasons for supposing that it can solve most of the disputes that arise, or at least clarify them so they are tolerable.

The second aspect of choice requiring some additional comment is the precise status of affective reactions. Without some human capacity for affect, choice would probably be impossible or pointless, and affective reactions are clearly evidence relating to choices. But the affective response is not itself an expression of preference. The statement "I like chocolate ice cream" is only a factual report on subjective states. It is not equivalent to the statement "I prefer chocolate ice cream to banana ice cream." The latter is a preference for which the former serves as evidence. The reasons offered in support of priorities will combine affective reactions with intellectual assessments of the implications of accepting one set of priorities rather than another—for the individual, for the collectivity, for present and future, and so on. The assessments are grounded in a judgment about the quality of life that is available to human populations touched by the choice, directly or indirectly. What will actually be the "best" reason depends on the particular case; there is no general justification for accepting a priority structure or a theory. Current practice and past history provide the only point of departure for answering priority questions. Much work needs to be done in the sociology of values, providing evidence for justifying or rejecting specific priorities. Until the priorities that have been employed by individuals and collectivities are established, and their consequences examined systematically in history and in the world as it is presently, evidence for or against them is extremely difficult to obtain. Philosophers are in many cases usefully suggestive, indicating aspects of individual and social life that have a significant impact on the overall quality of life, but they cannot be treated as evidence. In this area, even more than in respect of social and political theory, the social critic can find very little dependable assistance.

Reasoned choice entails the application of priorities to specific cases. Applications occur through rules of choice. At that point, reasoned choice makes contact with policymaking. For policies are quite reasonably identified with the rules needed to fit priorities to specific situations—and that is a very useful extension of the critical apparatus, which is explored at greater length in Chapter 6.

ARGUMENT

The concepts, measurements, descriptions, forecasts, theories, and priorities used to fulfill human purposes in the environment, and thereby improve the human condition or quality of life, normally appear in the form of propositions. Those propositions comprise the meaning or content of a message, relating to sentences in much the same way that a telephone message relates to the electric impulses that convey it. Every proposition incorporates some general or class terms, relating them to specific observations. All propositions are in some degree uncertain or problematic, no proposition is self-evident, no proposition is true in the same sense as a statement in formal logic. Reasons must therefore be provided for accepting or rejecting a proposition. Such reasons constitute an *argument* in the technical sense needed here.[5] The content of the argument will depend on the kind of proposition being justified.

Basically, there are only four types of propositions for which arguments must be developed: descriptions, forecasts, theories, and choices. Before they can be argued, the propositions must be recognized by form and content. That may be difficult where complex sets of propositions are included in a single sentence. A descriptive proposition is a record of observations made at a particular time and place using one or more concepts—"There was a dog in that yard at ten o'clock this morning." In some cases, elements of the description, such as time or place, are suppressed or implied but can be determined from content; otherwise, the description is simply incomplete or inadequate. A forecast states an expectation about the future or the unobserved past and gives a reason for it. It must contain at least two observables; otherwise, it is simply prophecy. For example, "If the temperature drops below 32° F. tonight, that water will freeze" is a forecast (which makes use of a theory); "it will snow tonight" is prophecy. Theories are recognizable by the implicit or explicit intervention strategy they must contain: "Do X, expect Y," is the base pattern, though "If Y, X preceded" states the same rule. Choices assign priorities to members of a fully articulated set: $A > B > C > D$. In some cases, only the top priority is indicated; the remainder of the set is lumped. Imperatives state priorities but in extreme form, since they force a specific choice regardless of the alternatives. Empirically and historically, there seems to be no option that can always and universally be chosen in that way; hence, their appearance is suspect in any priority system.

The content of reasoned argument, in the technical sense employed here, does not correspond to the expectations normally associated with the term. For in everyday language, an argument approximates a debate, and the goal of the debater is to gain support for a position. As the term is used here, the goal of argument is a full statement of the reasons that can be offered for or against accepting a particular proposition. The aim is to develop consensus on a conclusion among informed critics. The argument may include two types of materials: first, evidence relating to the implications of accepting a particular proposition; second, evidence and reasoning relating to the validity of the proposition. The separation is analytic, and in everyday cases the two are thoroughly intermingled.

An example may clarify the two aspects of argument. If a small child was seen preparing to leap from a balcony several stories above the ground, an effort would certainly be made to prevent it.

If the child was halted but demanded to know why the game had been interrupted, the argument for the proposition (Remain where you are and do not jump) could begin with the proposition: you (the child) would be badly hurt or even killed by the fall. The child may respond in two ways: first, questioning the priority, asking why being hurt should be avoided; second, querying the assertion that serious injury would follow the leap. In the first case, the argument would focus on the results expected to follow (assuming the projection to be correct) and point to the pain, high costs, possible permanent damage to the body and resulting handicap, and so on. Secondary effects on the family could be brought to the child's attention. All of these outcomes would be contrasted as sharply as possible with the alternative—conditions as they presently were. There is, of course, no guarantee that the child, or even an adult, would agree. Old-fashioned households might then be tempted to generate relatively severe pain in some accessible but not readily damaged portion of the child's anatomy to underscore some of the characteristics of the first alternative and what it might feel like to live with it, but it is at least feasible that the child, stubborn to the end, would refuse to agree. Would that mean that the normative process had failed? If the child returned to the balcony and prepared for a second launch, would the family provide escort service and stand aside? Certainly not. The child's behavior would be quite rightly ticketed an aberration, a clear case of the Caligula syndrome, and the choice would be interrupted once again.

If the child agreed that it would not care to be badly damaged or killed but asked why the fall would produce that result, the argument would run differently. The rate of acceleration of freely falling bodies (approximate) would be cited and applied, indicating that the child would strike the ground at a speed of, say, more than sixty miles per hour. Other evidence could be cited to show that human bodies hitting solid surfaces at that speed invariably are severely damaged. In time, if the child were not being perverse, the reasons would become too formidable to resist. There are various ways of amassing evidence and argument, depending on the kind of proposition being considered. They are considered in some detail in the following chapters.

NOTES

1. Norton E. Long, "Foreword," to Eugene J. Meehan, *Explanation in Social Science: A System Paradigm* (Dorsey Press, 1968).

2. Cf. Eugene J. Meehan, *Education for Critical Thinking*, forthcoming.

3. Karl R. Popper has put forward what is perhaps the strongest claim for testing or falsification as the basic scientific procedure, particularly in *The Logic of Scientific Discovery* (Science Editions, 1961).

4. See Eugene J. Meehan, "Science, Values, and Policies," *American Behavioral Scientist*, Volume 17, No. 1, September/October, 1973.

5. The closest parallel to the approach to argument taken here is found in Stephen Toulmin, *The Uses of Argument* (Cambridge University Press, 1964). Most standard treatments of argument come from either philosophy or rhetoric. For the philosophic tradition, see C. A. Kirwan, *Logic and Argument* (New York University Press, 1976), Perry Weddle, *Argument: A Guide to Critical Thinking* (McGraw-Hill, 1977), and D. Rieke and Malcolm O. Sillars, *Argumentation and the Decision-Making Process* (John Wiley, 1975). For the use of argument in rhetoric, see Glen E. Mills, *Reason in Controversy: On General Argumentation*, 2d ed. (Allyn and Bacon, 1968).

Descriptive propositions are the most basic form of organized human experience, incorporating, with varying degrees of precision, the results of observation. The general form is very simple: "X is/was the case." The precise cognitive status of descriptions, however, is not quite as simple as everyday usage suggests. Descriptions are not perfectly analogous to photographs or snapshots. Rather, they are sets of propositions that must be assumed and then justified—they are not self-justifying. The reason lies in the interpretive gap between actual perception and the content of the descriptive proposition. The observer does not *perceive* a member of the class "cows" in a field; the perceptions are interpreted to support the proposition "there is a member of the class 'cows' in the field." In everyday usage, the two elements are merged, and in most cases that does little if any harm, but for analytic purposes, the distinction must be retained. Otherwise, the criteria used to criticize descriptions might prove inadequate.

INTRODUCTION

Structurally, a description consists

of three major elements: a set of concepts, one or more relational terms linking the conceptual elements, and the grammatical fillers required by language. To illustrate, the proposition "There is a cow in that field" makes use of two major concepts (cow and field) plus a locational term (in that field). The time, implied by use of the verb "is," must be "now" or "at present." The proposition claims that an observation made by a competent observer will support three points: first, there is a field, second, there is a cow, and third, the cow lies within the geographic bounds of the field. Three judgments have been made, two relating to class membership and one referring to location. Assuming the proposition, or asserting that it is correct, is normally justified by referring to an observation. Since the "things" observed are external to the person and public, that would seem to settle the matter. In fact, it does not. For the proposition refers to a specific time and place, located in the past. Hence, it cannot be replicated, strictly speaking, because the situation cannot be reconstructed. Indeed, if the point is pressed, two observers in the same area at the same time do not actually make "the same" observation, although many of the problems associated with such differences can be eliminated by careful structuring.

When descriptive statements are merged with evaluative, aesthetic, or prescriptive judgments, the descriptive form is retained. Such statements as "That is a lovely house," for example, take precisely the same form as "That is a square house." The difference between them obviously lies in the difference between "lovely" and "square." But if the criteria by which the term "lovely" could be applied to objects were agreed upon, would the statement then be descriptive? That is, if "lovely" is a class term and membership in the class could be determined, would the result be a purely descriptive statement? Such problems need not detain us here, but they suggest some of the complications that develop when the underlying structure of thinking is exposed systematically.

Justifications for descriptive propositions tend to be much more complex than common usage suggests. The strongest element in the justification will, of course, be the results of observation. Indeed, the credence attached to descriptive statements is a recognition of the strength derived from their close and direct relation to observation or perception. If observers indicate that their perceptions support the descriptive proposition, and if it can be shown that they understand the meaning of terms, have normal vision, and so on, evidence can be cumulated that makes it very difficult to refuse to accept the proposition. To some degree, however small, descriptive propositions remain problematic or uncertain. No proposition about the observed world can be established in the same absolute sense that a conclusion relates to a premise in logic. It is impossible to be certain that two or more observers mean precisely the same thing, even though they make use of the same concepts and language. The inferential gap between concept and application remains, and that allows room for error. Finally, there is always some level of precision at which measurement or descriptive accuracy fails and observation is indeterminate. Nevertheless, adequate reasons for accepting and using all sorts of descriptive propositions can be produced, and mankind has progressed a very long way indeed by accepting them. The purpose of the analysis is to produce awareness and to enjoin caution, and not to produce unlimited skepticism.

Further evidence for descriptive propositions can be obtained from an examination of their internal characteristics and from the congruence of the substance of the proposition and the available body of related knowledge. Descriptive statements must "make sense." To assert "There was a gugoligar behind the gymnasium this afternoon" is to make a nonsense statement. The point is not arguable because the term was newly invented for the occasion. Similarly, such assertions as "The armadillo spoke fluent Spanish" or "The elephant flew to the top of a nearby tree" cannot be accepted because they are incompatible with established knowledge. Individuals who asserted such propositions would have their credence and sanity questioned, and not gain immediate acceptance because a basis in observation was claimed. Even the nature of an observation may invalidate propositions claiming support from it: "I saw the goat bite that man on the arm in front of that farmhouse four miles down the road" is a situation of that kind. Finally, even such things as the self-serving character of a proposition may be used in argument for limited purposes, particularly as corollary to other evidence or to support withholding judgment pending further information. *Ad hominem* arguments are always weak and potentially invidious but not totally worthless in all cases.

The justification offered for a description must support two basic points: first, the *accuracy* of the proposition, which is a function of the concepts, definitions, measurements, and observational techniques employed; second, the *adequacy* of the description, which requires reference to the purpose for which the description is intended. The need to consider adequacy as well as accuracy is a function of the basic theory of knowledge. Every description is a selection from an infinite set of possible descriptive accounts. Complete description is in principle impossible for any situation. Each of the descriptive accounts that can be produced will serve some purposes and not others. A universal description that serves all purposes equally well is as unattainable as a universal map able to serve all potential map users equally well. Descriptions can be expanded and enriched to allow use for a wider range of purposes, and in systematic inquiry casting the net too narrowly can be very expensive. But overexpansion is self-defeating, for as the amount of detail increases, the cost of production and use rises to a point where it is cheaper to create a new description for the specific purpose in hand than to explore the complex structure already available.

When descriptions are related to purposes, the potential for bias implicit in the descriptive process is brought to light. While an accurate description seems an unlikely place for bias or invidious distinctions, the potential for distortion is found in the *selection* of dimensions included or excluded from the account and not the accuracy of the observations. A common error is well illustrated by the story of the ship's mate who was cited for drunkenness by the captain. In retaliation, the mate made a log entry during the next watch that read: "The Captain was sober this morning." Concern for purpose calls attention to omissions from descriptive accounts that may have significance for the user. Sherlock Holmes' dog that failed to bark in the night is a famous case in literature; the absence of looting during a police strike or blackout, or the absence of particular symptoms in a medical report, suggest the importance of omission in real life.

DESCRIPTIVE ACCURACY

The accuracy of a descriptive proposition is a function of the quality of the concepts employed, the precision of the measurements and the care with which observations are made and recorded. The character of the descriptive process greatly influences judgments of accuracy and adequacy, and is worth further emphasis. Descriptions result from and refer to perceptions; they do not refer to what is "really out there." The process by which perceptions are organized is not analogous to picture-taking. It more closely resembles the process by which sound waves are converted into electrical waves in a microphone; the two are analogous but not identical. Moreover, the observer is always an essential part of the observation, serving as both an instrument for measuring and as the object of perception, depending on circumstances. Observation is a subjective process, and the thing observed can also be part of subjective experience, as in the case of pain or happiness.

SUBJECTIVITY

The subjective character of observation greatly complicates the task of justifying or supplying evidence for descriptive propositions. Since the internal experience of one person is not open to direct inspection by others, should accounts of subjective experience be ignored? Is the structure wholly beyond test? In the last analysis, there is no way to be sure that any person's experience has been recorded accurately. The integrity of the observer is the ultimate guarantee of quality—hence, the importance attached to it in academic inquiry. Even in those cases where the objects being described are public, it is often both difficult and expensive to replicate a description. In the physical sciences, the influence of subjectivity can be reduced by using mechanical or electronic measuring devices. They produce a standardized product, which is less ambiguous to interpret than human perceptions. But that escape route is not too accessible in social science. And measuring tools create their own problems, for the instrument "observes" only those dimensions of the environment included in the design. If the design is faulty or inadequate, the results of using any tool will be flawed. Measuring tools suffer precisely the same defects as direct human observations; they are only as good as the selection of indicators. The human observer, considered as a measuring "instrument," has one unequaled virtue—enormous capacity and flexibility. No television camera can transmit everything that a trained and competent observer will see, given the opportunity. The use of artificial observers, like the use of such artificial "thinking" apparatus as the computer, trades the very complex and sophisticated for the simple and accurate and reliable. The gain is sometimes worth the cost and sometimes not.

When a description refers to events open to public inspection, some of the problems associated with subjectivity can be avoided or reduced. One person's observations can be tested against another person's observations. Agreement among competent observers is evidence not only for the proposition on which they agree but also for the competence of the observers, other things equal. The meaning of concepts can be narrowed, and the number of indicators multiplied. But such efforts, like the introduction of measuring tools, increase accuracy at a price. And when every precaution has been taken, there remains an irreducible element of uncertainty about accuracy and acceptability.

Criticism or evaluation of descriptive accounts that individuals provide of their own subjective experiences is so complex and difficult that some social scientists have tried to eliminate them from systematic inquiry. But there are good reasons to assume that every individual has subjective feelings or experiences and that in some respects at least they are the same from one person to the next. Such propositions can be extremely useful, both for evaluating individual performance and for measuring the consequences of action. Propositions that refer to individual beliefs, attitudes, or states of mind are peculiarly difficult to handle. When Smith asserts that at time "t" he believed X was the case, for example, how can supporting evidence be obtained? Very frequently, such propositions are made under circumstances that are self-serving in quite significant ways. The policeman who states that he believed his life was in danger when he fired at a suspect, or the president who claims that atomic weapons were employed against Japan in the belief that millions of lives would be saved, exemplifies the kind of problem involved. In some cases, indirect evidence may be relevant. The policeman who claims he feared for his life but failed to draw his weapon might be behaving inconsistently. Evidence provided by the president's chief military advisers could corroborate his decisions and beliefs partially but no more. Only the actor is in a position to be certain, and as historical biographers know, even that assumption is doubtful in some cases.

Finally, when one person seeks to produce a descriptive account of the subjective state, past or present, of another person, as in the case of a psychiatrist testifying to the sanity of a defendant in a courtroom, the quality of the data is extremely murky, expert witness or not. When lay persons testify to such internal states as anger or fear in others, the situation is even worse. Such concepts are vague and uncertain; their indicators are poor; the individual can dissimulate, can produce the external manifestations usually associated with such internal states as fear or anger. All sorts of experiments have shown that one person perceives fear where another sees nothing but anger, and so on, both in animals and humans. Yet, such information is at times of such great import that the claim and supporting evidence, such as they are, will probably continue to be offered for criticism.

The uncertainties associated with the use of difficult concepts, or with efforts to describe difficult and ephemeral phenomena, tend to emerge in descriptions as "hedged" accounts. The observer will say "I believe that . . . ," not meaning it literally (for that would be redundant) but in the sense that "It is likely or probable that. . . ." If a bird is observed at a distance, for example, and the observer is uncertain of the species, the description may take the form: "I believe it was a hairy woodpecker." If the context is unclear, such assertions create an interesting and annoying class of pseudoproblems. The descriptive problem lies in the application of the concept "hairy woodpecker" to a set of perceptions and not with the individual's belief structure. More skillful description can prevent such problems, of course, but that aspect of the descriptive process probably needs more emphasis than is normally provided in methodological exercises.

CONCEPTUALIZATION

Concepts are sets of rules for organizing perceptions, for discriminating between "things" in the environment, and for bounding them. They range from such "simples" as red or yellow to complex second-order organizing devices such as atoms and electrons, syndromes, and psychic states. In most cases, complex concepts must be used to identify other concepts, producing overall structures that are large, sophisticated, and sometimes very difficult to apply or test. There is no good classification of concepts available, but some of the major conceptual problems in systematic inquiry need to be explored, if only because of their impact on the quality of the intellectual tools produced in the discipline.[1]

Languages are not equally well supplied with the concepts needed for life in the contemporary world; that is a commonplace. Moreover, within any language, the supply of concepts fluctuates constantly as old terms are dropped, new terms invented, and special modifications introduced. The same conditions are found in any field of study. For that reason, development, improvement, and clarification of the conceptual apparatus are major needs in every discipline. The problem is particularly acute in the social sciences because the concepts employed tend to be everyday derivatives with a long history and a wide range of meanings. Strongly socialized usage is difficult to alter, whether in politics or elsewhere, and the introduction of technical language has not been very effective as a means of improving the conceptual apparatus. And since the conceptual apparatus in use must be used to correct the conceptual apparatus in use, that makes for much more difficult going in the underdeveloped fields. Nevertheless, the need has deepened since Confucius called for a "rectification of terms" more than two thousand years ago, and some improvements could be made fairly readily. Not every concept can be or need be altered. The critical aspects of conceptualization, where inadequacy is most likely to interfere with the achievement of purpose, can be tackled first. Ultimately, the quality of the conceptual structure is a reflection of the overall effectiveness of the modes of inquiry employed in the field of study. Concepts can be separated from the rest of inquiry analytically and thereby opened to systematic and useful criticism. But in the last analysis, the quality of the concept improves in use, in the effort to bring the environment under intellectual control.

Concepts identify classes and not particulars. That makes them valuable intellectual tools. It also creates many of the problems associated with their development and use. Since both the value and the weakness of concepts are largely a function of what they are and how they are developed, it is useful to trace that development, in imagination at least, for a specific case. The perceptions organized by a concept must *precede* conceptual development; observables not yet observed cannot be suitable objects of organization. Conceptual development begins, therefore, with the first appearance of the thing indicated by a concept, say, the first appearance of a dog in an isolated village. If the village had no prior experience with animals of any sort (except other humans), which is possible but unlikely, there would be no fund of information that might be transferred by analogy to the new creature unless similarities with the human race were perceived. Familiarity with other animals could provide a crude and uncertain base for dealing with the dog. For example, if the villagers were aware of the potential danger from animal attack, they would be alert against it. More generally, observation would produce information about the creature's attributes and behavior: what it ate, where it slept, how it related to other animals, and so on. Some information could be gathered simply by watching passively. In other cases, deliberate stimulation, such as feigned attack, might be used to determine the dog's reaction. Although the dog could not be classified, it could be labeled or named. The data acquired from observation would attach to the specific animal. It could be quite rich and even useful. That is, villagers could learn to use the dog as an early warning device if it barked when strangers approached, and so on. In some very interesting ways, early human development must partake of many of the features of learning about a new species. The child's information will be rich and particular rather than generalized and applicable to classes. Understandably, children sometimes have great difficulty with the transition to generalized information. Indeed, what is most amazing is how rapidly and efficiently the transition is made in most cases.

The classification process, as opposed to gathering information about a particular thing, is disclosed when a second dog makes an appearance in the village. Would it be recognized as "just like X" or would it be identified as "another one?" In the latter case, the transformation to classification has been made, for the "one" must refer to a class. Much depends on the degree of similarity between the two animals, of course, but if they were approximately the same in size and appearance, there are fairly good reasons to believe that the traits observed in the first animal would be assumed with respect to the second. Indeed, one of the difficulties in education is to inhibit overly rapid transfers of that kind, "hasty generalizations," as they are called in logic. The defining attributes of the class, when it has been properly developed, can include only those factors that are shared by every member of the class, the so-called distributed properties. The kinds of errors likely or possible in the development of the concept are fairly obvious. By tracing the steps by which a large class such as dogs is developed, articulated, subdivided, and made increasingly reliable, the reader can obtain more insight into conceptual problems than any amount of writing could produce. If the changes taking place in the meaning and use of the concept are linked to the kinds of descriptive accounts that would be produced if the concept was employed, that can serve to illuminate some of the problems involved in systematic criticism of descriptions.

Vagueness and Ambiguity. The two most common faults in conceptualization are vagueness and ambiguity. A concept is vague if the meaning cannot be determined very accurately. With an ambiguous concept, the meaning may be accurate, but there is more than one meaning and no basis for choosing among them. Both faults render the concept unusable as it stands, but ambiguity is perhaps the worse of the two errors. If the meaning of a concept is vague or uncertain, the meaning of propositions that make use of the concept will also be uncertain and impossible to test. That can actually be useful, at least temporarily, particularly in the development of a new area of inquiry. Indeed, some degree of vagueness is probably unavoidable when new sets of relations are being explored. Moreover, the vagueness is useful to the extent that it prevents premature closure of meaning or premature rejection of the inquiry. To take a hypothetical example, studies of factory productivity might show that a particular kind of worker-job relation, hard to define but present in some sense, had a significant impact on productivity. That relation could be labeled "alienation" and defined very roughly and crudely, perhaps as a "lack of commitment" or "feeling of isolation." In the early stages of inquiry, that could be appropriate and valuable. In time, however, the concept must acquire a more precise meaning and an appropriate set of indicators; otherwise, it will serve no useful function. If vagueness continues, the concept remains untestable, and valuable time can be squandered arguing about whether or not a particular case properly belongs to the class identified by the concept. It does no good to know that an alienated worker will not produce if the alienated worker cannot be identified. Similarly, it is not much use to be able to identify an alienated worker if the effects of alienation are not known.

Conceptual ambiguity is a far more serious problem for the critic, particularly over the short run. Until ambiguity is resolved, there is no specific meaning for a proposition; hence, it lies beyond reasoned criticism. Ambiguities appear in a variety of forms and guises; three types are particularly common and important in social science. In the simplest case, a concept has more than one meaning, and that meaning cannot be determined in the context supplied by the proposition in which it appears. Since most of the concepts used in social science have a long history and are in common use, they carry a variety of meanings. Understandably, slipping from one meaning to another in the course of an argument is easy to do and hard to avoid. Rigorous specification of meaning and careful adherence to a single limited meaning may help, but it can do little to prevent the reader from attaching different meanings to the term, depending on context. Since the writer fails if the meaning intended is not conveyed to the reader, that becomes a very serious problem—one, let it be said, on which too little information is available.

The most common suggestion for dealing with that form of ambiguity is to develop standardized or technical concepts on the model of physical science or medicine. While some measure of standardization of concepts would probably be useful, some serious practical and theoretical hurdles would have to be cleared before it could be carried out. For one thing, the organizational base needed for conceptual standardization simply is not available, whether for social science as a whole or for more limited areas such as political science. Yet, such organization is essential for developing the consensus among those working in the field needed to make standardization effective. Even if initial agreement were reached, maintaining current usage can be a serious problem. The work of the French *Academie Française* is ample testimony to the problems associated with maintaining the currency of a language.

Supposing that conceptual standardization could be achieved, there remains some question whether it would really be desirable. At a minimum, the use of standard concepts implies a commitment to studying particular events using a particular conceptual framework. But in the social sciences, such frameworks are lacking, and those that are available could hardly be considered a resounding success. How could the needed standards be created without grossly restricting inquiry on wholly inadequate grounds? Concepts organize perceptions by exclusion as well as by inclusion, and the social sciences are ill prepared to say that certain classes of perceptions could be excluded without significant loss. Moreover, past experience with academic ossification suggests the wisdom of avoiding closure in such matters as long as possible. Most of the great advances in human knowledge in the past have involved a major reconceptualization of the area of inquiry. Einstein's work in relativity illustrates the point almost perfectly. Standardization of concepts could seriously impede, or even eliminate, the freedom to experiment and speculate on which reconceptualization depends. That is not to argue against steady efforts to introduce common meanings for concepts but to urge against sweeping transformations for which the intellectual foundations are lacking.

The two remaining common or major ambiguities occur in the use of aggregate or collective concepts—football teams, watches, automobile accidents, or cancer, for example. One occurs when the distinction between the aggregate taken as a whole and the parts or elements of the aggregate is not maintained. Concepts that refer to classes of aggregates must be handled carefully because the classes are made up of elements or subclasses. The relations between an aggregate and its elements can vary widely. In some cases, such as watches, the elements are organized mechanically or logically. In other aggregates, such as "all persons with red hair," the class is created by an observer for purposes external to the actual members of the class. Every aggregate, organized or not, will have collective properties or features that are different from and not logically deducible from the properties of the elements. Both the members of the class and the various subclasses can be quite different. That is, watches differ one from the other, and the parts of watches are different, both within and among class members. The relations can be extremely convoluted, as I have tried to demonstrate very quickly in this paragraph. Yet, the class "watch" includes every object that shares the distributed properties of the class, and propositions that refer to the class must fit or be tested against each class member—unless such "weasel words" as "usually" are added, as is usually the case.

The practice of confusing the attributes of aggregates and the attributes of their elements is so common that logicians have special labels for each type of reasoning error.[2] When the properties of an element are attributed to an aggregate, that is called the fallacy of composition, and when the property of an aggregate is transferred to its elements, that is called a division fallacy. For example, if a shipment of ten white hogs and fifty black hogs arrives at the market, it may be accurate to say that the white hogs (individually) weigh more than the black hogs (individually) but wrong to claim that the white hogs (collectively) weigh more than the black hogs (collectively). Unless the potential ambiguity is avoided, the description may be grievously erroneous. A parallel error occurs in such statements as "Men are found everywhere on the globe." The proposition is descriptively accurate with respect to the class as a whole but mistaken if taken to mean men as individuals. A slightly different form of the same type of ambiguity occurs when the parts of a collectivity are confused with its features. A crowd may be noisy while some of its members are silent; a watch can "tell time," and its elements are organized for that purpose, but no amount of study of those parts can establish the meaning of "telling time." This type of ambiguity occurs very frequently when the behavior of indiviual members of collective bodies (courts, legislatures, and so on) is described. The meaning attached to the action of the collectivity may be almost totally unrelated to the meaning of the action taken by the individual member of that collectivity. A decision of the Supreme Court may be described in terms of freedom of religion, while the actions of an individual judge may have been based solely on considerations of freedom of speech.

The third type of conceptual ambiguity, particularly common in social science, occurs when aggregates whose elements are homogeneous with respect to the effects of change in the environment are not differentiated from aggregates whose units are affected differentially by such changes. Detailed discussion of the point is reserved for Chapter 4, but the principle is important for conceptual criticism. If the consequences of social action, of intervention to achieve specified objectives, are to be projected accurately on the future, the class of persons to be affected by the intervention must be grouped in ways that will show the impact of the change. If the members of a given class are affected differentially by a common action, that class is useless for purposes of action. For example, a class of events such as "automobile accidents" cannot serve as a useful base for efforts to reduce the number of accidents. The class must first be unpacked to group together accidents that have a common cause, or that could be prevented by some common action. For actions that seek to reduce accidents due to drunken driving would have no effect on accidents due to mechanical failure or slippery roads. Precisely the same ambiguities arise when governments attempt to deal with poverty or to provide assistance for such vaguely defined classes as "the poor." Discussions of income maintenance programs, for example, are very difficult to evaluate because the effects of additional income on the different substrata of eligible populations are little known and cannot be assumed with any degree of confidence.[3] Deliberate efforts to modify the environment, whether to achieve individual or social purposes, occur within a conceptual framework supplied by descriptive accounts of the problem. When the concepts employed in the descriptive account are inappropriate for the task to be performed, there is no possibility of successful, improvable action.

DEFINITIONS

The meaning of any concept is contained in its definition. Unfortunately, definitions are also a major source of conceptual confusion. There are various ways of defining concepts or terms, and not all of them can be used for every purpose. It is often said, for example, that "I can define my terms as I please so long as I am consistent." The principle is acceptable with respect to some purposes but not others. Applied consistently across the board, that approach to definition can be guaranteed to create serious problems for the inquirer. Perhaps the most efficient way of handling the problem is to provide a quick survey of the more common types of definitions, indicating uses and limitations, and suggesting the points of particular concern to the systematic critic.

The most common source of definitions is probably the dictionary. The *lexical* definitions contained there record current usage, kept reasonably up to date by editors and publishers. Those who compile dictionaries are not responsible for their intellectual quality or usefulness. Usage is transferred from society to dictionary. Dictionary definitions are not usually very useful for systematic inquiry; several meanings are included, and none is very precise. When a concept already in use is adapted and limited, that is called a *precising* definition. For example, the student of political participation may find it useful to limit "participants" to those who make monetary contributions to a political party. That is perfectly acceptable, of course, as long as the restriction in meaning is stated clearly and used consistently—assuming the meaning is consistent with common usage and not aberrant. The danger here is that (1) the author will intermingle dictionary and restricted usage, creating an unresolvable ambiguity for the reader, or (2) the reader will forget the restricted meaning and read the everyday meaning each time the term occurs.

Wholly new concepts begin with a stipulative definition, which may be modified in due course. The label is created *after* the concept has been defined. For example, the ratio between the number of legal voters in an area and the number of votes actually cast in particular elections is a fairly precise, if not necessarily new and important, concept. It can be assigned a label, say "Local-Interest Ratio," and provided with an operational definition, a method for actually calculating the ratio. If the concept turns out to be valuable for some purpose it can be incorporated into the accepted vocabulary through use.

For criticism of descriptions and other intellectual tools, the most important definitional distinction to be made lies between *real* definitions and *nominal* definitions.[4] A great deal of the conceptual and theoretical inadequacy in social science, and perhaps most particularly in economics, is a result of the failure to distinguish one from the other. In part, that can be attributed to the complexity of the distinction, for it is not readily incorporated into working habits. More importantly, the importance of the distinction is not adequately appreciated, therefore it is not included in the standard texts nor in routine instruction in the schools. Yet it plays a major role in intellectual criticism, especially in social science, as I shall try to demonstrate.

A *real* definition refers to experience and observation, therefore it cannot be arbitrary or capricious. Every concept must have a real definition for a concept is a structure used to organize experience. Real definitions can be tested against experience and evidence can be offered for and against accepting them. The meaning of "robin" cannot be determined arbitrarily; it must correspond to the knowledge of the class that has been established by observation. Real definitions must develop in the same way that the meaning of "robin" has developed; their meaning cannot be postulated.

A *nominal* definition does not refer to observations, is not related to anything in the world of experience, and cannot be tested or disputed by reference to observations or experience. A nominal definition, to quote Robert Bierstedt, is "A declaration of intention to use a certain word or phrase as a substitute for another word or phrase."[5] There can be no dispute about the adequacy or accuracy of a nominal definition. It means nothing more than "I will substitute (this) for (that.)" Any concept that is used for talking about the world of observation *must* have a real definition; hence, it cannot be arbitrary. A nominal definition *cannot* be used to discuss the world of observation, for it has no meaning there. Perhaps the best known class of nominal definitions appears in geometry, where such terms as "line," "point," and "angle" are all defined without any reference to observables. Less obviously, most of the terms employed in modern economics are also defined nominally. That is, such terms as "market," "price," or "demand" are not defined by reference to observable events; they are conceptual equivalents to the lines and planes in geometry.

The restrictions that must be imposed on the use of nominal definitions are lethal for anyone seriously concerned with human affairs. Concepts that are nominally defined have no relation to observation and no basis in experience. They simply cannot be used to make statements about the observed world. A zoologist who defined a robin as a four-legged reptile would be attacked immediately by other zoologists for doing so. It would be a gross misuse of the term. If the zoologist then claimed that it was only a nominal definition, that would put an end to the criticism, but it would also mean that everything he had to say about robins would, quite properly, be ignored. Those concerned with observables must define their concepts in real terms. Or, to make the point technically, concepts and definitions must be reversible *simpliciter*. That is, the meaning of a proposition should not change, should remain empirically acceptable, if concept and definition are interchanged. Propositions that are empirically acceptable while they contain the phrase "robin" are likely to lose their capacity to convince if the phrase "four-legged reptile with a hard outer shell" is substituted for "robin" each time it occurs.

Given the dangers, why use nominal definitions at all? Cannot inquiry be limited to real definitions? Unfortunately, the limit would be too strong. The whole of logic and mathematics is built upon nominal definitions and could hardly be dispensed with. In addition, there are other uses for nominal definitions that could not be discarded. First, they are the only means available for introducing new words into the language and new concepts into scientific terminology. Second, they can provide a useful and convenient shorthand for stating complex propositions, making possible great economies in time and space, and simplifying the task of inquiry considerably. Finally, nominal definitions make possible the substitution of terms without pejorative or misleading overtones in propositions where their presence would be harmful. Nominal definitions, properly used, are valuable tools. The problems arise when they are confused with real definitions, or mistakenly employed, as in theory development. As Bierstedt points out, a conceptual scheme is a language and requires only stipulation; a substantive theory is propositional, made up of assertions about the real world. Propositional assertions must have empirical referents. The conclusions drawn from such propositions incorporate truth claims. Such claims are the ultimate goals of inquiry, and they rest, necessarily, on real definitions.

A brief illustration will suggest the kind of problem that confusing real and nominal definitions creates. Suppose that the term "great power conflict" is defined as a vote in the United Nations Security Council in which at least one major power votes on each side of a nonprocedural issue. In context, that *must* be a nominal definition. Otherwise, it is inadequate or wrong. For some of the issues on which the great powers voted against one another, though not procedural, would nonetheless not be considered great power conflicts. Other disagreements that would be classed as great power conflicts do not appear in the Security Council for vote. Nevertheless, suppose it were suggested that the number of such votes could be taken as evidence of an increase in the amount of great power conflicts. Clearly, that supposition would have to be rejected. As it stands, the term "disagreement" refers only to voting within the United Nations, and substitution of the two sets of terms produces statements about great power conflict that are empirically unacceptable. The source of the error is a confusion of real and nominal definitions.

MEASUREMENTS AND INDICATORS

A common source of descriptive inaccuracy is an inadequate relation between concepts and indicators. Every concept must have some observables for indicators that cue the correct use or application of the concept and provide a way of measuring its value. In some cases, indicators are simply properties of the class; the size, shape, and colors that identify a bird as a robin are all part of the attributes of the class. In other cases, class membership must be linked to an indicator by an appropriate set of theories. Thus, the splashes on the surface of a lake that indicate that fish are feeding are linked through a set of connections that include feeding maneuvers and their effects on the surface of the water. The meaning of a concept is always broader than the indicators that cue its use, as the meaning of temperature is different from the observations made on a thermometer that determines its value.

The development of good indicators may require considerable

ingenuity and fairly sophisticated theories. The concept "viscosity," for example, means the amount of friction between the molecules in a liquid. The indicator of viscosity is the rate of flow of the liquid through a tube of given diameter compared to the rate of flow of a standard substance such as water through a tube of the same diameter. The reasoning that establishes the indicator is roughly the following: viscosity is a measure of friction; friction should influence the rate of flow; if nothing interferes, the rate of flow should provide a comparative measure of the amount of viscosity among the molecules. A lie detector uses heartbeat, perspiration, and respiration as indicators of lying. Voice stress analyzers perform the same function by waveform analysis of voice patterns. In recent years, considerable attention has been given to the development of "social indicators"—in sets of observables that will provide an indication of the state of health of the society. Success has been limited, for it turns out to be a very difficult task either to design indicators or to obtain the needed information.[6] As medical practitioners have learned, the value of indicators in diagnosis varies greatly. Dozens of indicators, all precisely measured, may not suffice for diagnosis, while a single indicator, very roughly measured, may provide immediate and highly reliable diagnosis. The point is important in social science, for it is often assumed that increasing the number of factors considered automatically increases the validity of judgment or interpretation. The physician's diagnosis depends on the defining characteristics of a range of diseases as well as knowledge of the specifics that either rule in or rule out some possibilities. A symptom known to occur in only one type of cancer may be far more important in diagnosis than the total number of indicators examined. In Missouri, a bird some eighteen inches high, dark in color, and topped by a fiery knot of red feathers can be identified with near certainty as a pileated woodpecker. No other bird in the region has even remotely similar attributes. The "diagnosis" can rest on that one point.

The indicator serves as the measuring point for the concept. In very general terms, to "measure" means to organize or relate. In that sense, every concept is a measuring instrument, a structure that will discriminate, and every observation is a measurement. A description is a set of measures of the values taken by a set of concepts in a particular set of observations. In other terms, a measurement is the application of a measuring scale to a set of observations. The available scales are of very different quality; the scale used determines the amount of experience summarized in the description, the power or content of the proposition(s). The four major scales, graded from weakest to strongest, are nominal, ordinal, interval, and ratio. Since the scales used to produce a description determine the uses for which that description can be employed, a brief summary of their salient characteristics, which can simply be bypassed by those already familiar with them, may be useful.

Nominal scaling merely differentiates one thing from another without specifying the nature of the difference. "*A* is different from *B*" is a description resulting from nominal scaling. The difference remains unknown, with respect to both kind and amount. It could be vital or trivial. The amount of information in the description is minimal, and there is no external measure to be applied to the things measured—they are merely compared.

Ordinal scaling compares two or more things along a specified continuum—*A* is larger than *B*, for example. There is more information, since the dimension of difference is included, though the amount may be trivial or immense. Again, the measure is made by direct comparison. In a wider context, that information may be very useful. That is, if one of the objects has already been related to other circumstances, knowing that the second object is even larger may be quite useful and significant. Standing alone, the information contained in descriptions employing ordinal scaling is still slight.

If a standard unit of measurement can be developed for any continuum, then observable indicators can be placed on the continuum and measured. Direct comparisons are no longer needed. Two types of units of measurement are possible in principle. The simpler of them is an interval scale; the units here apply to the indicator but not to the concept directly. Each degree of temperature is the same as any other, but the thermometer cannot measure heat or hotness. A volume of water whose temperature is 50° F. is not twice as hot as a volume of water at 25° F. Interval scales do not have a zero point; measurements made with them cannot be expressed as ratios. If two birds were trained to perform specified tasks, and learning time is assumed to be a good indicator of intelligence, time would provide a standard unit of measurement. But it would make no sense to claim that a bird that took only one hour to learn a task was twice as intelligent as a bird that took two hours to learn the same task. The concept "zero point," point of no intelligence, is not appropriate to the situation.

If a standard unit of measurement can be created for a continuum for which it is appropriate to apply the notion of zero point, the result is a ratio scale. Measures made on these scales can legitimately be expressed as ratios. That is, a bird that weighs four pounds is twice as heavy as a bird that weighs only two pounds. Perhaps the most important characteristic of ratio scaling is that the resulting measurements can be treated arithmetically without distortion.

The key to differentiating interval and ratio scales is to focus on the continuum being measured. The characteristics of the continuum determine the kind of unit of measurement that can be produced, the kind of scaling that is possible. If the value of the concept incorporated in the continuum can be measured counting from a zero point, a ratio scale can be produced. Otherwise, only an interval scale is possible for that particular continuum.

Since the distinction between interval and ratio scaling causes much difficulty in discussions of measurements and their uses or limitations, an illustration of the difference may help clarify the questions involved. Suppose that two piles of identical blocks are placed on top of a table in the following way:

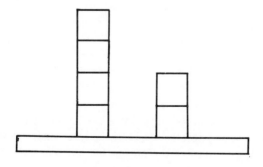

Since the blocks are identical, each can be considered a standard unit of length. There are two blocks in one pile and four blocks in the other; the surface of the table provides a zero point. There can be a "pile" with no blocks in it. It is, therefore, legitimate to assert that one pile of blocks is twice as long as the other. Moreover, if the size of each pile is halved, the ratio will remain constant, if the size is doubled, the ratio will continue, and so on. Because the table top provides a zero point, the piles have measured on a ratio scale.

The effect of eliminating the zero point from the measurement can be achieved by observing the two piles of blocks through a window in a way that blocks the observer's view of the table. Each block in the pile remains as a standard unit of measurement, but the overall quality of the observation is now quite different.

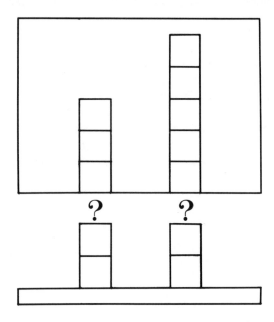

Looking through the window, the observer sees three blocks in one pile and five blocks in the other. The blocks are of the same size. But he can make no statement about the total length of either pile (he has no zero point) and, therefore, cannot make assertions about the ratio of lengths between the two piles. The lack of a zero point seriously reduces the amount of information available to the observer.

The relative value of being able to measure using the four different scales can be expressed in various ways. The two most important implications of type of scale are the amount of information that observation provides and the kinds of calculations or manipulations that can be carried out with the resulting data. The amount of information that can be inferred from propositions that incorporate those measurements is different. Clearly, those factors have a major impact on the quality of the descriptions that can be produced and indirectly affect the human capacity to achieve the purposes of inquiry, generate reliable expectations and control over the environment, and to produce reasoned and defensible choices. Nominal and ordinal scalings are very weak; the information supplied is minimal. In effect, they are little more than comparisons made directly between two or more observables. Such comparisons are not useless. It is worth while to know that bird *A* tastes better than bird *B* when cooked, or that one child is more impetuous than another. Valid comparisons of that order are useful contributions to knowledge. But the really powerful tools in the knowledge supply incorporate additive measures; they make use of interval or ratio scales, particularly the latter. Indeed, some writers do not use the term "measurement" for nominal and ordinal scaling, and others reserve the use of "quantification" for ratio and interval scaling. There is no harm in either practice if consistently followed.

To produce additive measures, the requirements for arithmetical manipulation must be satisfied by the continuum on which measurements are made. Otherwise, arithmetic or statistical manipulation will lead to perverse results. Abraham Kaplan has provided four useful rules for testing the results of measurement to determine whether or not the requirements for additive measurement have been satisfied.[7] First, the outcome of any combination of measures must be the same regardless of the point at which combination begins. Second, the results of combination should be unaffected by the arrangement of the objects counted. Third, when equivalents are combined with equivalents, the results must also be equivalent. Fourth, when one of two equivalents is combined with a third object, the result is no longer equivalent to the original. Measurements that can satisfy these criteria are genuine additives. In effect, the standard units developed for the continuum can be used to measure from a zero point.

The desirability of additive measurements is beyond argument. They facilitate mathematical treatment of the results of inquiry, maximize accuracy, and increase the content of the propositions in which they appear. Unfortunately, the development of additive measures is not a matter of simple choice. The concept to be measured must be amenable to such scaling; suitable indicators must be found; and a standard unit of measurement must be devised. The problem is not a shortage of observables, for any number can be found. But there is a genuine shortage of useful concepts, possibly because of the absence of serious commitment to the achievement of human purposes in the environment. Even more importantly, there are few sound theories available for linking concept to indicator in a reliable way. Psychological testing illustrates the problem very aptly. There is no end of easily quantified information available relating to individual responses to questions of the kind used in intelligence testing. What is difficult is linking that body of information to a meaningful concept. The data can be used to forecast such behavior as success in school or even at work, but the meaning of "intelligence" remains obscure, and the unit of measurement is at best unclear. Moreover, the need for a connecting theory cannot be reduced or eliminated by restricting the meaning of concepts more and more closely to the meaning of indicators. Strict empiricism of that kind poses some not altogether expected hazards. As Wassily Leontief has noted, the empiricist works by abstracting from observation in stages, omitting some factors, averaging results, and aggregating data. This seemingly safe and reasonable practice leads to a genuine and inescapable dilemma:

[the result is the] . . . essentially unsolvable problem of so-called index-number theory. He [the investigator] winds up either with a system of quantitatively well-defined relationships between qualitatively ill-defined variables or with a set of qualitatively indeterminate . . . relationships between sharply defined variables.

Pragmatic pursuit of human purposes helps the inquirer to optimize his choices in that situation, but it cannot eliminate the basic problem.

DESCRIPTIVE ADEQUACY

The accuracy of an observation depends on the quality of the concepts and indicators employed, the type of measurement or scaling available, and the care taken by the observer. Accuracy is important, of course, but accuracy alone is not enough. If descriptive propositions were advertised on the intellectual market solely with respect to accuracy, there would be no buyers. That would be like purchasing a phonograph record because of surface quality without knowing the content. A useful and valuable description will usually reflect all of the information obtained by applying an adequate conceptual framework to a particular situation. Those who employ the conceptual framework should then find the description adequate, other things equal.

The two most fundamental limits on the content of a description are, of course, the availability of concepts and the actual content of the environment. If there are no daisies in a field, or, more precisely, if a competent observer has no perceptions that would justify the assertion "There are daisies in that field," then that proposition cannot be included in a description. On the other hand, the observer may have appropriate perceptions, yet choose not to include the proposition in the description. Whether or not a perception is incorporated into an articulated description depends on the significance attached to the perception. That in turn is a function of the conceptual framework used by the observer, on the purposes for which the description is intended. If the description has no purpose, no good reason could be offered for either including or excluding the information. Again, if the observer does not have a concept of "daisies" or is unfamiliar with them, the presence of the flowers cannot be recorded *as daisies*. The absence of a concept will not determine whether or not the flowers are present in the field, and the observer could note that he had seen some type of flower in the field and describe them using other concepts. If the description is accurate, another person familiar with the class "daisies" should be able to recognize them from the description.

Descriptions contain a record of similarities and differences. Successive sets of descriptions of "the same" situation record differences in sets of differences, and that provides a justification for assuming change. A world without differences could not be described, not least because there would be no describer. An empirical situation in which there were differences but no changes is conceivable in imagination and perhaps approximated in some limited areas for limited times but would be impossible over the long run—equivalent to a zero entropy world, which is not achievable if present cosmological theories are correct. Observed differences that have no known past simply *are*; there is nothing to attract attention if there is no change in the past that could account for differences in the present. The point is very useful for evaluating the work of historians. A history that contains no record of change, no dynamics, would be quite useless for anything but satisfaction of curiosity. Histories that do incorporate dynamics but focus on the "wrong" variables (in terms of the reader's purposes) are very frustrating. Indeed, a social scientist seeking information about the effects of economic innovation on poor populations and finding only information about wars and dynastic successions might come to hold historians in very low repute—unfairly, if the reward system in history is skewed to support studies of war and dynastic succession.

Since every description is an incomplete account of observation, a selection of perceptions from an enormous range of possibilities, the selection requires justification for the description to be taken seriously. Usually, that is based on normative judgments (the significance of the events recorded for human affairs) or on theoretical grounds. In the well-developed sciences, it is often possible to show that certain kinds of observations are needed to fill lacunae in a theory or to show that certain characteristics are part of the defining terms of a given class. In the social sciences, the absence of strong theories tends to reinforce the importance of normative considerations in judging the adequacy of descriptive or historical accounts. One of the more valuable side-effects of encouraging the social sciences to pursue human purposes in their inquiries would be a major improvement in the relevance criteria employed in evaluating research proposals. That practice could also help to eliminate some of the more glaring examples of normative myopia, such as the historian who applauds the growth of industry while ignoring the human degradation or accumulation of waste which such growth involves. The concept of "adequacy" serves to reinforce that tendency. When perceptions are recorded without reference to human purposes or theories, they may be interesting but they do not contribute much to knowledge. On the other hand, descriptions made in the context of a particular theory serve to test the theory; at the very least, they examine the relatedness of particular variables or factors in the environment. Otherwise, description is little more than a casual excursion into verbal photography with a partly covered lens.

CONCEPTUAL FRAMEWORKS

No observer, not excluding the poet, goes into the world with an utterly random set of concepts to record perceptions. That is a human impossibility. Observations, even those of a casual nature, tend to be organized and structured. Releasing consciousness from that structure is an exceptionally difficult task and perhaps impossible without drugs or some other external agent. Human observers do not store their concepts in isolated units, matching them more or less haphazardly against the incoming flow of perceptions. Instead, concepts are clustered or grouped to form *conceptual frameworks*, sets of concepts or variables that come to be used together in the pursuit of certain sets of purposes in the environment. What identifies an individual as physician, electrician, biologist, and so on is primarily the conceptual framework employed in daily work. The framework is closely related to the theoretical assumptions on which the daily work depends, focusing on the factors that relate to occupational purposes and excluding other things. Even casual observation, such as scanning a newspaper, tends to seek "attention-capturing" materials in the headlines, and they are usefully construed as signals that bring into play a particular conceptual framework. Needless to say, those who put the newspaper together make use of a conceptual framework that incorporates the assumed conceptual framework of the reader to assign position and status to different items included in the paper.

Conceptual frameworks provide the observer with sets of spectacles for viewing or screening the flow of incoming perceptions; each is ground to a particular prescription, dictated by experience. The framework calls attention to some events and excludes others, more or less automatically. However, every person makes use of a very large repertoire of frameworks, developed for use in different situations. Incoming perceptions (or intentional actions) cue the use of a different structure. The effect of a very pretty young woman passing a construction site, for example, suggests the manner in which such switching operates.

Curiously enough, relatively little attention has been given to the particular conceptual frameworks employed in different cultures, how they develop, modify, and improve. Their role in everyday life is, of course, enormous. Without them, the individual would be literally swamped with incoming perceptions and unable to differentiate them or react appropriately—like the unfortunate wild animal newly placed in a cage and displayed to a crowd. The initial phase in the intellectual development of the child is acquisition of frameworks in which the major danger signals relevant to its environment can be located, along with the major sources of comfort, happiness, and security. By maturity, the individual acquires an astonishing range of conceptual frameworks, ranging from complex systems engendered by mathematical or scientific training to the structures appropriate for participation in minor social encounters. Each is cued by appropriate perceptions or by an internal mechanism that brings the apparatus into focus or into control of conscious concern.

The significance of any perception is a function of the conceptual framework in which it is observed. The physician responds immediately to the sight of arterial blood spurting from a wound, the ornithologist to the rare bird, the skillful hunter to the sight of disturbed vegetation. Unfortunately, there are few good parallels to those situations in the social sciences. The sight of a rare bird means nothing to the individual who does not know it is rare. Following Stephen Toulmin, such unusual or eye-catching events can be labeled *phenomena*, setting them apart from routine or expected perceptions—events that current knowledge can account for readily.[9] Conceptual frameworks are also needed to call attention to the nonevent, the failure of the expected. A framework that can call attention to unusual events or nonevents will usually incorporate sets of relations that are actually rudimentary theories or explanations. Use of the framework over time serves to strengthen and clarify those relations and in due course to spin off recognized and well-articulated theories. The absence of frameworks that are widely used to explore various classes of events is usually a good sign of a theoretically undeveloped discipline. The conceptual frameworks, or "approaches," are likely to develop before theories become available in a field. Indeed, if the sociology of knowledge were adequately buttressed by historical evidence, it might be possible to urge the development of conceptual frameworks as an essential prerequisite to theory development.

In the social sciences, where theories are weak and the supply of conceptual frameworks limited, some of the effects of weakness are readily observed. The focus of inquiry tends to be governed by tradition or fad rather than by theoretical considerations or normative purposes. The results of inquiry are only rarely useful for the achievement of individual or social purposes. Political scientists, for example, can provide some valuable information for those seeking to win election to Congress, but they have little to offer those concerned with improvements in community housing, transportation, health, and other major dimensions of community life. Moreover, the conceptual frameworks that are used to deal with specific problems such as housing or transportation have not been integrated, either in academia or in government. In consequence, the poor are placed in new housing without supplying the habits, knowledge, or resources needed to maintain it properly; transport systems are created that actually contribute to congestion and pollution without alleviating traffic problems; urban renewal programs displace the poor, destroy a large part of the stock of cheap and solid housing, and create Indian reservations in the older central cities that are almost totally dependent on transfer payments.[10] Such results are at least partly the result of conceptual inadequacy, though that inadequacy may itself be a reflection of underlying normative commitments.

An examination of the conceptual frameworks employed within a society for individual and collective purposes is a useful technique for uncovering faults, distortions, and inadequacies. One major function of the educational system, for example, is to supply those passing through with the conceptual apparatus needed for dealing with individual and social problems. Or, put another way, the manner in which such problems are handled will be determined very largely by the conceptual/theoretical apparatus supplied the individual by the educational system. Much can be learned about both the adequacy of education and the aberrations in the conceptual apparatus being generated in the young, by an examination of the substance of these structures. More generally still, the kinds of conceptual apparatus available in society provide a good index to the society's capacity to generate and use knowledge. Detailed and complex conceptual frameworks, requiring years to master and apply, imply social conditions which not every society can meet: availability of surplus resources, division of labor and specialization, availability of sophisticated capital equipment, and so on.

Powerful tools can be dangerous as well as beneficial; conceptual frameworks are no exception to the rule. Once a conceptual framework has been internalized, modification becomes increasingly difficult and elimination virtually impossible. In thinking as in walking, the well-worn trails that mark a successful past effort and promise least present resistance are most often walked. That may suggest why the young, who have not yet carved the grooves of the mind for major purposive action, tend to contribute most in areas where creativity is greatest. I am informed that no one over the age of thirty has made a really major contribution to mathematics, for example. As users become more and more habituated to their conceptual frameworks, they cease to be aware of them. Lack of self-consciousness increases still more the rigidity of the apparatus and the danger of bias. Moreover, each framework contains a potential bias, virtually impossible to anticipate and eliminate, arising out of the reactions it produces in others. For example, assume that all of the children in the first grade of an inner city school system were found to suffer from some degree of malnutrition. Then consider the implications of reporting that information in a variety of conceptual frameworks or descriptive contexts.

First, by using the conceptual framework of a nutritionist, the condition of the children will be described in terms of dietary deficiencies. Recommended remedial action will be articulated as diet modifications. The descriptive account implies no blame, and remedial actions are divorced from the responsibilities associated with any particular person involved with the situation. The report is affectively neutral. Described from the point of view of a social worker concerned primarily with parental neglect and its implications for physical development, the information will tend to foster hostility toward the parents for failing to care properly for their children. Again, if the information is supplied in the context of a discussion of the manner in which public authorities handle social problems, that will tend to generate hostility toward public authority, sympathy for parents, and perhaps a demand for public action. Such built-in biases can have serious repercussions for everyone involved with the situation—children, parents, and public agencies alike.

What emerges from a systematic examination of the relations that hold among descriptions, concepts, theories, and human purposes is the close connection and constant interplay of observation and theory, patterns and perceptions, possibilities and purposes, as knowledge systems develop. If the available concepts cannot be fitted to actual perceptions, they are useless, whether they refer to normative or empirical matters. And a society can "grow out of" its conceptual apparatus as surely as a child grows out of its clothing. The importance of maintaining a close link between observation and the fulfillment of purpose, between the academic enterprise and the human enterprise, could hardly be greater. And the set of interests, concerns, and purposes that currently guides the society needs much closer scrutiny if it is to provide the direction that systematic inquiry requires. When actions must be taken under conditions of extreme uncertainty, which is probably unavoidable given the course of human affairs, they can at least be taken in a state of awareness that will generate learning—a nontrivial side benefit. For social science as for agriculture, human consumption of the product should appear in the bottom line, as the final judgment of what has been accomplished.

NOTES

1. See Carl G. Hempel, *Fundamentals of Concept Formation in the Empirical Sciences*, Vol. II, No. 7, *International Encyclopedia of Unified Science* (University of Chicago Press, 1952), and *Aspects of Scientific Explanation* (Free Press, 1965), esp. Ch. 6.; Paul F. Lazarsfeld, "Concept Formation and Measurement in the Behavioral Sciences: Some Historical Observations," in Gordon J. Direnzo, ed., *Concepts, Theory, and Explanation in the Behavioral Sciences* (Random House, 1966); and Stephen Toulmin, *Human Understanding*, Vol. I (Princeton University Press, 1972).

2. Typically, Irving M. Copi, *Introduction to Logic*, 2d ed. (Macmillan, 1961), Ch. 3.

3. U.S. Department of Housing and Urban Development, *Housing Allowances: The 1976 Report to Congress* (U.S. Government Printing Office, 1976), Tulsa Housing Authority, *Experimental Housing Allowance Program: Final Report* (October 1975), or Vernon K. Smith, *Welfare Work Incentives: The Earnings Exemption and Its Impact upon AFDC Employment, Earnings, and Program Cost* (Michigan Department of Social Services, 1974).

4. The discussion follows Robert Bierstedt, "Nominal and Real Definitions in Sociological Theory," in L. Gross, ed., *Symposium on Sociological Theory* (Harper and Row, 1959).

5. Ibid., p. 126.

6. See Eugene J. Meehan, "The Social Indicator Movement," *Frontiers of Economics*, 1975, and "Social Indicators and Policy Analysis," in Frank P. Scioli, Jr., and Thomas J. Cook, eds., *Methodologies for Analyzing Public Policies* (Lexington Books, 1975). For example, see *Measuring Social Well-Being, A Progress Report on the Development of Social Indicators* (Organization for Economic Cooperation and Development, 1976), and *Perspective Canada II, A Compendium of Social Statistics 1977* (Ministry of Supply and Services, Canada, 1977). *Social Indicators 1973* (U.S. Government Printing Office, 1973), Morris D. Morris, *Measuring the Condition of the World's Poor: The Physical Quality of Life Index* (Pergamon Press, 1979), *Science Indicators 1978, Report of the National Science Board* (U.S. Government Printing Office, 1979), or Philip B. Price, et al. *Measurement and Predictors of Physician Performance: Two Decades of Intermittently Sustained Research* (Aaron Press, 1971). But see also *Personal Privacy in an Information Society*, The Report of the Privacy Protection Study Commission (U.S. Government Printing Office, 1977).

7. Abraham Kaplan, *The Conduct of Inquiry: Methodology for Behavioral Science* (Chandler Publishing Co., 1964), pp. 184-185.

8. Wassily Leontief, "The Problem of Quality and Quantity in Economics," in Daniel Lerner, ed., *Quantity and Quality* (Free Press, 1961), pp. 127-28.

9. Stephen Toulmin, *Foresight and Understanding: An Enquiry into the Aims of Science* (Harper and Row, 1963).

10. Norton E. Long, *The Unwalled City: Reconstituting the Urban Community* (Basic Books, 1972).

Expectations

In normal usage, to expect or to anticipate means to look forward to or to predict an event that has not yet been observed. The implicit claim in a statement of expectations is that an observation made at some time and place to be specified will produce a particular description. The expectation usually refers to the future, but it is sometimes reasonable and useful to develop expectations about the unobserved past—to assume that yesterday's heavy rains will have flooded a particular creek and made the road impassable, for example. Expectations cannot legitimately refer to observations already known to the person making the prediction. It would be an abuse of language to speak of "expecting" rain after it has fallen or "expecting" a horse to win a race when the outcome is known. The language used to state expectations need not be confined to the verb "expect." Such phrases as "It should rain tomorrow," "I expect that it will rain tomorrow," "I believe it will rain tomorrow," or simply "It will rain tomorrow" all state the same expectation. The strength of the expectation will vary, but the certainty implied by the use of "will" cannot be justified. The strongest claim that can be made is a probability that closely approximates 100 percent, perhaps strengthened by a willingness to wager a substantial portion of resources available on the outcome. In most cases, the substance of the expectation will be a change or the absence of change: The mountain will be there tomorrow; the pond will be frozen over by morning. In some cases, the expectation is independent of human action, a statement about the drift course of events, and can be produced by a forecast. In other cases, the expectation refers to the consequences of human action and must be produced by a theory.

Stated more precisely and technically, an expectation is contained in a proposition that specifies the content of a description produced from observations not yet made or available. Analytically, the content of the expectation is precisely equivalent to the description. A very simple notation can produce an accurate summary of descriptive content. Each element in the description, each variable (written V), falls within a set of square brackets that identify the selection of concepts used to make the observations. The values of those variables are determined by measurement. The value of the variable "color," for example, may be "red" or "green" and so on. The relational terms employed in the description, which link the variables in a static pattern, are included within the set in the following way:

$$[\quad V_1 \ V_2 \ V_3 \ldots V_n \quad Rel_1 \ Rel_2 \ldots Rel_n \quad]$$

The square brackets indicate an "open" set or selection, that is, a structure that cannot be calculated. The notation helps to suggest the precise kind of argument or justification that expectations or predictions require.

The conception of "expectations" employed here is relatively loose; hence, it is easy to verbalize an expectation as long as justifications are not demanded or offered. A reasoned or justified expectation, however, must be supported by reasons and argument. The man who predicts rain for the following day but is unable to give reasons why he should be believed is indulging in prophecy rather than reasoned forecasting. Such expectations are beyond criticism or reasoned discussion because they carry with them no justification for acceptance or belief. Of course, when the lifetime resident of an area announces that rain can be expected on the following day, and the local natives emerge the next morning carrying umbrellas, it may be wise to follow suit. The prophet's track record may provide the reasons for attending his prophecies that the prophet's reasoning lacks. In one limited sense, the quality of a forecast or prediction is independent of the forecaster's ability to justify accepting it. But without knowing the grounds on which the expectation is based, there is no way to convince others. The quality of the forecast is untestable. It is therefore beyond improvement and can only be argued *ad hominem*. Of course, experienced persons may be able to produce reliable forecasts without knowing how the task is accomplished, as a good "natural" golfer may swing his club correctly without knowing how he does it. But the knowledge on which such activities depend usually dies with the person. If a weather forecast is needed for the morrow, and the oldest living resident has the best track record in the area, it may be wise to accept his forecast, even in the absence of reasons, and particularly in the absence of reasons to the contrary. For developing and improving forecasting capacity, however, those conditions are unsatisfactory.

If expectations are produced using the generalized procedure proposed in Chapter 1, they are open to testing and justification. A pattern must be assumed which links one set of observables (the cue) to a second set of observables (the expectation) by rule under specified limiting conditions. The rules incorporated into the pattern must link the content of two descriptions separated in time. Since each description consists of a set of variables whose values are determined by observation, plus the appropriate relational statements, the rules contained in the pattern will link the values taken by the variables. The selection of variables is controlled by reducing the value of a variable to zero, thus eliminating it from the set. The dynamics are simple: if a bird is observed, and some pattern is available which generates an expectation that the bird will migrate south in autumn; the pattern must somehow link that bird to the act of migration. Both observables must lie within the pattern and be connected by rule. Two basic forms can be used to generate and justify expectations. With respect to each form, two prime questions must be asked by the critic or answered in reasoned argument: first, the logical question whether the expectation is justified given the initial cue and the pattern that has been applied; second, whether the pattern itself can be justified, and whether it has been applied correctly to the situation.

A Digression on "Change." The central feature in purposeful inquiry is almost invariably change, or perhaps the absence of change. But change as object of inquiry is a major source of confusion, perhaps philosophically more than empirically. Change is not directly observed; changes cannot appear in descriptions. Change must be assumed (some philosophers and logicians prefer to say "inferred"); the assumption can then be supported by reference to successive descriptions of the same set of observables. If the color of a man's hair is brown at age forty and white at age sixty, it is usual to say that his hair has changed color. Descriptively, the value of the man's "color of hair" variable would be brown at age forty; the value of that same variable at age sixty would be white. The potential difficulty in the process arises out of the need to assume that it is the same man. For if it is uncertain that the "same thing" has been observed and described on successive occasions, there is no basis for claiming that change has occurred. In a famous example, every original piece of wool in a sock was replaced over time as the sock was darned; if the sock was also converted in color, would it be proper to claim that "the sock" had changed color? If every cell in the human body (excepting bone) is replaced several times in a lifetime, is it proper to speak of the "same person" when all of the constituent elements in the body have been altered?

When changes are identified in an individual, a finite geographic area, or even a set of institutional arrangements, few insurmountable conceptual problems are created by the usage. But when corporate bodies such as the Supreme Court, the Senate, or a large corporation are treated in the aggregate, the result may be seriously misleading. Yet, it is quite usual to find such collectivities treated as entities, or even as personalities, in the media or in texts. When the newspapers announce that "The Chase Manhattan Bank today raised the prime interest rate," the precise meaning is clear enough—the management of the bank acted through its regular procedures in a particular way. But what is to be made of such propositions as "Between 1945 and 1975, the Supreme Court changed its mind about the meaning of the First Amendment to the Constitution"? Are such propositions analogous to confusing the attributes of two different persons? Do they involve a suppressed composition fallacy? Certainly as the proposition is stated, it could not be researched. If it is assumed that the author intended to ask, "Why did the Supreme Court decisions made in 1945 incorporate a different meaning for the First Amendment than the decisions made in 1970?," then the question is answerable, but such interpretation is technically improper. None of the problems associated with the use of aggregates, or with the study of change, is insoluble, but they need to be handled with particular care because they are so easily mishandled.

GENERATING EXPECTATIONS USING CLASSIFICATIONS

A reasoned expectation is cued by a description, generated by a known pattern, and incorporated into a second description. Once the pattern is assumed to hold, observing the cue justifies the expectation. A very simple example may help to clarify the process and the justification. Assume a substance that is known to burn as soon as it makes contact with oxygen. If a small amount of that substance is observed being taken from water and placed on an open dish, it can be expected that the substance will ignite and burn spontaneously. Justification for that expectation must be provided in two stages. First, accepting the initial assumption, it must be shown that the expectation is correct. If the substance is assumed to burn when it makes contact with oxygen, does that justify assuming that it will burn when taken from water and exposed to air? In this case, the inference is clearly proper because the air contains free oxygen. The initial assumption takes the form: Substance + Oxygen $\longrightarrow$ Burning. The cue must be an observation of the substance in oxygen; what was observed was Substance + Air, but the air includes oxygen; therefore, the cue was adequate. It follows that once the pattern is assumed, Burning is to be expected. The logic is correct. In the next stage of justification, the pattern itself is questioned. If the pattern is already well established in physical science or elsewhere, that will be considered sufficient warrant for assuming adequate justification. In social science, where the supply of well-established patterns is very limited, the quality of the pattern will have to be examined. Indeed, justification of the pattern is likely to be more important than affirming the correctness of the logical reasoning used to generate the expectations.

CLASSIFICATIONS

One of the two instruments that can be used to generate justified expectations is the classification or concept. Classifications are general in form, not limited in time and space; they include all of the established properties shared by every member of the class. In effect, classifications are stored human experience, suitably generalized. Structurally, a classification consists of a selection of variables and a set of rules that specify the limits of the values for each variable that defines the class. The class "robins" will be defined by size, shape, color, feeding habits, migratory patterns, bone structure and so on. Identifiable subclasses, such as young robins, may have distinctive features, such as spotted breasts of a different color from mature birds. Moreover, there will always be a few birds that differ from the norm, perhaps significantly. They will lack essentials or have characteristics unusual for members of the class. One of the more difficult judgments required in classification arises from the need to treat such exceptions or aberrations. When they are infrequent and minor, no problem arises, but at some point, reclassification or subclassification may be required to maintain useful concepts. In medicine, that can be a very important matter: classifications provide the basis for much routine treatment, even of serious cases, and knowing when a patient is likely to respond to normal treatment and when special treatment is required may be a matter of life and death. In all cases, classifications are modified to fit what is observed, and not the converse. Otherwise, endless examples of highly developed but utterly useless classification could be produced in a relatively short period of time.

The structure of classifications can be used to demonstrate the way in which they are used to generate reliable expectations. Each classification consists of a set of variables and the rules that stipulate the range of values they can take. The selection is an important part of the classification, and the set is contained in closed or curved brackets:

$$(\quad V_1 \ V_2 \ V_3 \ V_4 \ V_5 \ldots V_n \quad R_1 \ R_2 \ R_3 \ R_4 \ R_5 \ldots R_n \quad)$$

The substance or content of the pattern, it must be emphasized, is established independently out of the results of observation over time. Everything observed that has all of the attributes included in the set is a member of the class as defined. All members of the set have all of those attributes, barring occasional abberations.

If a classification has already been established, and its content is known, an expectation can be generated in a relatively simple three-step process or sequence. First, something in the environment must be observed to have some of the defining attributes of the members of the class—say both V_1 and V_2 fall within the range prescribed by R_1 and R_2. Second, it must be assumed on the basis of that observation that the thing observed in fact *is* a member of the class. Third, a set of expectations, consisting in the remaining attributes of that class, is developed logically out of the structure. The logic of the process is elemental:

> All members of class C have properties P
> X is a member of class C
> $\therefore$ X will have properties P

The expectation is the sum of the established but not yet observed properties of the class, plus or minus any conditions peculiar to the situation. For example, in some parts of the United States, robins do not migrate in winter.

Most of the fundamentals of developing expectations through classifications can be illustrated within that elementary context. First, the entire process is contingent on the availability of a classification, already established or justified. An observed "cue" actually is part of the classification and is not independent of it. Second, the power of the classification depends on the residual properties available after identification. If a class had only four properties and a member of the class could not be identified reliably until all four had been observed, the classification could not be used to generate expectations. It would be otiose. Third, the identification could be mistaken, in which case expectations would be frustrated. Finally, the classification itself could be poor, the attributes not really applicable, and the results of action grossly different from expectations. Each of these aspects of the process can be tested and improved in application.

WHY CLASSIFICATIONS WORK

The reasons why good classifications produce reliable predictions are found in the way classifications are created and justified. If the metaphor is not pursued too strongly, a classification can be likened to a battery in which knowledge and experience are organized and stored. The way in which the battery is designed and built determines what can be obtained from it later. A brief illustration of the way in which a classification might develop will suggest the major factors contributing to the quality of the end product. The example is drawn from ornithology, but any observable would serve. Since birds are common and wholly disconnected from the kinds of affective responses that might be aroused by political or social examples, they are useful for illustrating the process.

Classifications begin with, and are limited to, what has been observed. Before birds can be classified there must be birds and birds must be observed. Classification also requires a human classifier, an appropriate set of concepts, a language, and a conception of what classification involves—how it is done, why they are needed, and so on. Classifications are based on real and not nominal definitions. Such things may seem obvious, but a great many classifications are produced without any particular purpose in mind. Others do not actually begin with observations and do not consist in the organization of observables. Some are simply generated from an overarching conceptual framework through formal logic—or even created ad hoc using the language of some conceptual framework.

The classification process begins with a collection of birds that have not previously been observed by the individual who will perform the classifying. Assume that all of the birds are either black or white, long-tailed or short-tailed, and have a straight beak or a curved beak. Direct observation is presumed to be limited to these three variables: color, length of tail, and shape of beak. Each variable can have two and only two values. The set of permutations that exhausts the logical possibilities is readily established:

1. black, long tail, straight beak
2. black, long tail, curved beak
3. black, short tail, straight beak
4. etc. etc.

While the permutations might be useful in preparing for the inquiry, classification depends on observed differences and not logical potential. Enough classes are needed to organize the birds actually observed, no more. Somewhere in the universe, there may be a bird with white feathers, short wings, and a curved beak, but if it is not observed where the classification is being made, there is no point in reserving a place for them. The "rule of parsimony" stated by William of Occam in the fourteenth century remains sound advice: do not multiply entities needlessly.

For simplicity, assume next that all of the birds observed fall into one of three groups or classes, identified by reference to color, tail size, and beak shape:

1. black, long tail, straight beak
2. black, short tail, curved beak
3. white, short tail, straight beak

The three classes can be named or labeled: (1) GOK, (2) MOK, and (3) SOK. The class names are purely nominal definitions. It would be pointless to ask whether a black bird with a long tail and straight beak was really a GOK—that is all that the symbol GOK means.

This simple, three-element classification scheme allows for quick and accurate identification of any bird seen. Every white bird is a SOK; every bird with a curved beak is a MOK: every bird with a long tail is a GOK. Moreover, the structure can generate reliable expectations. A white bird observed at a distance is readily identified as a SOK, and it can safely be assumed that it will have a short tail and a straight beak. Every bird with a curved beak will also be black and have a short tail. The classification is accurate and easy to use. Is it, then, a high-quality classification? Clearly not! The structure can produce expectations, but they are unlikely to interest a human observer unless that person was for some reason trying to fill in a list of "birds spotted" as a matter of personal achievement. The classification has little discernible relation to any human purpose, save, perhaps, the wealth and distinction obtained from successful authorship of a classification. In fact, the classification could be greatly enriched, extended to include nesting habits, number and type of feathers, visual capacity, and so on and yet remain virtually useless.

Classifications intended for serious use must have a purpose; that purpose will determine the significant attributes of class members. If birds are classified in ways that will be useful to a farmer, or anyone else, those aspects of the class that relate directly to members of the human species become a matter of prime concern. If MOKs are tasty when broiled, easy to snare, and highly nutritious, that is worth knowing, particularly if MOKs are plentiful. If SOKs are dedicated and voracious consumers of insects that injure countless millions of dollars worth of crops each year, that is a matter of considerable interest to farmers who may wish to protect, nurture, and even deliberately foster the species. One of the curiosities of natural history is the extent to which the natural historians have managed to escape all responsibility for the widespread ignorance among farmers and ranchers of the value to man of the various birds and animals they have slaughtered with such recklessness—coyotes, eagles, wolves, and so on.

The use of classifications to generate expectations provides a perfect example of the power of tautologous expressions, that is, expressions in the form $A = A$. If a black bird with a long tail and straight beak is a GOK, then asserting that a GOK is black or has a long tail is tautologous, true by definition. But the definition of a GOK is real and not nominal, and that gives it power. For it justifies the assumption that a bird with a long tail and straight beak has been seen *before* those attributes are observed. While the assumption is uncertain or problematic in some degree, the process solves the knowledge problem in principle, and that is all that an ongoing enterprise requires.

While classifications are produced from observations and are most easily illustrated by reference to "natural" phenomena such as birds, they can be developed for human artifacts and for humans themselves. A bird is no more "natural" than a house or a family; both are classified by the same procedures; the classifications are justified and used in the same way. A distinction between what appeared in the environment before man entered and what man has created or modified is sometimes useful, but that is another matter.

The classification process, like any other human procedure, can be misused or abused, resulting in classifications of very poor quality. While the social sicences do not often generate good classifications, there is no reason in principle why they should not. Unfortunately, the quality of the available supply of classifications or concepts lends some credence to the arguments of those who believe that the instruments and processes employed in physical science are wholly inappropriate to social science. Efforts to produce typologies based on such factors as head shape, climactic conditions, race, ethnicity, or religious affiliation and to link those attributes to such diverse behaviors as creativity, criminal activity, or laziness do nothing to improve the reputation of the disciplines involved. The answer to such nonsense is to know the minimum requirements for sound classification and to insist on them rather than deny the validity of the whole effort to classify.

ARGUING EXPECTATIONS BASED ON CLASSIFICATIONS

Analytically, three major assumptions are required to justify an expectation. The pattern or instrument employed must be acceptable; the pattern must fit or apply to the situation in hand; and the expectation must be a forced conclusion, a logical implication, of the pattern. A common example will illustrate the process by which expectations are argued or justified. Suppose that Smith sees Jones bitten by a snake. Smith assumes from what he has seen that the reptile was a copperhead; he assumes further from what he has heard that the bite of the copperhead is always fatal to man. From those two assumptions, he infers that Jones is going to die. Jones, who must either say his prayers or seek assistance, is understandably concerned about the quality of Smith's reasoning. He asks to have the argument deployed.

Three points in the argument are crucial. First, did Smith identify the class correctly? Was the reptile really a copperhead? Second, what is the content of the classification? What attributes have been established for the snake? Is the bite of a copperhead always fatal for humans? Third, has the logic been correctly applied? If the first and second points are as Smith has stated them, does it follow logically that Jones will die?

Put another way, argument and justification will focus on three questions: Was the classification correctly applied? Were the class attributes correctly stated? Were the logical calculations carried out properly? The formal and logical dimensions of argument will not be examined at any length here, of course, but their inclusion serves as a useful reminder of the importance of logical competence in systematic inquiry and criticism. The significance of the three questions is readily established. If the snake was not a copperhead, the expectation is unwarranted whether or not the classification is accurate and the logic correct. If the class is identified correctly but the attributes of the class are wrongly stated, the conclusion is again unjustified. Finally, if the classification is both identified and defined correctly, does it follow that Jones is doomed? The logic is simple: If copperhead bites are deadly (All A is B), and Jones has been bitten by a copperhead (X is A), then Jones is certainly on his way out (X is B). Note particularly that Jones' death does not confirm the reasoning simply because it corresponds to the conclusion. Unless all three steps in the argument are correct, the whole is flawed and unacceptable.

The formal and logical aspects of argument and justification will now be left aside, and the considerations involved in the application of a classification to the environment, or the development of the attributes of a class, will be examined more closely.

Applying Classifications. How to know one when it appears? Identification of class membership is one of the basic problems in social science, if only because any observable is in principle open to classification in a number of ways. One of the first problems in criticism is to find clues in the context that can narrow the search. In the case of snake-bite, the critical concern is clearly the danger to man. Had Jones been on the verge of starvation, the conceptual pattern applied to the reptile might have been quite different.

If *all* the attributes of a class appear in observation, a member of the class has been observed. If identification cannot be made until that point is reached, the quality of the classification may be less than it should be. Usually, identification is assumed before all class attributes have been observed; otherwise, the identification would not be of any use. There is always some measure of uncertainty in the assumption. The complexity of the process depends on the nature of the concepts and the kinds of indicators that have been supplied. Experts can disagree on the question of whether or not a recession has begun, whether or not a given person is psychotic, whether war is imminent, or whether criminals have been rehabilitated. Such concerns are not trivial, and they have been studied exhaustively; they remain uncertain. Even in such areas as medicine, different types of diagnoses are subject to different levels of uncertainty, and in some cases, fortunately rare, the diagnostic capacity of the profession is very low indeed.

In general, the question what constitutes an adequate indicator for a class, what justifies the assumption that a particular observable belongs in a class, is answered out of experience, and the answer is improved through experience with answering the question. If an assumption is based on one cluster of attributes, use of that cluster provides a test of the viability of the cluster as a warranted or justified indicator. If one set of cues is tried and fails, it must be augmented or modified and tried again. Over time, systematic experimentation can establish the relative validity of different sets of cues, and that information becomes the basis for arguing in favor of an application or diagnosis. When conditions are difficult, as in emergency situations, diagnosis may be acceptable that would otherwise be considered inadequately based. Indeed, one of the best means available for pursuing the question is to work out the kind of argument that could be offered in a court of law to defend reliance upon a particular diagnosis in different medical circumstances.

Identifying Class Attributes. The question what attributes should be considered part of the attributes of a class raises in microcosm nearly all of the fundamentals that a theory of inquiry must resolve. The attributes of a class, for example, develop out of observations of particular members of that class. The elements of the class are both historically and analytically prior to the classification. Every element in the class is in some respects unique and different from all of the others, if only positionally. In most cases, not every member of a class can be observed; of the classes that can be enumerated exhaustively, few are interesting. Yet, class attributes can only include those properties that are distributed within the population and shared by every member of the class. Moreover, knowledge of the class, speaking very strictly, is limited to those attributes. It is quite improper to transfer what is known of a particular member of a class, say my standard schnauzer, to the class as a whole, although we all sin in this way at some time or another. The attributes of a class are therefore assumptions, often rather vague and imprecise in content, and not infrequently mistaken, misleading, or at least much more uncertain than they appear in formal statements.

Consider the situation described earlier in which Jones was bitten by a reptile identified as a copperhead. Is the bite fatal? Taken literally, the question is probably unanswerable. Observation and experience are not always decisive or even very clear. Copperhead bites, examined randomly or objectively, might be fatal in the first fifty cases observed and not fatal in the next twenty. If observation stopped after forty, fifty, sixty, or seventy cases, the judgment of fatality would be different in each case. No matter how many observations were made of "copperhead bites" in that gross sense, the residual error is likely to be substantial. The class of events labeled "copperhead bites" is also heterogeneous, for much depends on where the bite was located, how deeply the teeth penetrated, and so on.

If the problem is attacked in a more roundabout way, a rather more accurate set of attributes can be developed. If chemical data relating to the effects of the venom on the human body can be obtained, perhaps differentiated to show the amount of venom injected, the location of the injection, and the size and state of health of the person, that could lead to a much more precise classification of "copperhead bite" and its effects. Careful experimentation could establish the limiting conditions in which the expectations would hold. Jones may acquire immunity in some manner; the venom may lose some of its power under certain circumstances. The end result might be a classification that would generate expectations in the form: if a mature male in good health is bitten by a full-grown copperhead but the venom is not injected directly into the bloodstream, the individual can be expected to survive if specified actions can be taken within a given time period.

The key to improvement in classifications, as with most intellectual tools, is continued observation and use. Since any observable that meets all of the defining characteristics of a class is a member of that class, the results of use are probably the best overall index to the accuracy of the classification and to its usefulness. Classifications are created by selecting observables on the basis of their similarities. In very general terms, the object of classification is economy. Treating each "thing" in the environment as an individual unit places an impossible burden on the individual; things must be generalized and treated as classes. But that means that the things brought together must be homogeneous with respect to specified traits, whether that involves an expectation about the behavior of things within the class or an expectation about the way members of a class will react to some specific stimulus or action. That characteristic of classifications gives us the essential clue to improvement. If too few variables are included in the classification, it will not distinguish adequately between members and non-members, and the class is likely to be very heterogeneous—an undesirable feature. By increasing the number of class attributes, which is dependent upon the classifier's judgment and not on nature (every observable could in principle be classified by an infinite set of attributes), heterogeneity is reduced and the classification is made more accurate. However, the applicability of the class is then much restricted. In effect, the same index problem noted with respect to measures arises in classification (see above, p. 54. If defining terms are multiplied, any class can be reduced to a single member, which is pointless—except, perhaps for sportscasters seeking a "new angle" on every commonplace they report. At the other extreme, a class so loosely defined that every observable belongs to it does not discriminate at all and is worthless. Where the line is drawn depends on the purposes of the user and the amenability of the subject matter. A classification of microbes that is adequate for a general practitioner in medicine may be grossly inadequate for an immunologist. But an inadequate classification may be the best classification possible, in which case there is little option to using it.

GENERATING EXPECTATIONS WITH FORECASTS (OR THEORIES)

Classifications generate expectations by grouping observables according to their shared attributes and applying that generalized body of information to new situations. The patterns are static; the rules incorporated into the structure place limits on the values that attribute variables can take. The major weakness in classifications, which is a function of the way in which they are created, is their inability to deal with change over time. For generating expectations about change, two instruments are available—forecasts and theories. They are identical in structure but rest on different assumptions and can therefore perform different functions. Each produces forecasts in the same way, however; hence, they can be considered together. The principal difference between them is the ability of theories to predict the effects of human action.

Although the meanings attached to "theory" and "forecast" here correspond fairly closely to current scientific usage, it is more important to be clear about structures, processes, and limitations than to argue labels. Both forecasts and theories consist of a set of two or more variables whose values are linked by rule, plus a set of limiting conditions. The heart of the structure is the set of rules, for the variables are embedded in them. Forecasts are based upon covariance in the past and can be used only to generate predictions. They do not provide a basis for intervention and cannot be tested in use. Theories have precisely the same structure but incorporate a causal assumption relating the variables. Therefore, they do provide an intervention strategy, and they can be tested and improved in use. For purposes of prediction, the two instruments can be collapsed and treated together.

DEVELOPMENT AND USE

Forecasts commonly take one of two basic forms: static and dynamic. In the static form, the rule links specific values of the variables included in the structure. For example, if the value of X is at M, the value of B will be at N, or if the price of cotton is high, then the price of land in Texas will also be high. In the dynamic form, which has the same cognitive status, and is produced and justified in the same way, the rule links changes in the values of the variables. For example, if the value of variable A increases, then the value of variable B will increase, or if the price of cotton increases, the price of land in Texas will increase. No causal connection is implied or required for such propositions. On the other hand, the possibility of a causal relation is not denied. If the average daily temperature can be used to forecast demand for ice cream, that does not imply that the higher temperature caused the increase in demand. On the other hand, the higher temperatures may in fact cause increased demand for ice cream. The absence of a causal assumption is important because covariance is much easier to locate and justify than a genuine causal relation.

Forecasts are simple instruments, easy to construct and apply, and very widely used, though not always consciously.[1] Forecasts vary with respect to the number of variables employed and the complexity of the calculations involved, but they all depend on a simple principle—projection of past trends onto the future. How easily that can be done is best illustrated by tracing the development of a specific, if imaginary, case. Assume that a businessman wishes an estimate of sales for some future time period so that personnel levels can be set, equipment and supplies purchased, capital obtained, and so on. It makes little difference whether the businessman involved manufactures trousers, operates an airport, or embalms and buries bodies. The principles on which forecasting depends are the same.

Development of a forecast begins with the variable whose value is to be projected on the future, in this case, anticipated level of sales. The forecaster must find some other variable that can serve as a basis for the projection and an appropriate rule for making the estimate. The simplest and most common base for such projections is, of course, last year's level of activity, suitably adjusted. Several years' data may be organized to provide trend lines that can be used to adjust for the coming year. If sales have been increasing about 10 percent annually for the past five years, last year's monthly sales increased by 10 percent, is likely to be a useful forecast. Another common practice is to locate a bellwether, an observable whose values follow those of the desired prediction (sales levels) but antecede them in time. If some factor can be found whose value changes in the same direction and amount as sales, but one month earlier, that factor can be used as a base for projecting next month's sales—assuming that one month of advance warning is sufficient. All that is required for the manufacturer's purposes is a formula that can be applied to some set of figures to produce future values for the variables that concern him. Once the formula is put into practice, it can be adjusted periodically to eliminate major discrepancies. If the forecast is unreliable, it can be improved by increasing the number of factors involved, making parallel predictions, and rationalizing the results. Whether the two variables are related conceptually is irrelevant in forecasts; if anticipated demand for coveralls manufactured in Chicago could be projected from the number of traffic accidents in San Francisco, the user would be unconcerned. For psychological reasons, a user might sleep more soundly if a closely related indicator were used in the forecast, but that change might not improve its reliability.

Structurally, a forecast consists of two or more variables linked by rule or formula. In some cases, a complete forecast will actually include several parallel structures, each making an independent prediction of the future value of the critical variables. Whatever the structure, one variable, obviously, must appear in each part of it. In use, the values of some of the variables are established from observation. The value of the desired prediction can then be calculated using the rule incorporated in the set.

ARGUMENT ABOUT FORECASTS

Argument or justification of forecasts is conditioned by two important characteristics of the instrument. First, a forecast cannot be tested by acting upon it; the only test available is against the historical records. Second, from the point of view of the user, the quality of the instrument must be estimated *before* the forecast is used. The critical question, then, is the kinds of reasons that can be offered in support of a forecast before actual application. Obviously, the argument will center upon historical experience. Specific questions may vary, but the kind of information available is actually quite limited.

If it can be shown from the records that a forecast would have produced reliable and accurate results had it been applied to past history, that is perhaps the strongest argument that can be provided for using it. While it can be strengthened, the means employed is basically "more of the same." For example, the longer the time period covered, and the larger the number of cases involved, the stronger the justification—other things equal. If there have been no counterexamples, no situations in which the relationship established in the forecast did *not* hold, that can be considered evidence in favor of the instrument.

Beyond such simple extensions and the use of parallel forecasts, some evidence can be obtained by exploring known or suspected causal connections. Forecasts of wheat prices may have to be adjusted drastically if an unexpected crop failure is reported in the media. Again, if two factors are assumed to be influenced by a common factor, one may be used as a predictor for the other or an early-warning device for unexpected changes. If the demand for both textbooks and clothing is affected in the same direction by changes in the number of students enrolling in college, for example, but the change in demand appears sooner in the clothing industry, textbook manufacturers can use sales levels in the clothing industry as an early-warning device and modify production plans accordingly. Again, a forecast used to project traffic accidents is more likely to be accurate if road and weather conditions are taken into account than if they are ignored. Good forecasting goes beyond mechanical calculation of one set of values from another to explore potential sources of error and try to adjust for them. What is done specifically will depend, of course, on the use to be made of the forecast, the knowledge available that can be linked to the events being forecast, and various other contingencies.

NOTE

1. William Ascher, *Forecasting: An Appraisal for Policy-Makers and Planners* (Johns Hopkins University Press, 1978).

4   Controlling the Environment

The importance to mankind of being able to control the environment deliberately, to bring about or inhibit change by reasoned action, is literally beyond exaggeration. Without some capacity for directing the course of events, human survival would be extremely unlikely. The basis of that capacity is, of course, intellectual. Nearly all of the known potential for exercising reasoned control over events is vested in the human species. Few other creatures can much exceed the instructions encoded in the genes. That human potential for reasoned action is expressed in everything from simple foodgathering or flight from danger, which is shared with some other animals, through complex and sophisticated feats of engineering such as the moon landings, feats that had few equals as prolonged, detailed, and precise exercises in environmental control. How that intellectual potential is brought to fulfillment, what types of instruments it is exercised through, and how those instruments can be developed and improved provide the central foci of this chapter.

In order to achieve deliberate and intentional control over events, an instrument must be created from human experience that can provide an unbroken chain of connections between specific human actions and foreseeable consequences in the observed world. The actions may cause a change or suppress it; in either case, they have the effect of making the world different. In effect, reasoned action depends on the intellectual ability to supply reliable answers to three basic types of questions: What caused a particular change to occur? How can a particular aspect of the environment be changed? What will follow if a specific action or change is introduced into the world? A theory of knowledge supplies a set of working assumptions from which the nature of an adequate response to each question can be determined and from which appropriate techniques for criticizing, justifying, arguing, and improving the response can be developed.

The intellectual instrument that can supply answers for those questions, that provides a base for reasoned and corrigible human actions, is the *theory*. Although the meaning of theory, as it is used here, corresponds fairly well to current usage in physical science, it has actually been developed from a different direction—beginning with the human purposes to be served—and in that respect is different.[1] As in the case of classifications and forecasts, the discussion of theories and their applications concentrates on the conditions that must be satisfied before a theory will perform properly, on the ways in which theories are developed, generalized, and improved, and on the kinds of arguments that are required to criticize or justify a theory.

HOW AND WHY THEORIES WORK

Reasoned control over events is obtained through the same basic procedures used to produce justified expectations: a pattern of structured relations (a theory) is assumed and acted upon, and the results of action serve as a test of the theory and provide grounds for improvement. Structurally, a theory is identical to a forecast, for each consists of a set of rules linking two or more variables plus appropriate limiting conditions. But for exercising control other events, a causal relation must be assumed between the variables. To control events means to produce or inhibit them. The structure must therefore enable an actor to produce foreseeable results by deliberate action. Once the causal assumption is made, it follows that acting to change the value of one variable in a theory will produce changes in the rest of the structure that can be anticipated using the rules. That makes control over the environment possible in principle. In effect, a theory provides an unbroken chain of causal connections between at least two variables and specifies the limiting conditions under which the rule relating them will hold.

Both of the basic forms of causal relations can be used in theory development. If the *necessary* conditions for an event to occur can be established, a theory can be created in the form "No *X* unless *Y* under conditions *C*." If the much stronger, but more difficult to establish, *sufficient* conditions for an event to occur can be determined, that produces a more powerful theory in the form "If *X* then *Y* under conditions *C*." The limiting conditions (*C*) are an essential part of every theory, though they are usually suppressed when theories are stated. Theories based on the necessary conditions for change can be used only to prevent change—eliminating oxygen to stop a fire or returning a fish to water to keep it alive. When the sufficient conditions for change are known, an intervention strategy can be developed that produces the change. Patients are cured of specific diseases by prescribed modes of treatment, for example. Any assertion to the effect that an individual "knows how to do" something implies knowledge of the sufficient conditions for that "something" to occur, whether it is winning an election, curing a patient, or simply making ice.

Because theories incorporate a causal assumption, they always provide a basis for action, an intervention strategy, for achieving purposes that lie within the boundaries of the theory. That is, the purpose must be identifiable with an attainable set of values for the variables included in the structure. The technology needed to implement the strategy need not be available to validate the theory. The theory must, however, be applicable in principle; otherwise, it could not be tested. Testability is essential for any structure intended to serve as a basis for action. Put another way, a theory that cannot be tested cannot be acted upon, and a theory that cannot be acted upon (in principle at least) cannot be tested.

STRUCTURES AND PROCESSES

Structurally, a theory consists of a finite set of variables, linked through their values by a set of rules expected to hold under specified conditions. The change that a theory can be used to produce or suppress is usually referred to as a phenomenon and will be symbolized as ($\emptyset$). The phenomenon must appear within the boundaries of the theory, although it can be shown as an entailment. That is, the phenomenon must be identified with some combination of variables and values that lie within the set. From another vantage point, any achievable state of the structure, any combination of variables and values not forbidden by the rules, is a phenomenon that can be handled by the theory. In short, the theory handles all of the interactions that can occur among the set of variables that it includes.

The dynamic aspect of theory, the element that supplies the processes that can occur within the theory, is a logic or calculus. Theorizing is a special kind of applied logic or mathematics.[2] Once the basic assumptions of a calculus are accepted, it has the power to force agreement with its internal operations on threat of self-contradiction. However, that power extends only to the boundaries of the formal system. In order to harness the power of the calculus to the pursuit of human purposes, the formal structure must be fitted to observations, linked or applied to the observed world. The ultimate justification for efforts to produce that linkage is pragmatic success in attaining human purposes, but good reasons can be offered for accepting some and rejecting others prior to applications. Some of the conditions prerequisite to success are known. Because the procedures and limitations required for legitimating the application of a calculus to observations are so crucial to the development and use of knowledge, they are examined below at some length.

A logic is nothing more than a set of symbols and the rules of manipulation that define their use. In the notation employed here, the basic structure of a logic is as follows:

$$\begin{pmatrix} V_1 \ V_2 \ V_3 \ \cdots \cdots \ V_n \\ R_1 \ R_2 \ R_3 \ \cdots \cdots \ R_n \end{pmatrix} \supset \emptyset$$

The round brackets indicate that the set is closed. In that case, any change in the value of one of the variables can be accounted for *completely* by a change in the value of some other variable in the set, in combination with the rules. Once the initial change is specified, all other changes that will follow logically can be fully calculated. The logic or calculus may be part of simple arithmetic or algebra, a very sophisticated and complex branch of mathematics, or a new logic invented specially for the occasion. In the remaining discussion, the accuracy of logical reasoning is taken for granted; in real criticism, that would probably be unwise.

The basic goal in applied mathematics is to be able to transfer the logical or mathematical capacity contained in the logic to the observable world. Whether the purpose is to keep track of indebtedness and pay bills or to develop a very complex branch of physics, the basic procedures are the same, and the conditions required to validate the transfer are identical. The key to harnessing the logic is to fit the pattern to what is observed in the environment, to obtain isomorphism between the pattern and the observations. The first step is to assign empirical meaning to each of the symbols in the calculus, using what are usually called "rules of transformation." The user simply identifies each symbol or variable within the calculus with an observable in the environment. Both the variable that identifies the phenomenon and the variable(s) that identify its cause must, of course, be included in the set. In electricity, for example, the theory that is called Ohm's Law is symbolized as $E = IR$, where E is the voltage, I is the current or amperage, and R is the resistance in a given electrical circuit. Linking the symbols to observables is an easy task, however, compared to what must follow. The heart of a calculus, or a theory, is the set of rules that govern the relations among the values of the variables. Those rules and the various changes they entail must also be matched to what is observed in the environment. Only then can it be said that the structure is genuinely isomorphic to the situation in an adequate way.

The nature of the isomorphism required is immutable and unambiguous. *The whole structure must fit observation.* It does not suffice to show that some of the implications of the calculus appear in observation; that result can be produced using false assumptions. But assumptions that are known to be false and to be imperfectly isomorphic to observation cannot be incorporated into theories. They are useful only for producing forecasts or predictions. The point is vital, particularly for criticism of much of the work in economics and econometrics. It may be the case that on a planet with half of the earth's gravitational attraction, *some* events occur with moving bodies that are identical to events observed here on earth. Nevertheless, a theory of motion on earth that assumed a gravitational force half as large as the one that has been established would be worthless, even though it can be agreed that some of its predictions would be accurate. The problem arises out of the need to assess reliability in theory *prior* to use. When the axioms or assumptions in a theory are known to be false, there is no way to predict in advance which of its implications, if any, will correspond to observation. Once the theory has been applied, it may be discovered that some of its implications actually fit observations. But the instrument is nothing more than a post hoc rationalizing device when used in that way. For use in a theory, a calculus or logic structure must be isomorphic to observation with respect to both variables and rules of interaction. The power of the structure actually lies in the rules.

Theories must be fully and completely calculable; the logic must be closed and complete. Probabilistic statements in the form "*n* percent of *A* is *B*" are a common source of confusion in this regard. Such propositions can occur within a logic only in a few very special and limited cases that appertain to very long sequences or very large collections.[3] The content of a sample of the earth's atmosphere can be deduced from the composition of the whole, given certain assumptions that are appropriate there. In virtually every case, all of the logical operations performed within a calculus have the same level of absolute certainty, regardless of the branch of mathematics.[4]

The Fudge Factor. For a logic to operate properly, it must be wholly self-contained; for a theory to function, it must be isomorphic to the environment. But no set of factors in the observable world can be separated completely and perfectly from the rest of the environment, even under the most stringent of laboratory conditions. There are always some external influences on the set, however slight or periodic. Moreover, as the precision of measurement is increased, the capacity to measure eventually breaks down and isomorphism is indeterminate—at that level. In effect, no theory is perfectly isomorphic to the environment. Hence, the transfer of assumptions from the theory to the world of observation is always problematic, and there is some error.

A very practical and efficient way of dealing with such external influences is to add a "Fudge Factor" (FF) to the theory, lumping together all of the external factors that influence the variables within the theory in any way. The amount of influence exercised by the factors within the FF, which need only be specified in the aggregate, is a measure of the reliability or accuracy of the theory. The technique allows the theorist to calculate reliability without having to specify all of the external factors that influence the elements of the theory or determine their individual influence, which is a much easier job. If the theory is not accurate or reliable enough for the user's purposes, some of the influences within the FF will have to be identified, and their interaction with the variables within the theory determined—or they can be added to the specification of limiting conditions. The FF performs something of the same function in theorizing that the royal prerogative plays in British government. That is, it provides an unanalyzed reservoir of capacity that can be discussed or manipulated as a whole without forcing further, and perhaps impossible, analysis.

Every theory must have a Fudge Factor to cover slippage. No theory fits observation and measurements perfectly; if it did, measurement error would destroy the symmetry. That is particularly true because logical limits preclude the development of large and cumbersome theories that contain a great many variables. Most of the complex structures that have been produced in the computer era are actually very weak and unreliable, and their internal operations are simplistic. Good theories are likely to contain only two or three variables, perhaps with an elaborate set of limiting conditions. If the system is characterized by interactions among the variables (feedback), those limits must be maintained. Calculi containing four variables with feedback are for all practical purposes impossible to calculate. If that number is increased to five, calculation becomes impossible in principle. That argues strongly against the development of theories containing dozens of interacting variables.[5]

But two- and three-variable theories are unlikely to fit the course of events very precisely, particularly in the social sciences. For example, assume a simple three-variable structure in which A varies inversely with B and C varies directly with A. If that pattern is roughly isomorphic to the relation between the amount of good will toward the company found among members of the general public (A), the price of the company's goods (B) and the profit made by the company (C), the structure can be very useful. For example, it suggests that a reduction in price, other things equal, should produce an increase in good will and a corollary increase in profits—presumably through increased sales, though that need not be specified for the theory to be acceptable. However, it is commonplace that various conditions might interfere with the operation of the theory. For example, if wages were rising more rapidly than prices, a small price increase might actually produce substantial amounts of good will and increased profits—though perhaps not enough to keep up with inflation. Must the theory be abandoned because the fit with observations is weak? That is certainly one option. But the theory can also be maintained, reliability can be determined from use, discrepancies can be attributed to the Fudge Factor, and the whole system remains free of anomaly. For the social sciences, where theories are likely to remain weak and isomorphism with observation poor, the Fudge Factor provides a badly needed margin for error without disturbing the epistemological or theoretical stability of the discipline.

DEVELOPING THEORIES: AN ILLUSTRATION

Coping with the environment requires tools that can generate reasoned and justifiable expectations about unobserved events and control over some aspects of the future. Classifications, forecasts, and theories can produce the needed expectations; only theories provide a way of controlling the environment. It follows that any claim to exercise control over the flow of events, or any suggestion that particular modes of intervention in the environment will produce a desired outcome, depends unavoidably on a theory. While that sounds formidable, theories are readily available within human capacity. Powerful, sophisticated, and highly reliable theories of the sort found in physical science are very difficult to produce in social science. They are also difficult to produce in physical science. Simple, crude, and imprecise tools may be both effective and adequate for a wide range of essential tasks. It is not necessary to generate a scalpel in order to cut a loaf of bread. A brief illustration, borrowed and adapted from literature, should help to clarify the structures and processes involved in theorizing and suggest how theories are improved. It may also serve to dissolve some of the mystique and the consequently exaggerated expectations associated with "theorizing" in social or in physical science.

In genuine cases, the phenomenon that a theory is meant to control will be a real event, already observed in a concrete setting. Hypothetical cases cannot produce theory. The constraints which the theory is intended to overcome would remain unknown. Moreover, the process of theorizing begins with a particular case and not a class of cases. For the most part, aggregates are useful for calling attention to problems and not for solving them. For example, information relating to the total number of automobile accidents may be useful for suggesting the scope and significance of the problem and development of an impetus to action. But a search for theory (or theories) that can be used to control automobile accidents must focus on the individual case, seeking a theory that will account for and suggest a way of controlling that case. The solution to the particular case, suitably generalized, becomes a proposed solution for the class of cases exemplified in the particular case that has been solved. A theory can only be applied to the class of cases that is homogeneous with respect to the content of the theory. There is little point in developing homogeneous classes of events before a solution or theory is available. A seemingly homogeneous class of unsolvable problems may actually be heterogeneous when solutions are found. In any case, a homogeneous class is developed by examining each case in turn. If careful study of a particular automobile accident suggests that the cause was driver intoxication, that the accident would not have occurred had the driver been sober, then a fairly simple structure linking intoxication to automobile accidents provides an appropriate theory and suggests at least one intervention strategy—elimination of intoxicated drivers would certainly eliminate all accidents due to intoxication. But if that strategy could be rigorously applied, some automobile accidents would continue to occur. This would be a signal that the class was not homogeneous, that the theory was not properly limited, and so on. Other theories would be needed to deal with different causes of automobile accidents. The search for theories could be expected to continue to a point where the costs of continuing would be considered greater than the anticipated benefits and where other priorities would take precedence in the allocation of resources. Automobile accidents, considered as a class, illustrate the homogeneity problem very well. So does the disease of cancer in medicine: there are many varieties and a wide range of treatments, each appropriate to one of the subclasses of the disease.

The structures and processes required for theorizing, and some of the possibilities and limitations that may not be wholly obvious, can be illustrated very effectively by Charles Lamb's short story about the discovery of cooked meat in China—*A Dissertation upon Roast Pig*. In the story, a Chinese family living in the era when meat was eaten raw returned home one day to find that their house had burned to the ground, destroying, among other things, a litter of young pigs. As soon as the embers were partially cooled, the rubble was searched for valuables that could be salvaged. One member of the family, screening the ashes through his fingers, chanced to grasp one of the burned pigs. Since it was still quite hot, his fingers were burned. The reaction to the burning was spontaneous: the fingers were placed in the mouth to cool. There followed the first contact with cooked meat. Yummy!! The sequence of events that followed is readily imagined: exploration, reinforcement of the initial reaction, the summoning of other members of the family, the consumption of the young pig, and the search for others. When the orgy was ended, the family was hooked on roast pork. The essential precondition to a search for theory was now satisfied: there was a phenomenon (roast pork), a human evaluation, and an urgent desire to replicate the phenomenon or to control the environment in a way that would make such replication possible.

How to get more? The desired phenomenon was clear enough: conversion of raw pig into roast suckling pig. How could that conversion be brought about? What had caused it? More important still, how could it be caused? There was no prior experience with the phenomenon; only the one case for evidence. It seemed clear that burning the house somehow produced the result. The family was familiar with fire and heat; the pig had been hot when cooked. No one can say how the two things were put together or when, but the information available was put together (in the story, of course) to produce a simple but adequate theory or explanation:

$$house\ containing\ pigs\ +\ fire\ =\ delicious\ food$$

A set of nominal definitions quickly converts that equation into a somewhat more abstract formula:

$$HP\ +\ F\ =\ RP$$

The Chinese family now had a theory. The theory suggested an intervention strategy, a way of exercising control over the condition of pigs—they need only be placed in a house and burned. The essential variables were a house made of wood, which was speedily rebuilt, a new litter of pigs from the fields, and a fire applied to the house. The theory was plausible given past experience; and the strategy was readily tested. Would it work? Doubtless there were last minute discussions about the efficacy of the procedure and the propriety of proceeding, but if action was carried through and the results were gastronomically gratifying, the family had tested and confirmed its theory.

Once armed with a tested theory, it might be presumed that the family's production of roast pork was limited mainly by desire and the availability of resources. However, the quality of the theory was weak, and the procedure was relatively inefficient. If production was maximized, a variety of problems could be expected to surface in due course, just as present-day automobile engineers are discovering and trying to remedy the basic inadequacies in the approach to automobile design taken in the early twentieth century. The theory needed improvement with respect to reliability, cost, quality control, side-effects, and time consumed, among other things. Each roast pork dinner required construction of a new dwelling. The quality of the product varied widely. In some cases, the meat was nearly raw and in other cases, burned beyond recognition and inedible. The frequent conflagrations excited much attention in the area. With repetition, sympathy gave way to fear, and some who feared they had brought a curse on the area circulated a petition to have them driven from the place. The children found it increasingly difficult to maintain social relations with their peers. The theory was too rough and the level of control inadequate. The family was being forced to choose between ceasing production, moving to another village, or find a better theory.

Was another theory actually produced by the family? What stages did the new theory develop through? Were there technological changes that triggered the new theory? Such questions, though interesting and important, cannot be answered; the source is only a story and not history. One major point emerges from the situation, however: the problem had to be reconceptualized before a better theory was possible. As long as the theory was stated in terms of houses and burning, improvement was unlikely to be major. A simple transformation from "house burning" to "fire" would revolutionize the possibilities. A further conversion from "fire" to "heat" would open the way to using ovens or boiling water to produce the desired change. Concurrently, the problem could be attacked by focusing on the pig, designing an apparatus that would prevent escape or movement and eventually producing more modern concepts of food preparation. The origins of the technique are in any case trivial. What is significant is that all of the essentials of theory can be found in so crude a case.

Much can be learned about theory development from the illustration. The role of the phenomenon and of normative evaluation (based on affective reaction in this case) is prime. Without a desire for roast pig, there would be no reason to seek a means for producing it, and without the prior experience, there would be nothing to suggest that the desired effect could be produced by burning a house. Imagine the predicament of a neighbor supplied with a sample of the product but not informed of the method of preparation. Initial contact with cooked meat was accidental, of course, but the scope of human experience is so enormous, particularly in literate cultures where vicarious experience is the primary source of information, that there should be no shortage of such first encounters. Even in the case cited, in which cooking meat is connected to burning houses, the conceptual leap and cognitive processes required to move from the initial experience to subsequent action would be enormous relative to the state of knowledge of the time. Countless other factors in the environment might have been assumed as the cause of the event. Indeed, ascription of cause to a spirit or deity might be likely given the circumstances. Had the cause been identified in different terms, different courses of action might have been tried—and failed—or perhaps no action whatever would have seemed reasonable. In the latter case, that particular set of experiments could have been closed permanently.

The Charles Lamb story can also be used to demonstrate the basic structures and processes involved in theorizing. The practical effect of any theory is to separate some set of variables from the rest of the environment, on the assumption that they are more closely related to one another than to the rest. It must be assumed, analytically at least, that the conversion of pig to roast pork relates so strongly to the burning house that the influence of other factors in the environment can be ignored. Otherwise, the theory would not hold, and action based on the theory would not produce the desired outcome. The first step in developing the structure is to link the phenomenon to its cause by appropriate rules. In the case of the pigs, burning the house is assumed to be the sole cause of the transformation. As a limiting condition, the pigs must somehow be confined within the burning building. Structurally, the theory comprises a two-variable set with a single rule of interaction and can be diagrammed as follows:

$$\left(V_h \ V_m \ R_1 \right) \quad \supset \quad \varnothing$$

Where: V_h = condition of the house
V_m = state of the meat (raw and roast)
R_1 = As V_h changes from wood to ashes, V_m changes from raw to cooked.

The rule, which contains the essence of the theory, takes precisely the same form as the rule in physics that states: As the temperature drops below $32°$ F., the physical state of water changes from liquid to solid. The measures are, of course, much less precise.

In the structured theory, the selection of variables is closed and calculable; application of the rule $(R)_1$) entails the phenomenon. The phenomenon actually lies within the boundaries of the set since the change in value of V_m is the phenomenon sought. Other things equal, the meat will change from raw to cooked any time the house burns, whether from natural causes or the actions of a human agent. That is a function of the causal assumption built into the structure. Without it, the act of burning the house to produce cooked meat would be utterly irrational.

As the family learned from experience, the results of acting on the theory varied grossly. The influence of the factors included in the Fudge Factor was large. Neighbors might come to put out the fire; the pigs could escape from the house unscathed; rain might interrupt the cooking. If the theory worked well on five occasions in ten, that level of reliability might be acceptable to the user, particularly if it worked well on the first deliberate attempt. But if the reliability of the theory was only one in ten or one in twenty, efforts could be made to strengthen it. Of course, such actions are in real life extremely sophisticated, and the continuation of the example depends very much on poetic license. If one attempt fizzled, future efforts could be confined to dry days (a new limiting factor is added). If the neighbors interfered, they could be drawn away by threats, promises, or diversions. If the pigs escaped, careful tethering or even prior slaughtering might be called for. By such procedures, the original theory is augmented, limiting conditions are made increasingly precise, and other actions are taken (using still further theories) to create the conditions in which the actions entailed by the theory could be expected to succeed. Once the user is satisfied with the costs and benefits, compared to the costs and benefits of any available alternative, theory development can stop, for there is no reason to underwrite the additional costs.

The importance of conceptualization, particularly conceptual innovation, is well demonstrated in the story. In principle, any phenomenon can be controlled through a variety of theories, each couched in different sets of concepts. Cooking can be carried out under a wide range of circumstances using many different techniques. The basic structure remains the same: a theory is a set of variables, rules of interaction, and limiting conditions, bolstered by a Fudge Factor. But different theories produce different associated costs and side-effects. Those differences make reasoned choice and policies based on them a genuine and significant possibility. That is, theories can provide alternative ways of achieving desired outcomes in the environment, thereby providing different sets of costs and benefits from which choices can be made. That is usually the prime value of technological innovation.

A theory applies to observation any time that the set of factors it contains occur. The theory adopted for producing roast pork, for example, could be expected to hold on any and every occasion where pigs and burning houses were found in combination and the limiting conditions were satisfied. In general, any time the variables contained in a theory are observed and stated limits are met, the theory must operate. That is why a two-variable theory is likely to include a very large FF or a large set of limiting conditions. Most discussions of scientific theory tend to ignore limits or to take them for granted. In the social sciences in particular, theories are more likely to be improved through more precise specification of limiting conditions than by reconceptualization, which is a creative action not usually generated on demand, or by including more and more variables, which very quickly leads to a system that cannot be calculated.

THE SEARCH FOR CAUSALITY: MILL'S METHODS

The importance of causal relations has been realized for centuries. Not surprisingly, various efforts have been made to improve the procedures by which they are found or produced. Probably the most famous of them, the work of John Stuart Mill, appeared in the nineteenth century.[6] Mill's "methods," as they are usually called, provide a good illustration of the uses and weaknesses of procedural solutions to essentially creative problems.

The aim of the methods is to locate causal relations among observables. The procedures depend on the availability of a number of cases in which a phenomenon ($\emptyset$) occurs. Those cases are examined systematically to determine what other factor in the environment caused the phenomenon to occur. Since theories are not usefully developed for nonrecurring events, other examples of the event should be available in history. Otherwise, they are unlikely to be considered important enough to be concerned about their causes. As long as such methods are used as devices for *suggesting* causal relations and are not regarded as *proof* of causal relations, they can be invaluable. The methods that Mill devised do not help the investigator to select the factors or variables that should be considered as potential causes. That question lies outside their scope. Within the limits of the selections made, they are a very efficient device for eliminating factors as potential causes or for strengthening the belief that the cause of the phenomenon is one factor rather than the others.

The procedures are simple and sensible, and easily followed when several cases in which the phenomenon occurs can be examined together. For example, if six cases are known and only one factor of six occurs in all six, that factor is the best contender available for identification as the cause of the phenomenon. A visual structuring of the cases will suggest the process on which the methods depends:

Case 1	$A,$	$B,$	$C,$	$D,$	$E,$	$\varnothing$
Case 2	$A,$	$C,$	$D,$	$E,$	$F,$	$\varnothing$
Case 3	$A,$	$D,$	$E,$	$F,$	$G,$	$\varnothing$
Case 4	$A,$	$E,$	$F,$	$G,$	$B,$	$\varnothing$
Case 5	$A,$	$F,$	$G,$	$H,$	C	$\varnothing$
Case 6	$A,$	$G,$	$H,$	$C,$	$D,$	$\varnothing$

Clearly, the only member of that set of variables that *could be* the cause of $\varnothing$ is A, which appears in every case. Of course, the cause could be another factor not included in the set; that is the limit on the power of the methods. Moreover, the concepts themselves may be aggregates, and the causal agent can be one of the subclasses of the aggregate. Such conditions are also lost by the method.

The example given above refers to what Mill called the method of agreement. Other methods employ similar strategies. If the cases are arrayed together with one case where the phenomenon did *not* occur, the factor absent on that occasion is a probable or possible cause of the phenomenon (method of differences). The two techniques can be combined with reference to a single phenomenon, producing what Mill chose to call the joint method of agreement difference. If all of the factors in the situation that are known not to be causes of the phenomenon are eliminated, the cause must lie in the remainder—the method of residues. Finally, in the method of concomitant variation, Mill focuses on changes taking place in both the phenomenon and the factors in the environment that might cause it, seeking those that vary in the same way. For example, if a cornfield is divided into four units and seeded identically throughout, but different amounts of fertilizer are applied to each of the subunits, differences in production from the different pieces of land will show the effect of differences in the amount of fertilizer applied.

Suitably limited, Mill's methods are a useful adjunct to the search for causal relations and theories. They must not be regarded as a source of proof. The methods serve to rule out factors as causal agents rather than establish them positively. In effect, they suggest limited focuses for future inquiries into cause. At best, they can indicate the most likely causal agent in a given selection of factors. The adequacy of the selection cannot be tested by the methods; such problems require different techniques. The psychoanalyst who persisted in searching for the cause of a pig's transformation to roast pork in the psychic states of the pig because the conceptual framework available contained no other variables would typify the individual wedded to a dogmatic version of the methods.

Of course, methods cannot be criticized because they do not make use of a particular set of concepts. Some social scientists seem to believe that human behavior is properly explained only when psychological concepts are employed. Others insist on reference to motives, intentions, or similarly limited dimensions of action. Some have claimed that all social theories will ultimately be couched in "system" terms or make use of functional analysis.[7] But there is no way of prejudging the conceptual case. The value of a concept depends on the results obtained in use. At present, there are very few good reasons for insisting, or even suggesting, that a particular set of concepts is more likely to produce theory than any other.

Similarly, the fact that Mill's methods cannot be used to determine primary or "first" causes for a phenomenon is *not* a valid criticism of the procedures. Pressed strongly, every effort to establish causal links proceeds to an endless regression. That is the primary reason why satisfaction of purpose, the pragmatic criterion, is needed for systematic inquiry. As long as the chain of relations can be extended far enough to provide a way of controlling the phenomenon, the theory is useful. Human knowledge consists in enormous numbers of patterns or relations, built over time, and very thinly integrated into networks. There is no overall structure. Some areas are fairly thickly populated with patterns, and others are virtually empty. The availability of theory is probably the most important factor in criticizing new claims to knowledge. Where patterns or theories are scarce, new patterns are hard to test. The structure is "loose," incomplete, and unintegrated.

Understandably, there is no simple or final test for theories. While it is true that every theory must correspond to observation, that is not enough, in itself, to guarantee the theory. The theory must hold when examined in the light of other relevant theories, or it must be so exceptional that the failure to correspond is taken as a criticism of the others. A theory that fails occasionally is not necessarily abandoned. Evidence is often very difficult to obtain, particularly for theoretical notions that deal indirectly with observables. The pigs who perished in the burning house may have furthered their own destruction because they felt deserted by the homeowner, but how could evidence be obtained for such notions? Sailors long believed that dolphins try to help humans lost at sea by pushing them toward the shore; given that belief, any case in which the individual is pushed toward land is positive evidence. But as has been noted before, there can be no evidence if the dolphin chooses to push humans in the other direction. The belief is virtually untestable. And can that untestability be taken as evidence of the craft and cunning of the dolphin?

GENERALIZING THEORIES

Theories begin and end with specific cases. The goal is a tool that provides adequate control over specific cases at acceptable risk and cost. Given the diversity of human interests, theories dealing with a wide range of phenomena under a variety of circumstances can be expected to appear at quite diverse places at very different times.

Some are local and particular, and others have wide applications. Knowledge essential for functioning within a single family, for example, is usually of little value to nonmembers; other kinds of knowledge, such as survival techniques in polar regions, are of limited utility but wider application; and some knowledge is valuable to all humans, wherever they reside. As the amount and diversity of available knowledge increase, the problem of intergenerational transmission grows more serious, and even within one generation it may be difficult to stay abreast of what is being created. A good analogy can be made to a machine shop which develops a new tool for each job undertaken by the company. Even if the tools could be paid for from profits, consolidation and integration are clearly desirable for both intellectual and financial reasons.

In the field of knowledge, the need to merge and integrate individual and particular theories, to merge them into composites that can be applied to a wider range of phenomena, is equally great. In the physical sciences, where the problem is more acute than in social science, that process of generalization or reduction goes on constantly.[8] Other things equal, the more general the tool the more useful and efficient it is. In some cases, generalization has actually been accompanied by increased precision in application. The need for generalization of knowledge is increasing; unless ways of merging and compressing are found, the burden will soon be unbearable. Scholarship is concerned, among other things, with editing the available knowledge supply and transmitting a more efficient corpus to the next generation. Some things can be eliminated, some are replaced, much is compressed and generalized, and reorganization is often useful. An example will illustrate the value of the process. The case comes from elementary physical science and should be familiar to nearly everyone. No theory in social science would make the point half as efficiently.

The phenomenon to be explained by the theory is a change in the amount of light coming from a light bulb at two different times (t_1 and t_2). Since the phenomenon is clearly "electrical," an appropriate conceptual framework can be selected using such concepts as wires, batteries, and bulbs. To simplify, assume the bulb was connected to one battery at time t_1 and to two batteries at time

t_2 and nothing else changed. That provides the second change which theory or explanation requires. If the light changed but nothing else was observed to change, no explanation would be possible. On the other hand, many other factors in the situation could change between t_1 and t_2; people could move about, tap water might run, the sun could go behind a cloud, and so on. The conceptual framework identified as "electrical" excludes such factors and assumes they are unrelated to electrical changes. Since the conceptual framework is well established, it is safe to accept that limit. In an area only weakly supplied with theory, it might be desirable to include a much wider range of factors.

The first step, then, is a simple descriptive account of the event. That requires two cross-sections, first at t_1 and again at t_2. Any information that relates to the phenomenon should be included. Electrical experiments do not work under water; boiling temperatures must be standardized at sea level pressures. When an explanation is being constructed, it is often very difficult to know which of the observed conditions in the environment have to do with the outcome under investigation. There is usually a temptation to include too much, since discarding is usually easier than rerunning the experiment or finding another natural state experiment. Notice that it would be pointless to look for additional cases at this initial descriptive stage of theory development. The initial task is to find a way of explaining the particular case and to find a pattern that will fit the observations actually made there. At this point in the inquiry, the variables included in the pattern have not yet been selected or separated from the rest of the environment. That selection is the first decision. Until then, it would be pointless to seek a second case.

In the illustration that follows, the phenomenon is the amount of light coming from the bulb; the cause of the light is assumed to be the battery attached to it. While it might be convenient to use symbols for each of these variables, everyday language is perfectly acceptable as long as meaning is clear, and it opens the way for the critic to use any information about the relationship available in everyday language. The two descriptions taken together provide support for a relational proposition in the form "As the number of batteries increased, the amount of light coming from the bulb increased." That proposition is descriptive and historical; the verb tense employed shows that it is not a generalized rule of interaction.

Summarizing in symbolic form, if V_1 is identified with the number of batteries connected to the bulb and V_2 is defined as the amount of illumination coming from the bulb, a descriptive relational statement can be justified from observation: As V_1 increased in value from one to two, the value of V_2 increased. The proposition is particular; the implied change is an assumption. A very simple transformation can then be carried out which will convert the descriptive accounts of a particular case into a generalized statement of relations or pattern. "The amount of light coming from a bulb varies directly with the number of batteries attached to it," or "V_2 varies directly with V_1" result from the transformation. The structure of the generalized proposition can be symbolized as follows:

$$(\quad V_1 \ V_2 \ R_1 \quad) \quad \supset \quad \varnothing$$

Where: V_1 = the number of batteries in the circuit
V_2 = the amount of light coming from the bulb
R_1 = V_2 varies directly with V_1

The phenomenon to be controlled (V_2) appears within the closed set; the formal requirements are satisfied. If the theory is correct, increasing or decreasing the number of batteries in a circuit will increase or decrease the amount of light coming from the bulb. While this may seem an inordinately and even unnecessarily complex way of describing a very simple process, the apparatus is designed for use with situations of any level of complexity.

A descriptive account of a particular phenomenon has already been generalized. The pattern that has been created, by a very simple transformation of terms, fits the description with respect to both variables and rules of change, and it accounts for the phenomenon. Other tests are readily applied to it. Is it internally consistent? Is it consonant with other knowledge? Are there any known cases to the contrary? Can it be tested experimentally? Experience with using the theory should soon suggest the limits of application—bulb sensitivity at low voltages, or the inability of the bulb to produce more than a certain amount of light. Such limits are added to the content of the theoretical structure.

The greatest limit on the theory as stated, however, is conceptual. The concepts used in the theory severely limit its applications. The theory could not, as it stands, be applied to situations in which lighting did not depend on batteries and bulbs. With effort, those other situations might also be dealt with in the same manner, leaving the field of inquiry with a variety of different theories for dealing with a variety of phenomena. If all of those phenomena could be handled with a single comprehensive theory, *if the theories involved could be generalized*, the results would be much more economical and efficient. Again, there is no way to formalize procedures for actually producing such an integration of theories or generalization of existing structures. But the manner in which it evolves can be suggested by reference to the example as long as it is not construed as a model for or limit on the actual process.

If precisely the same situation in the environment is taken as a point of departure and descriptions are produced from the same observation point but the conceptual framework is modified significantly, the effects of integration can be demonstrated quite dramatically. Moreover, the importance of the basic conceptual apparatus is highlighted in a very useful way. The concepts that are now used in electrical work are easily understood if the flow of electricity is taken to be analogous to water flowing through a metal pipe. The pressure exerted by the water at the end of the pipe is called voltage; the amount of electricity flowing through the pipe is called amperage; and the friction or drag exerted on the water by the pipe is called resistance. Modern instruments allow very precise measurements of these three aspects of electricity. The amount of illumination coming from the bulb can also be measured accurately in lumens.

The situation can now be described using the new concepts. The value of each variable can actually be measured on a ratio scale; hence, all sorts of arithmetical relations can be explored accurately and quickly. The description is richer and more difficult to produce but much more productive as well. The variables to be used in the new description are as follows:

V_1 = amount of voltage in the circuit (volts)
V_2 = amount of current in the circuit (amperes)
V_3 = amount of resistance in the circuit (ohms)
V_4 = temperature of the bulb filament (degrees C.)
V_5 = illumination provided by the bulb (lumens)

The two descriptions used in the first example (times t_1 and t_2) can now be transformed (using imaginary magnitudes).

Variable		Time t_1	Time t_2
V_1	voltage	20 volts	40 volts
V_2	current	5 amperes	10 amperes
V_3	resistance	4 ohms	4 ohms
V_4	filament temperature	100° C.	200° C.
V_5	amount of light	10 lumens	20 lumens

From these two descriptions, a relational proposition can be produced which states that as voltage changed from 20 to 40 volts, amperage changed from 5 to 10 amperes, temperature increased from 100° C. to 200° C., and illumination increased from 10 to 20 lumens. Rules of interaction (a pattern) must now be created to connect the set and explain the phenomenon. Three rules will suffice; two are purely imaginary and the third is Ohm's law:

$$R_1: \quad V_1 = V_2 \times V_3 \quad \text{(Ohm's Law)}$$
$$R_2: \quad V_4 = 5 \ V_1$$
$$R_3: \quad V_4 = 10 \ V_5$$

Any variable that appears inside the selection but is not incorporated into the rules of change is otiose and can be eliminated. Variables that appear in the descriptive accounts must be added before the theory can be tested. By using the rules, the value of V_5 (the phenomenon) can be calculated once the values of the first three variables are known.

The superiority of the generalized theory is obvious. The concepts are far more precise and can be measured with much greater accuracy. Moreover, the theory itself produces much greater accuracy in prediction and control. In addition, it can be used to deal with any form of illumination that makes use of electrical energy. Hence, it is no longer restricted to battery-powered circuits. Finally, the more general theory offers a wider range of intervention strategies and more ways of controlling the phenomenon, since any of the variables it includes could be used as a point for controlling the situation. The explanation is more roundabout and uses more intervening variables, but the chain of relations between phenomenon and individual variable is unbroken, and each of the variables is an essential part of the total structure.

In its more generalized form, the theory can be applied any time the full set of variables contained within its boundaries appears in the environment. For the theory can be translated to mean: "Any time this set of variables appears in the environment, and the limiting conditions attached to it are satisfied, the values of the elements in the set will change according to the following rules. . . ." Any such occasion provides an opportunity to test and improve the theory; any situation where it fails to work indicates an inadequacy. Precisely where correction is required may not be easily and readily determined. Conceptualization, rules of interaction, statements of limiting conditions, or all of these things, may have to be adjusted to produce an instrument of increasing accuracy and flexibility. Whether those efforts are carried out will depend on resources available, costs and benefits, and the use made of the structure. Improvements in a massive computing system are more likely to be pursued than improvements in a child's toy.

ARGUING THEORIES

Arguments directed at proposals for controlling the environment, at recommended ways of intervening to bring about or inhibit specified changes, will relate to theories and their applications. No other instrument can perform those functions. Justification or criticism will involve discussion of three basic questions: (1) Has the theory been used for an appropriate purpose, are the aims of inquiry such that they could be satisfied if an appropriate theory were available? (2) Has the theory been correctly applied, has the situation been correctly diagnosed? (3) Is the theory itself acceptable with respect to accuracy, adequacy, and justification? The strictly logical aspect of the process of applying theories is bypassed; the proposed action will be assumed as a proper inference from the theory. In a real case, that aspect of usage would have to be examined carefully, for *non sequiturs* are common, as are many of the formal and informal reasoning fallacies, particularly in everyday affairs, public or private.

IS THE PURPOSE APPROPRIATE?

The first point of criticism with reference to applications of theory is whether the purpose that is sought in the environment can, in principle at least, be achieved by any theory. A theory cannot be asked to do what no theory is in principle capable of doing. Therefore, if the purpose of the user is not directed to controlling the environment, if the phenomenon sought is not a change to be brought about or inhibited, the enterprise is misdirected. Of course, a theory can be used to make a prediction, but that situation is properly examined as a case of forecasting rather than the application of a theory. It is merely foolish to ask "Why is a cow?" or to try and answer such questions. No explanation can be offered for baseball or chickpeas; nouns do not refer to changes or processes and are therefore not appropriate targets for theories. If a theory has not been used to explain why a change occurred, how to produce a change, or what effects will follow on a change, then the application cannot be subjected to systematic criticism. The tool has been misused.

If the purpose of the user requires a theory for satisfaction, the question remains whether any of the theories available can deal with the specifics of the application. Any number of theories may be available for explaining a given phenomenon, but they may not have the strength, precision, or reliability needed to satisfy the specific purpose for which theory has been used. No theory can do more than it can do, given its structure and content. Until the question a theory must answer is fully specified, the value of application remains moot. For example, suppose that a government agency must try to provide for a small group of very badly undernourished children and seeks advice from a learned professor of nutrition. The kind of advice received, the theories that will be applied, will depend on the purposes identified by the agency, implicitly at least, in its questions. To ask "How can the nutritional state of the children be altered?" would be grossly inadequate. In that context, acceptable answers would include (1) starving the children without mercy, (2) feeding a balanced and tasty diet, or (3) plying them liberally with alcohol. Each of those actions would produce a specified change of nutritional state; each can be derived from a respectable theory. Unless purposes are stated precisely, it is impossible to determine whether the supply of available theories can handle the problem, or more likely, what the best solution available is, given the current state of theory in the field.

The more precisely purposes are stated and the more difficult it becomes to achieve them, the more demanding the theoretical requirements will be. Many theories can be used to suggest ways of changing the physical condition of living humans if the direction of change is not specified and side-effects are ignored. Changes of unspecified direction that refer to specific aspects of the human physique—sight, hearing, or coordination, for example—can be brought about by a subclass of the larger set. But if the value of such variables must be changed in a particular direction, if hearing or strength must be improved or increased, then theoretical requirements are significantly stronger, the concepts employed in the theories will be more narrow and the justification more complex. Limitations placed on side-effects have the same impact. As in engineering, it is not sufficient to specify the positive conditions that design must satisfy. The constraints in which the design problem is solved must be incorporated into the statement of purpose. The door cannot be left open to curing the cancer by killing the patient.

Finally, the troublesome question "Is the purpose worth achieving?" needs to be examined. That aspect of the use of theories is left for discussion in Chapter 5, but on the understanding that with reference to inquiry in general, that may well be the most significant aspect of the entire argument.

THE DIAGNOSIS PROBLEM

Given a well-conceptualized phenomenon and an appropriate and clearly identified purpose, the focus of argument about theory can move to the relation between structure, process, and observation—to the isomorphism of theory and environment. The application of theory to environment to achieve fulfillment of purpose depends on the assumption that the theory is appropriate. Otherwise, it could not be expected to work, and the application would not serve as a test. In general, a theory can be applied to any situation in which all of the variables in the theory appear, and the limits incorporated into the structure are satisfied. If the theory is sound, the dynamics of the situation will then be reflected in the rules of interaction. If, however, the structure and limits have not been specified adequately, the theory will not work. The rules will not hold for situation dynamics. The fact that a theory can be fitted to the observables and therefore used to generate implications for the situation is not enough. The observables must also interact in ways predicted by the rules incorporated into the theory. Moreover, even if outcomes agree with predictions, it is still possible that the assumptions on which the structure depends are mistaken.

An example may serve to illustrate the kind of situation that may arise. Assume that the following observations were made at noon of a specific day of the year:

1. A stick placed vertical to the earth's surface on the equator produced no shadow.
2. Another stick, also vertical to the earth's surface but located one thousand miles to the south, cast a shadow about 14½ degrees from vertical.

How can the difference in the two shadows be accounted for? What is the appropriate pattern or theory for explaining it? The answer is simple enough, given current knowledge of the solar system. Knowing that (1) the earth is round and (2) the sun is very distant, that outcome is to be expected. Given the vast distance from sun to earth, the sun's rays are almost parallel when they reach earth. If the sun is directly above the stick placed on the equator, its rays are striking the equator at the perpendicular. The curvature of the earth will account for the shadow:

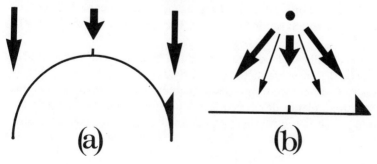

(a)   (b)

In fact, since an angle of 14½ degrees is about 1/25th of a circle, it follows that the earth has a circumference of about 25,000 miles if the 1,000 mile difference between the sticks is accurate.

So far, so good. But suppose the observer assumes that (1) the earth is flat and (2) the sun is very close to the surface. In that case, the sun's rays are not parallel, and the shadow is again to be expected. But the implications of the shadow are different; the 25,000 miles is now the distance between sun and earth rather than a measure of the earth's circumference. Both sets of assumptions are wholly consistent with the two observations. Although one set can be rejected on the basis of external knowledge now generally available, suppose those data were offered as a justification for assuming that the earth is flat and the sun is close? How could the reasoning be refuted or rejected? Do the observations constitute evidence for the set of assumptions? If nothing more is known that relates to the situation, it certainly does. Is the evidence conclusive? No, for no body of evidence is conclusive. Where is the weakness in the evidence? It simply corresponds to observation; no action has been taken on the basis of the initial assumptions that would serve to test them in other ways.

The relative scarcity of good theories in the social sciences is widely remarked, although there is probably some tendency to underestimate the number of theories significantly by failing to count a great many perfectly useful if minor structures. Nevertheless, the possibility that any given set of assumptions fits the observed data in much the same way that assuming a flat earth and a close sun fitted the observations in the earlier example cannot be discounted automatically or even readily. When knowledge of a field is weak, the danger of overestimating the significance of a single test against observation is often substantial. Alternative theories may be weak and poorly articulated, and choosing between them is virtually impossible given the knowledge available in the field.

How easily such questions arise and how they can be resolved in one of the more highly developed fields can be demonstrated most easily by reference to medicine. Suppose that a previously healthy person suddenly developed the following rather alarming symptoms: high fever, severe abdominal pains, frequent vomiting, and, obviously, a severe case of "feeling terrible." What diagnosis is appropriate to the case? Clearly, a three-element pattern in which fever, abdominal pains, and vomiting are linked by rule would be inadequate. For adequate diagnosis, the three symptoms must be linked to a fourth factor; if not, one of the three must emerge as the cause of the others. The ways in which a physician can be sure that the three factors are symptoms rather than causes are too complex to be elaborated here, and the level of confidence attached to the judgment would depend very much on the actual symptoms involved. But the case illustrates rather dramatically the impact of knowledge on diagnosis, and indirectly on action, for both specialist and average citizen. Faced with these symptoms, the average American is most likely to consult a physician or to go to a local drug store for medication. In some parts of Central America, family remedies might be employed; there are still areas in which the services of a witch doctor would be secured. And under some knowledge conditions, the symptoms might be completely ignored, and the impact on the individual suppressed as far as possible. Although it may be wrong, each context must produce some diagnosis before an appropriate response can be determined. In that sense, the general level of knowledge within a culture is an important determinant of the quality of life of its members, though there may be gross disparities with respect to a whole host of continua within what is considered a "single" culture.

For the Western-trained physician, the symptoms described could be part of a number of different patterns or theories. For clarity, only two diagnoses are considered. The first ascribes the trouble to indigestion or intestinal blockage; pain, fever, and vomiting are usually linked to the presence of obstructions in the digestive passage. A second diagnosis links the same set of symptoms to an infected appendix, to appendicitis. The result is a dilemma very close to that facing the person seeking to interpret the meaning of the shadows cast by the sticks in the earlier example. Each diagnosis accounts for the symptoms. Unfortunately, they suggest entirely different modes of treatment. For indigestion, a laxative is needed; for an infected appendix removal of the appendix is usually required. The dilemma is clear: alternative and incompatible theories can account for what is observed; the data available are not sufficient to justify a reasoned choice between them.

When the information needed to make a reliable diagnosis or to apply a theory is not available, a common strategy is to select one of the available alternatives, apply it to the situation, and use the results of application to improve future diagnosis. But if the consequences of error are potentially serious, as in the example, that procedure is not advisable. Administering a laxative to a person with indigestion will clear up the problem, but if the cause of the problem is appendicitis, a laxative could lead to a ruptured appendix, peritonitis, and serious illness, or even death. On the other hand, removal of the appendix, though not usually fatal, is expensive and inconvenient, and does not aid the digestive system. Moreover, the American Medical Association takes a dim view of appendectomies that do not lead to removal of a diseased appendix. Actually, the evidence that has been supplied thus far is so thin that the unfortunate patient could actually have *both* indigestion and appendicitis.

Two basic procedures are available for resolving this kind of dilemma. First, the complexity of the indicators used to identify both "indigestion" and "appendicitis" can be increased. In particular, diagnositicans look for indicators that are associated with one illness and not with others. Second, additional information can be obtained through further observation. Note that the process of complicating the theory is undertaken first; merely to accumulate new information might obscure the problem even more if there were no basis for evaluating it. Of course, the physician's confidence in the diagnosis is not a matter of maximizing the number of indicators. If the available theory is strong, a single indicator may lead to a reliable diagnosis. Moreover, some level of uncertainty will remain, even under ideal conditions. And a skilled diagnostician may not be able to articulate fully and completely the information used to make the diagnosis. Medical training tends to reflect these characteristics of the problem. Diagnostic training places heavy emphasis on supervised work with real patients. That brings into play the extraordinary human capacity to note and register very complex details of observation and then to recognize them when they recur, even though the full content of the pattern is nowhere articulated completely and may never appear full blown in the individual's consciousness. This is a typical example of the use of the full human observer as a "measuring instrument" of a very special kind. While that practice has limits, it is also indispensable for some purposes.

An important dimension of the diagnosis problem emerges if it is assumed that the symptoms appeared in an era when physicians knew nothing of appendicitis but were familiar with indigestion. There is then no question of correct diagnosis: the physician must assume indigestion and prescribe accordingly. Presumably, some patients will have indigestion, and the prescribed laxative will solve the problem. But in other cases, the patient will have appendicitis, will become seriously ill, and may die. What will the physician do in such cases? Change to another type of laxative? Shrug off the loss as "normal?" Will the loss be "normal?" In fact, it will. Indeed, the whole conception of indigestion, its symptoms, and its effects, will be quite different, for it must combine the effects of indigestion and appendicitis in one package. In some known percentage of cases, death will not appear as an alarm signal but as an expected consequence of the illness.

How very difficult it would be for a physician to question such diagnoses is surely apparent. Yet, somehow the training of persons who will work in such circumstances, whether in medicine or any other field of inquiry, must alert the individual to possible improvements.[9] Sensitivity to error, whether in assumptions, conceptualization, or application of theory, must be incorporated into the techniques and methods used to develop and apply theory in the field. In an era of increasing specialization, when theory development tends more and more to be separated from application (the research lab grows more and more removed from the clinic), that sort of sensitivity will become increasingly difficult to produce. The value of a firm commitment to application, to the use of knowledge to achieve purpose, is here apparent. While it cannot guarantee improvement, it does create the minimum conditions for learning.

DOES THE THEORY HOLD?

Thus far, discussion of the kinds of arguments involved in theorizing has focused on the purposes for which theories are used and on the application of theory (diagnosis) to specific situations. The quality of the theory has been taken for granted. Yet if the theory is inadequate, the application will come to nothing or miscarry badly. A sound theory should function properly when it is used for suitable purposes and properly applied, regardless of the person who does the applying. But there are no wholly general criteria of adequacy that can be applied to every theory. Theories are evaluated with respect to their internal characteristics, to their congruence with other theories, and to the results of acting on them. There is no general standard of acceptability that can be applied to theories.

Some valuable insights into the adequacy of theoretical formulations can be obtained by regarding theories as analogous to maps.[10] By using conventional symbols that have been assigned empirical meanings, maps produce a record of observation that locates observables in physical space and relates them to one another, again in physical space, with varying degrees of accuracy. No map records everything that is observed. Like theories, maps organize observations from a particular perspective or conceptual framework. The data included on the map relate, presumably at least, to the purposes for which the map will be used. Maps may serve a number of purposes economically; universal maps that can serve all purposes of all users are impossible. Given a specific purpose and some knowledge of the ways in which maps are constructed and used, the adequacy of a map can be tested prior to use by reference to its internal characteristics. Without a knowledge of the uses for which it is required, only accuracy can be checked. Internally, the map must be consistent, free of ambiguities, accurate, and so on; the selection of factors included on the map can only be measured against purpose. Ultimately, the map is taken to the environment and used to attain the purposes for which it was intended. In the process, new uses for the map may be discovered; ways of improving the map may be found. The process will by now be familiar to the reader.

Internal Characteristics. Several of the internal dimensions of theories are open to criticism prior to use. The clarity and precision of the variables or concepts can be examined. The selection of variables can be criticized with respect to both relevance and sufficiency by reference to the purpose for which it will be used and the theories available that impinge on that purpose. The rules of interaction and the statement of limiting conditions must be sufficiently detailed. Otherwise, the theory may resemble a road map that has gaps in the highway network. The symbols must be clearly and unambiguously linked to observables. None of the variables included in the set should be otiose, and the rules should connect each variable to every other variable. The logic must be adequate for calculating the full implications change within the structure. The assumptions underlying the theory and, as far as can be determined, the implications of those assumptions, must be consistent with accepted knowledge in the field. No theory in psychology would be acceptable, for example, if it was contradictory to established principles of neurology or cytology. Finally, the theory must be available for use by any trained person; it cannot be reserved for the use of special persons whose qualifications cannot be duplicated or transferred to others. These points can, for the most part, be established by direct inspection of the theory.

The concept of "theory" employed in this approach to knowledge is relatively weak or loose. It is fairly easy to satisfy the minimum requirements for theory—a valuable characteristic for theories intended for use in the social sciences. The price of a weak definition of this kind, of course, is wide variation in quality. As long as purposes are specified, the quality of a theory can be linked to its reliability for achieving set purposes under known circumstances. The best analog is found in diving, where judgment is based on a combination of the dive attempted and execution. Good execution of a simple dive may count for less than imperfect execution of a very difficult undertaking. Much the same situation is found in the realm of applied knowledge. Some purposes cannot be achieved without powerful theories of very high quality; others can be satisfied by relatively weak structures. As long as purpose is matched or overmatched by capacity, that causes no particular problems. The capacity of the theory may far exceed the requirements of the purpose for which it is used—a giant computer can be used to do a child's homework—but the converse is not acceptable.

Compatibility with Current Knowledge. In many popular accounts of science, the role of the crucial experiment, with its dramatic potential, plays an understandably central role. Scientists in smocks await the outcome of an experiment with bated breath; loud cheers greet a successful outcome. In such technological activities as rocket launches, where technical reliability rather than validity of knowledge is at issue, such attitudes may be appropriate. In the early stages of development of some fields, experimental results may be exceptionally important, but in most of the sciences, the situation is quite different. Theories can usually be tested quite thoroughly before they are tried simply by embedding them in the body of currently accepted theory in the field. Experiments tend to corroborate expectations and not produce new and startling insights. Most commonly, the insights precede and even produce the experiments. When theories involve difficult measurements, or actions that exceed technological capacity, compatibility with established knowledge may be the only major test available. But such situations should be rare, particularly in social science. As long as inquiry remains rooted in observation and tied to the achievement of purposes, most of the structures that emerge from the effort are likely to have applications where they can be tested.

The Appeal to History. When theories are put to the test, the social scientist is at a serious disadvantage compared to his colleague in physical science. The supply of well-established theories is small; experiments are difficult or even impossible; and control over the natural state experiment may not be permissible or desirable. The social consequences of theory testing may be too high a cost to pay for a tested theory. It is therefore much more difficult to establish a theory in social science than in physics or chemistry, even on the weaker conception of theory. In one area, however, the social sciences actually enjoy some advantage. The historical record contains much more information related to social phenomena than to the phenomena of physical science. History is the basic laboratory of social science, and if the data it contains are far less thorough and precise than one might wish, it is not a vacuum when intelligently used.

The laboratory analogy is in one sense misleading. Discrepancies between suggested theories and historical records are not necessarily fatal to the theory. The historical record is incomplete, often inaccurate, and frequently unreliable. Historians rarely inscribe the kind of data that social scientists would like to have, even in the present. Nor do curators of museums preserve the kinds of things that social scientists would like to know more about, for very similar reasons. Each field of inquiry has its own traditions, and they provide most of the criteria of selection employed. Finally, historical accounts, as successive generations of "revisionist" historians hasten to affirm, reflect the conceptual framework of the author, which reflects, in turn, the dominant values of the times. Historical evidence is not decisive and is much less convincing than laboratory evidence. Nevertheless, going to history with a conscious purpose is a useful investment of time and energy. At the very least, history is a mammoth suggestion box for concepts, relations, priorities, and consequences. History can provide illustrations, patterns, questions, and answers. It is a source of intellectual fertilization in which the empirical constraints are already incorporated, which makes it a vast improvement on literature for the purposes of social science. In an era seemingly bent on substituting formal technology for historical study, it may be useful to stress the importance of historical evidence, both in theorizing and in testing theory and recommend efforts to improve it. It will serve neither all purposes nor no purpose. Such extremes aside, there is nothing to consult but history. Even imagination must feed upon it or run dry. At the very least, examining the theories that have been employed, their quality, and their consequences, may provide a useful way of improving theories and conceptions of theories.

Experimentation. It is widely agreed that perhaps the best way to test any theory is to create a situation to which the theory applies, isolated as fully as possible from external influences, and to apply it. Experiments of this kind are particularly well suited to the study of patterns. In the natural environment, and even in everyday discourse, intellectual patterns are inextricably mingled, often within a single proposition. That very much complicates the task of the observer or critic and accounts largely for the need to rely primarily on written rather than verbal data. Experiments can provide a way of comparing the interactions of relatively isolated sets of variables with the interactions of the same set in the natural environment, thus facilitating their transfer to real-world use.

The principal weakness of the laboratory experiment is a product of the same isolation process that makes it valuable. The aim of theorizing is to cope with the real world and not with conditions found in the laboratory. Excessive reliance upon laboratory findings, best illustrated in some phases of psychology, can be misleading and even sterile. Success in the laboratory is not always a good indication of success in the environment, even in medicine. The laboratory eliminates some of the limits and restrictions that the natural environment enforces. To the extent that theories are developed in that "unnatural" context, they truly are hothouse hybrids. "Laboratory theories" are valid mainly or even solely within the laboratory. A genuine theory is intended for use in the world as it appears in observation and must work there.

While there has been some laboratory experimentation in the social sciences, the prime source of information and tests of theories remains the "natural state" experiment. Taking the theory to the environment and trying it, or finding a situation where it was tried, with or without awareness, is the basic technique for all fields seriously concerned with developing useful theory. That is the only place where information about unanticipated side-effects can be obtained and where the influence of variables not incorporated into the conceptual framework can be determined. Political scientists have been particularly slow to experiment, either in the laboratory or in the ongoing society. That may be partly the result of lack of opportunity; access to such experimental sites is usually controlled by government. In part, the attitude can be ascribed to the general antipathy to "social engineering" among American scholars, especially in social science. And it should be said that the criteria of successful inquiry that the academic community endorses have little to do with successful application. Until very recently, few political scientists regarded government, at any level, as an appropriate testing area for their products. Many still regard incursions into "policy analysis," or emphasis on pragmatic usefulness, with unconcealed distaste.[11] Yet, if academic inquiry is something more than art for art's sake, as most would claim, the opportunity that governments provide for improving the available knowledge supply in such critical areas as education, social melioration, conflict resolution, and institutional improvement seems too important to ignore.

No amount of testing, whether in the laboratory or in society, can eliminate risk and uncertainty from theories. No theory can be "proved"—and no theory can be utterly and finally "disproved" either. The status of theory is not fixed once and for all by any particular test or set of tests. New information or a change in theoretical assumptions within the field may lead to modification, rejection, or even readoption. The central question is whether best knowledge at the present time justifies accepting and using the theory at the present time. Even that principle can be dangerous. The drowning man, as everyone knows, clutches at straws, and he is not blamed for this. But if the man dies clutching at straws while heavy logs float by unnoticed, he has not acted very wisely. Poor theories may be worse than no theories if they are accompanied by illusions, if they lull the sense of watchfulness and opportunism that theorizing demands.

Beyond specific tests in use, any argument relating to the quality of theory will attend to various other aspects of the structures and their uses. The accuracy and reliability of the theory, the precision of the measurements it incorporates, and so on, each contributes to overall quality. Perhaps the most significant dimension of theories that remains to be touched, however briefly, is the scope or generality of the structure. In general, the wider the scope and the more general the concepts, the better the theory. A theory of violence, other things equal, has wider application than a theory that relates police action to strikers. But here as elsewhere, the index number problem serves as an ultimate limit on theoretical extension. As the concepts included in the theory are broadened, its applications increase. But the process serves to diversify the populations to which the theory applies and thus reduces precision of implication. The price of wider applicability is a loss in precision and reliability.

POSTSCRIPT

The need for better theories in social science is hardly debatable. This weakness in theory does not seem to be necessary; it is not a function of some innate difference in phenomena or methods required for handling them. Moreover, arguments that assume the special status of social science are unconvincing.[12] A short history and poor tradition are better ways of accounting for present weakness. Systematic social science is relatively new and virtually undeveloped. The most desperate need at present is to reach an agreement on the nature of the enterprise rather than any specific result of inquiry. If there can be agreement on purposes and how they might be achieved, that would accomplish more than any amount of agreement at the level of specific theory. For the quality of the available theory is a function of several closely related factors. Concentrating on any one aspect of theoretical development while ignoring the others would not be very helpful. It would be like providing housing for the poor without giving them the resources or knowledge to maintain it. Conceptual improvement requires better measures; testing depends on the quality of concepts and indicators. In the short run, the development of increased awareness of the purposes of inquiry and the methods of criticism is perhaps the most that can be hoped for.

The step most likely to contribute to improved theory in social science would be a firm commitment to purposeful inquiry—to a conception of social science modeled on the medical clinic, the agricultural extension station, or the physical education program. Granted that laboratories as well as clinics are needed, they should take their cues from clinic patients and not from laboratory needs.

NOTES

1. For comparison, see Herbert Feigl and May Brodbeck, eds., *Readings in the Philosophy of Science* (Appleton-Century-Crofts, 1953), Part IV; Ernest Nagel, *The Structure of Science: Problems in the Logic of Scientific Explanation* (Harcourt, Brace, and World, 1961), Ch. 6; Carl G. Hempel, *Aspects of Scientific Explanation* (Free Press, 1965), Part III; Carl G. Hempel, *Philosophy of Natural Science* (Prentice-Hall, 1966), Ch. 6; Karl R. Popper, *The Logic of Scientific Discovery* (Science Editions, 1961), Ch. 3; Stephen Toulmin, *The Philosophy of Science: An Introduction* (Harper and Row, 1960); and Richard B. Braithwaite, *Scientific Explanation: A Study of the Function of Theory, Probability, and Law in Science* (Harper and Brothers, 1960), esp. Chs. 10 and 11.

2. Wesley C. Salmon, *The Foundations of Scientific Inference* (University of Pittsburgh Press, 1966) examines the underlying structure in a very useful way.

3. For a valuable treatment of plurative or pleonotetic logic, the logic of majorities, see P. T. Geach, *Reason and Argument* (University of California Press, 1976). Marvin Minsky and Seymour Papert, *Perceptrons: An Introduction to Computational Geometry* (MIT Press, 1969) offer a useful, if more technical, perspective on another intriguing line of development.

4. For the exception, see Ernest Nagel and James R. Newman, *Gödel's Proof* (New York University Press, 1958). Gödel demonstrated that "it is impossible to establish the internal logical consistency of a very large class of deductive systems—elementary arithmetic, for example—unless one adopts principles of reasoning so complex that their internal consistency is as open to doubt as that of the systems themselves" (p. 6).

5. See W. Ross Ashby, *An Introduction to Cybernetics* (Science Editions, 1963). Ashby, a strong proponent of cybernetic systems, was nevertheless acutely aware of the problems associated with them. For example: "When there are only two parts joined so that each affects the other, the properties of the feedback give important and useful information about the properties of the whole. But when the parts rise to even as few as four, if every one affects the other three, then twenty circuits can be traced through them; and knowing the properties of all twenty circuits does *not* give complete information about the system. Such complex systems cannot be treated as interlaced sets of more or less independent feedback circuits, but only as a whole" (p. 54). The implications for those seeking a multivariable "theory" for dealing with individual human behavior are fairly obvious.

6. John Stuart Mill, *A System of Logic* (Methuen, n.d.). See also Hubert M. Blalock, Jr., *Causal Inference in Nonexperimental Research* (University of North Carolina Press, 1964).

7. For a technical and critical account, see David Berlinski, *On Systems Analysis* (MIT Press, 1976). See also Nagel, *The Structure of Science*, Ch. 14; Hempel, "The Logic of Functional Analysis," in *Aspects of Scientific Explanation*; or Eugene J. Meehan, *Contemporary Political Thought: A Critical Study* (Dorsey Press, 1967), Ch. 3, for related criticism of functionalism.

8. Nagel, *The Structure of Science*, Ch. 11.

9. For a detailed treatment of the entire area of inquiry raised by such questions, see Larry D. Spence, *The Politics of Social Knowledge* (Pennsylvania State University Press, 1978), and for a more narrow treatment, see *Behavioral Sciences and Medical Education: A Report of Four Conferences*, U.S. Department of Health, Education, and Welfare, DHEW Publication No. (NIH) 72-41.

10. Toulmin, *The Philosophy of Science*, Ch. 4.

11. The most striking example known to me occurs in Edward C. Banfield and James Q. Wilson's *City Politics* (Harvard University Press, 1963),

p. 4, where the authors state: "The ultimate justification for the study of city politics, however, is certainly not a practical one. Perhaps the most intrinsically satisfying of man's activities is trying to understand the world he lives in. Politics, being one of the most difficult things to understand, is therefore particularly challenging. Responding to the challenge is, we think, its own justification and reward."

12. For examples of such criticism, see John G. Gunnell, *Philosophy, Science, and Political Inquiry* (General Learning Press, 1975), Maurice Natanson, ed., *Philosophy of the Social Sciences* (Random House, 1963) or Maurice Natanson, ed., *Phenomenology and the Social Sciences* (Northwestern University Press, 1973), Michael Polanyi, *Personal Knowledge* (Harper and Row, 1964), or Thomas Spragens, *The Dilemma of Contemporary Political Theory: Toward a Post-Behavioral Science of Politics* (Dunwellen Press, 1973). Compare Eugene J. Meehan, *Contemporary Political Thought*, Ch. 6, Spence, *The Politics of Social Knowledge*, or Maria J. Falco, ed., *Through the Looking-Glass: Epistemology and the Conduct of Inquiry* (University Press of America, 1979), Panels I and II.

5 Choices

The humanist plea that "Science is not enough" is correct on at least two counts. Knowing what to expect or how to make things happen does not suggest the appropriate reaction to expectations or the proper use to be made of the capacity to control the flow of events. Further, there would be little reason to create the instruments that can generate expectations about the world or control events unless those instruments could somehow be used for human purposes. Time and history tend to blur the dependence of tool upon purpose, particularly in intellectual matters, but the fundamental contingency remains. Every human action is an expression of value and not merely an application of science. The need to choose, and thereby to express preferences, provides the underlying impetus and rationale for systematic inquiry. The quest for knowledge is only another expression of the human desire and need to continue improving the quality of human life. The central problem in a theory of knowledge is not to produce a "science" but to find the means for placing human actions on a reasoned and corrigible foundation and to suggest the ways in which actions can be justified and defended.

Traditional moral philosophy or ethics is not very useful for that purpose. Neither the kind of questions asked nor the kind of reasoning employed to answer them relates very closely to the choices that must be made in everyday life, individual or collective. The nature and purpose of the moral enterprise, the means by which improvements are achieved, and the criteria on which a claim to improvement can be based are subject to widespread dispute among philosophers.[1] No acceptable basis for justifiable and improvable choice can be found within philosophy as practiced. Nor can much assistance be obtained from such newer fields as "public choice" or "decision theory," although some of that work has great promise.[2] An independent intellectual base must be created for the enterprise.

The generalized solution to the problem of knowledge developed in Chapter 1 holds for normative as well as empirical matters. If human experience can be organized in an appropriate form, the resulting structures provide a corrigible basis for action. The experience is generalized in a pattern; the results of using the pattern serve as evidence for justifying or improving the pattern; the practice of informed users indicates whether the result should be considered improvement or merely change. The critical base is supplied by the human capacity to react affectively to different aspects of the environment and to modify those reactions on cognitive grounds. How that process is carried out and applied will be explored in detail below. The aim is to demonstrate a way of criticizing or justifying choices that lies within human capacity, is grounded in human experience, and will satisfy human needs or purposes. The focus is methodological and not substantive; the argument is directed mainly at modes of argument and not at the substance of any particular action or choice.

REASONED CHOICE

The centrality of choice or action in human affairs is indisputable. Individuals have the capacity to act and must act to survive; actions produce differences in the environment, and differences are an indication of choice. Actions are precisely equivalent to choices. The need to act cannot be evaded by doing nothing, for if the capacity is present, failure to act has precisely the same effect as positive action—the world is different than it might otherwise be. The need to choose cannot be avoided by choosing everything, for the world is characterized by scarcity, and some resources such as time are both limited and indivisible. If it sometimes appears that choices are made "naturally," as in the case where people head for higher ground when they learn that the dam has burst, close inspection does not bear out the interpretation. Choices are unavoidable, often difficult, sometimes dangerous, and occasionally lethal. The problem is to bring them under intellectual control.

The structures and processes involved in reasoned choice are complex, difficult to apply, and uncertain in application. From the point of view of either the actor or the critic, reasoned choice is tedious, time-consuming, hazardous, and unrewarding. There are no short-cuts available; there are few models in which the process is exemplified and therefore easily studied; and there is no guarantee of success. Arguments on either side of significant issues are likely to be weak; emotional commitment is likely to be strong in inverse ratio. Even in quite commonplace circumstances, humans reach diametrically opposite solutions to simple matters of choice and then dispute with and even kill one another over the disagreement. Nevertheless, a set of assumptions, structures, and processes can be developed that will narrow and clarify the issues involved, maximize the likelihood that agreement will be reached, and provide grounds for improvement over time and for justification of the belief that an improvement has been made. How those structures and processes can be combined to provide a solution to choice problems is developed first. The arguments that are needed to produce and support those decisions and judgments are considered in the remainder of this chapter.

SOME PRELIMINARIES

The meaning of action or choice is most accurately stated by referring to structured descriptions. Choices produce change and are indicated by change. The substance of change is specified by references to the values of some finite set of variables at two or more points in time. The results of choice, including "nonchoice" or inaction, can always be stated in the form: "This set of values for these variables *rather than* that set of values for the same variables." Where the selection of variables is important, it can be shown in the form by contrasting positive values with zero value for the same variable. In effect, the substance of choice is a set of alternative descriptions; the consequence of choice is to produce one of those descriptions rather than the others. However, the descriptions in this case actually refer to the future. They must be projected by an appropriate theory, and their reliability will be less than perfect. On this way of conceptualizing action, the consequences of action can be determined objectively, using theory and observations. The actor's intentions and beliefs are not relevant to the consequences of action. There is therefore no need to inquire into the actor's conceptual framework or to engage in amateur psychoanalysis. The focus of criticism is the choice: the actor must be identified only in order to determine the content of the alternatives.

Obviously, not every human choice is reasoned. Moreover, a clear distinction is needed between reasoned choice and affective response or reaction. Affect can and does generate behavior, of course, but the response engendered is characteristically direct and spontaneous. There is no element of calculation. What identifies reasoned choice is a deliberate effort to calculate costs and benefits, and not necessarily in monetary terms. The alternatives available for choice are weighed in terms of known criteria or priorities. That conception of reasoned choice is deliberately made weak. The quality of the choice may vary greatly: alternatives may be ignored, calculations may be inaccurate, and so on. The critical factor is the process, for it allows identification of the structures required to carry it out, and that in turn can be tied to the kinds of assumptions needed to put the whole procedure on a corrigible base. The justification or argument that is offered in support of a reasoned choice will refer to the direct and indirect consequences of that choice for all of the individuals actually affected.

In the approach to reasoned choice detailed below, development begins with the particular case, resolved by comparing the available alternatives in terms of the populations affected. Solutions to particular cases are generalized or aggregated in precisely the same way as theories. Justification is provided solely by reference to the consequences of use. The situation defines the choice; criticism begins with the situation. Comparison of possibilities must generate reasons for preferring one outcome to the others. If no reasons can be found, the choice is a matter of indifference given the accepted ethic. Over time, a priority system can be developed that will represent the generalized solutions found for the particular choice problems that have been resolved systematically. In one sense, the mores and norms of society represent the same type of outcome but are generated more or less uncritically. As in theorizing, the procedures by which priorities or preferences are created remain unknown. Argument focuses on the kinds of reasons that can be found (in the consequences) for continuing or modifying the initial assumption. The critic's task is to expose inconsistencies and ambiguities, to eliminate useless rules, to develop new priorities, to expose new dimensions of human life that should be taken into account when choices are made, and, if possible, to further the generalization of the total structure. Focusing on the particular case roots the enterprise in real consequences, avoiding the kind of disputation over principles with no concrete implications for action that characterizes so much of moral philosophy. A testable rule of action must *force* behavior in the situations where it applies; rules that are merely compatible with certain outcomes and not others cannot serve as guides to action.

THE CONTEXT OF CHOICE

Choices arise either in the context of a specific actor or as a problem requiring solution in a social context. The procedures used to make the choice are the same in either case, but the overall implications of the two contexts are different. If the actor has been identified, the problem in choice is to determine the best course of action at a given time and place. A set of theories is needed to explore the implications of the actor's capacity for action, indicating the benefits and costs associated with each of the options. A priority system will then provide a basis for action. The problem is straightforward; individual and collective implications of action coincide.

When some condition in the environment is attacked on normative grounds and when change is demanded in a specific situation, a number of actors may have the capacity to produce the required modification. That creates problems not encountered in criticism of individual actions. Since social criticism usually focuses on choice problems arising in such social contexts, some of the peculiarities inherent in them bear emphasis. In particular, choices made in social context may involve quite different sets of costs, for both individual and collective, depending on the institutional arrangements available for choosing the appropriate actor. If the hidden social costs of such actions are overlooked, as is often or even usually the case, an important part of society's institutional structure escapes criticism and potential improvement.

When change in some particular dimension of the observed environment is sought on reasoned normative grounds, the first step in the process is to locate an actor with the capacity to change the situation. Theories must be available that can link the particular situation to each of the potential actors. That does not automatically produce a solution to the problem, however. For each actor, that situation will be one of a range of situations in which there is capacity to act or intervene. A situation must rank at or near the top on *some* actor's list of priorities; otherwise, it will not be acted upon, however significant it may appear from a neutral vantage point. Moreover, even though some actor may act to produce change in the situation, the institutional sorting mechanism that produces the decision may not operate very efficiently. The total cost or social cost of the action involved will appear differently, depending on the actor involved. For each actor, the sets of options that determine those costs will be different. When the wrong actor makes a social choice, real social costs can be increased very dramatically.

The social critic who asks for action on some specific situation without specifying the actor may be asking for action that lies beyond the power of any available actor. That is analogous to feeling sympathy for the cancer victim while being unable to denounce the physician for failing to save the life. The problem tends to be masked in social affairs, however, because the request for action can be construed as a request to public authority to create a jurisdiction with the resources, knowledge, and priorities needed to assist the population whose unfortunate condition is the focus of concern. Such proposals play an important part in the extension of collective responsibility and jurisdiction, for the power to create new jurisdictions is an important element in the claim to sovereignty that is normally accepted (and demanded) for political agencies. Many of the more important changes in modern society have resulted from the creation of new legal rights and moral obligations against the collectivity. All too often, the cost of creating the machinery for choice is not included in the action that creates the machinery. A demand for extension of public authority is a request for a choice whose costs and benefits can be weighed in the same manner as any other choice.

Part of the difficulty encountered with this class of choices arises from a mistaken attribution of previous choice. That is, the action requested is regarded as a simple remedy for a previous error. Treating social choices in that way serves to hide the costs and benefits associated with the choice. The inadequacy of existing patterns of authority and jurisdiction in society usually emerges when either the distribution of resources produces palpable inequities among significant groups of persons or the social costs of collective action become excessive. In the traditional case, the rich man's dog drinks milk while the poor man's child does not have the milk needed for normal growth. For purposes of argument and illustration, assume that (1) a poor father in city X feeds his child on gruel and water because he can afford nothing better, and the child fails to develop normally; (2) a rich person in city X feeds milk and beef to his dog each day in quantities larger than the child requires for normal development. Specify that both events take place during the same time period. These observations can be taken to mean that a terrible choice has been made somewhere in the society. In fact, there has been no choice, and there is no conspiracy. The social institutions operating in the society may be inadequate (measured against the critic's priorities), but there is no past choice to be undone. Before the assumption of real prior choice could be justified, an adequate theory would be needed linking the present situation to an identifiable actor, individual or collective. If there is no actor, the accusation must lie against existing institutions for producing, or not inhibiting, development of the situation complained against.

That is the sense in which every individual choice has a social dimension.

Under other circumstances, an undesirable situation may be improved by social action, but at excessive cost. Assume, for example, that three public agencies can intervene to provide assistance to a group of elderly persons but that only one group will act because of their individual action priorities. If the cost of producing a desired modification in the conditions of life of the elderly persons is twice as great for the agency actually prepared to act as for either of the two alternative actors, the social costs of action have doubled as a result of the existing decision-making machinery. To the extent that each agency operates independently of the others, there is no way to optimize social costs. When social actions depend on procedures that can overlook or suppress significant costs, the society courts disaster over the long run. In some cases where the costs of both action and inaction are very high, centralized authority may be unavoidable. A good illustration is found in the way distress calls are handled by ships at sea. Obviously, the calls *must* be answered. One solution, analogous to mass vaccination, is for every ship that hears a distress call to head immediately for the site. That could be enormously wasteful, but if not followed, it could have lethal results for those on board. Without adequate communications, there is no option to waste. Contemporary technology provides a means for rapid and efficient optimization of the procedure, given central direction. Such problems could also be solved without an overriding authority, of course, if there was an agreed base for calculating actions and responsibilities—or if costs were simply ignored. If each captain knew the position, size, speed, and so on of all the other ships in the area and the needs of the foundering vessel, self-allocation of responsibility for decision could also lead to effective and efficient action. Indeed, an "overkill" could easily be built into the calculations. In the relatively crowded coastal and inland waters, allocating authority and information to the Coast Guard seems the most simple and most efficient solution to the problem. Without coordination, the system would be too dependent on altruism, projected self-interest (I may be next) and willingness to accept costs.

Choices made in a social context call attention to a dimension of action that is common to most individual and collective choices. For the most part, the range of options consciously considered actually includes only a small part of the real capacity of the actor. The young woman engaged in choosing between two dresses rarely considers use of those same resources to aid underprivileged youth or to provide assistance at a local public hospital. Similarly, governments do not usually examine overall expenditures in terms of overall need, shifting resources to where they are most needed, although the practice is common in families. For both individuals and governments, the result of such myopia is to strengthen tradition and established practice. In budgetary matters particularly, it fosters what has been called incrementalism—the practice of adding serially to established activities in proportion to past expenditures rather than through assessment of need or contribution.

ACTIONS

The term "action" tends to be regarded in physical or bodily terms, so that an "active" person is usually taken to mean someone who is physically "on the go" much of the time. But with relation to social affairs, physical actions are probably the least important means available for producing an effect or impact on another person. Since the effects of action depend on the context, the characteristics of the persons affected, and the type of action taken, excessive concentration on physical action could be quite misleading. Without attempting a definitive treatment of the dimensions of human action, some of the alternatives to physical actions are easily identified. Three alternatives seem particularly important in social affairs: communication, especially communication targeted at preprogrammed behavior patterns that have been internalized with the norms; allocation of resources; and creation of rights and obligations for specific populations. In addition, efforts to create or criticize action strategies are concerned with such characteristics of action as reversibility, duration of impact, and rate of taking effect (gradualism versus triggering effect or "all or none" actions). Finally, although *all* of the consequences must usually be taken into account when an action is criticized, in some special cases that is not required. The coach of a basketball team, for example, does not have to be concerned with parental disappointment when selecting members of a team. Similarly, an employer is not required to examine the effects of selecting employees outside the workplace. However, "affirmative action" asserts that once the requirements of the workplace have been satisfied, then the employer is obligated to take into account the socioeconomic conditions in society at large and how they are affected by the decision.

Action as Communication. As human interactions become increasingly complex, and as social institutions become more detailed and firmly embedded, the role of written and verbal communications expands rapidly. The importance of socialization also grows, for the effects of any communication depend on the meaning attached to it by the recipient, and not merely the intentions of the communicator. To rise in a crowded theatre and shout "Fire" as loudly as possible is to attempt communication with the other occupants. In this context, capacity is a function of vocal power and language in combination. If the message is not heard, it has no effect. If the message is heard but not understood, if the theatre audience is made up of people who are wholly ignorant of English, there will be no effect. The action is equivalent to shouting "Watch out" to a deaf person about to step off the curb in front of a moving vehicle. Moreover, language barriers are found within a common language as well as between languages. If cultural differences are wide enough, communication may be impossible. The concept of a "shared" language and culture can in some circumstances be seriously misleading.

The specific effects of communication depend on a complicated set of patterns that have been socialized into the person who receives the message. The habits, mores, values, beliefs, assumptions, and so on that have been acquired by the individual serve to link incoming messages to certain kinds of responses that experience deems "appropriate." Advertising consistently, if somewhat crudely, attempts both to construct such linkages and to make use of them to sell particular products. The same procedures are widely, and often just as crudely, used with respect to collective affairs. Conditions within society will depend greatly on who is able to trigger the functioning of such semi-automated responses and what purposes they are used for. That in turn depends on the role structures society has created and the manner in which they are allocated and used. What appears as a legitimate order in one context may seem unwarranted intervention in personal affairs in another. Which assumption is made depends very largely on the role structures assigned to the situation rather than on the personal attributes of the actors. A private citizen at the scene of an accident may be able to produce motorist behavior that a regular policeman could not achieve in normal conditions.

For purposes of social action, the range of preconditioned response patterns actually shared by most members of society provides one of the more important channels available for influencing the lives of individuals within the society. The occupants of certain key social roles, which are not necessarily "public" or part of the formal institutional arrangements of the society, usually have the capacity to produce such patterned responses. One major function of social science, obviously, is to determine the latent capacity of the socialization structure and how it can be employed. One major function of the social critic is to consider the various alternative purposes for which it might be used. Strictly speaking, these are empirical questions, but they have an enormous impact on the quality of life within the society. Hence, they are among the major objects of normative inquiry and argument.

Resource Allocation. The second major form of social action, public or private, is the transfer or allocation of resources. The effects of governmental resource allocation are particularly significant because of the magnitudes involved and because resources are both collected from and distributed to the same aggregate population, thereby generating enormous redistributional potential. Various aspects of the process can influence effects in a particular situation. Among them, the more salient include the amount of resources collected and dispersed, both in absolute terms and as a portion of total economic activity; the elements of the population where resources are gathered and the primary beneficiaries; the purposes for which resources are used; the form in which resource transfers are carried out; the constraints placed on the use of resources; and the manner in which access to transfers is specified. Systematic inquiry can be directed at both the effects of allocation, which is an empirical matter, and the purposes sought through allocation, which refers to the priority system in force in society.

The effects of taxation and spending are omnipresent in every modern society. The sheer volume of government purchases makes it a major factor in domestic and international markets. Indirect influence over the flow of goods and services through monetary and fiscal policies, subsidies of various kinds, and controls or regulations is simply enormous. While such matters are left primarily for the economists, they are subject to the same procedures and criteria of inquiry as any other dimension of action. For the social critic generally, the ameliorative and redistributive effects of governmental actions are especially important. Here it is useful to distinguish the potential value of resources provided in kind and direct transfer of funds to beneficiaries. Public housing, highways, public hospitals, and schools are examples of services and goods in kind; welfare payments exemplify direct resource transfers.

The major differences between the two types of actions or choices can be found in the amount of control provided over such things as cost, quality, and predictability of effects. Very large populations can be assured of necessities such as education, highways, or inoculations by provision of goods and services in kind. Since the quantities involved are likely to be very large, savings through large-scale purchasing are possible in principle. So are opportunities for large-scale waste and malfeasance. Providing liquid resources directly to the individual reduces the donor's control over the use made of the funds, as a child provided with lunch money may choose to skip lunch and spend the money for something else. But if the funds are used intelligently, the match between particular individual need and preference and the goods or services provided can be much more precise and satisfying, and there are clear side-benefits for the individual. In general, provision in kind tends to maximize efficiency, concentrates authority in the hands of program directors, and reduces flexibility at the point of consumption. Direct money transfers maximize individual control over purchasing, increase individual unit cost by abjuring large-scale purchases, and take away much of the donor's control over the use of donations.

In practice, both modes of action will be found in every society, together with efforts to obtain the best of both worlds—use of food stamps, for example, as a quasi-currency with partially restricted use. There has been a marked tendency to centralization and provision of resources in kind, though it has been strongly resisted. Centralization is unavoidable if outcomes are sufficiently important to accept potential waste in order to ensure universal availability—education, medical attention, food and shelter, and so on. But some resources must be left to individual control, partly for reasons of efficiency and partly for psychological reasons, no matter what purposes are sought in action. Otherwise, the society risks a form of dependent quiescence that would be extraordinarily difficult to modify or amend.

Creation of Rights and Obligations. The third significant form of social action is the creation of rights and obligations for individuals and groups within the collectivity. The principal results of such actions are the laws of society, of course, but every individual and group has some limited capacity to create rights and obligations, for the self and for others. The young woman who allows herself to be kissed creates a right for the person doing the kissing and an obligation for herself. Her parents may countermand this set of rights and obligations on grounds of higher authority, and if the young woman is a dependent minor, the claim will have to be accepted. If the young woman is beyond the age of consent and independent, the parental claim can be resisted, and support would be forthcoming from the society as a whole.

What is unique about the national state and what makes the rights and obligations it creates particularly important is the claim to sovereign authority. Within a given geographical area, national states allow each other (legally at least) supreme authority with respect to rights and obligations. Constitutional and other limitations are internal devices, not part of the international order. The sovereign claim is in principle limitless. The state creates rights and obligations for individuals, and regulates the creation of such rights and obligations by subsidiary organizations, public or private, or by individuals. The individual can create rights against the self and personal property—for example, allow another person to use an automobile—but the individual cannot create rights with respect to another person. Outside the family, only the state can without interference create rights against an individual which must be accepted on threat of punishment.

Actions that create rights and obligations have effects ranging from vital to trivial. These effects are felt in such diverse areas as interpersonal relations, consumption habits, wages, disposal of wealth and income, treatment of the family, education of the young, and even religious practices. Since they are easily created and enforced with all of the paraphernalia of modern bureaucracy, the power to create rights and obligations places unimaginable potential in the hands of those who govern. There are limits on what government can enforce; *quid leges sans mores* is as true today as in Roman times. When law conflicts with the mores, the law usually loses. Nevertheless, modification of existing rights and obligations remains a very powerful technique for influencing the lives of very large populations in fundamental ways. When the potential effects of inaction are taken into account, the effects of failing to create rights and obligations or creating but not enforcing them, the potential for change inherent in government is nearly boundless. Indeed, the limits on that potential are themselves socialized norms subject to the same influences as other norms.

STRUCTURING THE ALTERNATIVES

For every human agent with a capacity to act, whether individual or collective, existence is comprised in endless, sequential decisions about the use of that capacity and the resources attached to it. Life is usefully considered a series of decision points. Most of the possibilities are ignored and the drift course of events is allowed to continue. It can be a very momentous decision. Some of the possibilities are merely trivial. Socialization alerts the actor to crucial decisions, those with extensive implications. Since it may omit some, overemphasize or deemphasize others, its influence deserves careful examination. At any of the decision nodes, the alternatives available to the actor can be identified and the consequences examined. Information relating to choices actually made can be used to criticize both the socialization process and the priority system used to deal with the choice. The way in which those alternatives are structured will tend to determine the choice made and the justification offered to support it. Since choices are made within the real constraints that environment provides and those constraints are particular, a general discussion of process cannot produce or substantiate concrete rules of choice or priorities. They depend on situation, knowledge available, technology, prior experience, and a range of other factors. Nevertheless, the base from which reasoned choice proceeds is a systematic structuring of the alternatives available to an identifiable actor at a given time and place.

Perhaps the best analog available to the alternatives from which a choice is actually made is a sequence of film clips, each commencing at the point of action or choice and incorporating the significant effects of action, as far as they can be foreseen. Each alternative is a future scenario, projected by an appropriate theory and brought into being by human action. Reasoned choice requires at least two alternatives; where there is only one option, there is no choice. The content of each option will be a future description, often extended over time. The consequences of the choice can be stated in the general form: Alternative A (described by some set of variables and their projected values) *rather than* alternatives B, C. . . . The meaning of the choice necessarily involves reference to the full set of options and not merely to the option chosen.

Because the options involved in choice are projected by theory, the outcome is always in some degree problematic. Each option has an attached probability, which is itself rough, approximate, and uncertain in many cases. The risk attached to the outcome and the likelihood that the theoretical structure will fail must certainly influence the choice. Given a choice between atomic war and an outbreak of measles, only a monster would choose war. But if the measles epidemic is a near certainty and the atomic war is a one-in-ten-trillion risk (if such numbers have any meaning), the choice of measles is much less likely. Compared to certain death, severe injury is trivial. The problem is to find reasons for supposing that death is really certain. Unfortunately, delay or temporizing does not suspend decision; it merely introduces another level of decision-making. Delay counts as action, and the costs and benefits of delay are calculated in the same way as other action costs. Procrastination has its price.

The level of risk attached to the different outcomes involved in choice can itself be a source of normative disagreement. People differ markedly in their willingness to accept risk; both cowardice and foolhardiness are common. Even though agreement is reached on the outcomes possible and on their relative desirability, differences in willingness to accept risk can prevent action.

Chain Reactions. Structurally, human actions can be construed as the triggering device for a sequence of chain reactions. The action changes the value of one variable; that change produces further changes in a second set of variables; they in turn produce changes in yet another set; and so on until the theoretical capacity of the actor or critic is exhausted. Several theories may be used to explore the full implications of action, producing a structure closely resembling a nuclear chain reaction:

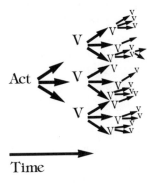

Time

Where does the chain end? There is no simple answer to the question. The state of knowledge of the time is one major limit; the chain cannot extend beyond the theoretical capacity to extend it. But other considerations, such as the pressure of time and prior experience with this or an analogous situation, will influence the extent to which the structure is elaborated before choice is actually made. Wherever analysis ends, the result is always partial and incomplete. Where the effects of action "really" end is always indeterminate.

The rapidity with which such chain reactions grow complex and fade is a powerful reminder of the limits on the human capacity to deal with the future in a reliable way. The film clips from which choices are made may be sharp, clear, and detailed in the beginning, but they blur and evaporate within a very short time. There is no cause for alarm in that, for the condition is unavoidable. Indeed, the danger in theorizing lies in expecting too much rather than too little. By necessity and not choice, the human species lives very close to the present. The antecedents to the present are speedily obscured by time and the flow of events: books become chapters, then paragraphs, then sentences, and finally disappear entirely. The implications of the present cannot be projected very far into the future with accuracy or reliability. That annoys perfectionists, but is simply one of the defining conditions of being human, and it may be a blessing—too much memory could be a burden. As long as theories offer a short-term guide to action that is better than random action, the astrologer's tent, or even the economist's crystal ball, their use can be profitable. The critical factor is corrigibility over time. Much can be done with weak and ineffective tools, given time and patience.

The ongoing character of the human situation provides the escape clause for humanity, taken in the aggregate. As long as *some* base for action can be found and used, experience can refine, elaborate, and extend the structure. Moreover, a large part of the social repertoire is made up of negatives, actions, and outcomes to be avoided. Such high-priority dangers as death, physical maiming, or psychic destruction can usually be linked to broad classes of actions (such as handling weapons, transportion devices, and certain kinds of toys), and suitable avoidance strategies can be devised and used to train children. A prime function of socialization, in other words, is to provide the young with cues and strategies for minimizing or avoiding highly undesirable outcomes. Youngsters who learn to hunt with their elders, for example, soon learn to avoid certain classes of actions that are tabooed while hunting. In periods of rapid social and technological change, such early training may prove inadequate or even counterproductive. It is a commonplace that yesterday's essentials can disappear overnight, and some of today's essentials were wholly unknown only a few years ago. The changes wrought by replacing the horse by the automobile, for example, or the train by the airplane are staggering. So are such things as the introduction of drugs into a youth culture. In stable eras, when life-styles are relatively constant between generations, both the dangers and the situations in which they arise become well defined. When social conditions are changing rapidly, transitional generations may be adversely affected by strongly inculcated but inappropriate priorities or by a structured inability to adapt individually to circumstances. The dilemma is inescapable. Youth need to learn warning signals available in the culture; what is available may prove inadequate. The lesson, clearly is to teach the young how to do their own reasoning rather than what priorities to accept—easier by far to state than to carry out.

The Normative Variables. All decisions are based on a limited set of factors; that set can be extended if it proves inadequate. The actor (or critic) is socialized to consider certain dimensions of the results of action or choice, using them to rule out certain options and to underscore or weight others. In effect, reasoned choices are usually argued in terms of the values of certain key factors or variables. They identify the "normative" dimensions of life affected by the action.

A modified diagram will suggest the way in which the normative variables (*NV*) are incorporated in the structure of choice. Assume a choice with two options, each producing a different effect on those involved:

	(b)	(c)	(d)	(h)		
(a)	V_1	V_2	VN^1	VN	R_a	
	V	V	V	V		
	VN	V	V	R_h		
	V	R_c	V		(f)	
R_b	(e)		V	VN	V	R_e
			R_d		V	
					VN	
					R_f	

A

$$(k) \quad \overline{V_1 \quad V \quad VN^1 \quad V \quad R_k}$$

$$V$$

$$VN \qquad\qquad (n)$$

$$(m) \quad \overline{V \quad V \quad VN \quad V \quad R_m}$$

$$R_1 \qquad\qquad VN$$

$$V$$

$$R_n$$

B

The actor's primary purpose is to change the value of the normative variable (*VN*) identified as (1) in the primary set. The desired change can be produced by two actions, identified as (*a*) and (*k*). Each action can generate its own set of consequences, shown as (*A*) and (*B*). The size and complexity of the structure depend on the type of action taken, the situation in which action occurs, and the theories available for projecting consequences. To the extent that they can be determined within existing capacity, the values for each normative variable that appears within the structure must be specified for all outcomes. If the values of some variables remain unknown in some outcomes, that must be included in the calculation of preference. For example, the fact that certain kinds of consequences for the patient cannot be projected by available knowledge may be of great importance to a physician. The normative variables contain the primary costs and benefits of action, the dimensions of human life that are affected by the action and considered to have the greatest amount of normative significance. *All* of the foreseeable effects of action are included in the structure. Although certain effects are excluded from judgments by the norms that guide particular kinds of choices (the reaction of parents to coaching decisions, for example), including those costs serves to call attention to the price of maintaining such norms. Partial enumeration of the effects of action destroys the value of the procedure. If none of the available means for intervening to change the situation is acceptable and if negative effects outweigh benefits in the judgment of actor or critic, alternative theories must be sought that can provide a different set of benefits and costs. If action is delayed, however, that delay must also be assessed by the same procedures.

To the extent that costs and benefits are limited to what theoretical capacity can project, the diagrams are correct but potentially misleading. For at the boundaries of knowledge, there are usually suspected but unsubstantiated effects and relations. However vague, uncertain, and imprecise such suspicions may be, they can have significant implications for action, depending on content and situation. For example, general agreement among experts that certain substances are a likely source of damage to children's development might, in the absence of convincing evidence, warrant exclusion of that material from baby food pending further inquiry. Much depends on the nature of the situation and the source of the suggested relation. A semidemented parent's belief that school lunches are producing sterilization in children will be ignored. A similar judgment from well-established medical authorities is likely to be heeded, at least to the extent of conducting further inquiries, perhaps while suspending use of the materials. The structure of choices can easily be extended to take such considerations into account.

When the set of outcomes from which a choice must be made has been structured as fully as the available theory permits, the normative variables that appear in those outcomes can be brought together in a matrix to demonstrate the normatively significant content of the outcomes in a very economical way. The values of every normative variable must be shown for each of the options:

Normative Variables	*Alternative Outcomes*	
	1	**2**
NV_1	a_1	a_2

Normative Variables	*Alternative Outcomes*	
NV_2	b_1	b_2
NV_3	unknown	c_2
. .		
NV_n	n_1	n_2

Since each normative variable refers to a significant attribute of some person or class of persons, and the values taken by those variables are projected on the future by theory, the task of the actor or critic is to prioritize the different conditions of life of some identifiable population that can be produced by the actions of a known human agent. The actor must find reasons for preferring either alternative (1) or alternative (2). The full set must be selected; the priority is attached to the whole set, taken together, and not to individual parts of the set. The reasons used to justify preference may be either positive or negative, that is, refer to conditions of life to be avoided at all costs or to conditions of life so favorable they should be sought at all costs. How those preferences can be argued and justified will be considered below.

THE NORMATIVE VARIABLES

Choices are criticized or justified by comparing the situation or condition produced by action with the alternative situations that could have been produced by the same actor at the time of action. Since every situation can in principle be conceptualized in endless different ways, some selection of variables must be used to structure the options, otherwise the description could not be completed and the arguments would not intersect. Formally, comparison requires two or more things to be compared and some continuum on which both can be measured. The continua needed for reasoned choice are supplied by the normative variables. They identify the differences that make a difference in human life, the dimensions of life that are normatively significant.

Structurally, a normative variable is quite complex. The operating assumptions on which the theory of knowledge depends requires that all normative variables refer to some aspect of human life. The individual life will actually serve as a common denominator since it is also assumed that *qua* life, one is the equal of any other. The first step in the development of the structure is to identify the conditions that an adequate set of normative variables must satisfy. The exact dimensions of life that will be included in the normative variables may vary with time and culture but the structures and processes required by reasoned choice will be the same in all cases. The discussion will therefore concentrate on those aspects of the normative variables.

Every person can be described fully, though not exhaustively, in terms of the observed values of a finite set of variables at a specific time. The variables, drawn from an infinite set (in principle, at least) can refer to any dimension of the person, from purely physical attributes such as weight through the gamut of psychic states, learned capacities, legal rights and obligations, possessions, relations with others, and life styles. Not all of these aspects of individual life have equal normative significance, of course; some may have virtually none under some circumstances. For reasoned choice, a set of variables is needed that will identify the critical aspects of life, the factors to be weighed before acting or choosing. To put the point another way, the normative variables must identify the dimensions of life that can be used to measure the effects of action on the individual, or to compare the conditions of the life of the individual before and after action has occurred.

One person affects another by inducing some change in the set of attributes that describe that person, or by preventing a change in those attributes that would otherwise take place. The consequences of action can therefore be stated as one descriptive account of the individual rather than one or more different descriptive accounts. The justification for the action will refer to the conditions of life contained in each of the alternative descriptions. Happily, there is no need to produce an absolute measure of the quality of any particular alternative. Choices are made by comparing two or more outcomes. Nevertheless, the normative variables needed for comparing the human situation in two or more different conditions will be composite structures, miniature theories whose rules of interaction actually generate the value taken by the composite normative variable. The complexity is unavoidable, as can be demonstrated readily by examining the function that the variable performs.

Structuring the Normative Variables. The structural features of the normative variables can be demonstrated through sequential development, using relatively simple diagrams. The purpose of the normative variable is to provide a base for comparison between two or more outcomes attainable by action. The root meaning of the variables, the thing that is being measured or compared, is the quality of the life that is affected by choice or action. Hence, development begins with the set of variables used to describe the individual at some point in time. The selection is enclosed in square brackets to indicate that it cannot be calculated. Such structures are used to record observations to produce a description.

$$[\quad V_1 \ V_2 \ V_3 \ V_4 \ V_5 \ldots \ldots \ V_n \quad]$$

For any actor to have an effect on the individual described in the brackets, or the class of persons to whom the description applied, a change will have to be made in the value of at least one of those variables. The actor must be able to change one of the individual's attributes or to prevent such changes.

The individual attributes that can be altered by another actor will be called *indicators* and symbolized as (VI). The values of these variables, which remain attributes of the individual, must be linked to specific actions by appropriate theories before the structure can function. They are not intrinsic measures of impact. The body may be badly mauled physically, for example, without a significant long-range impact on the individual. A hypodermic injection, on the other hand, may produce only a tiny hole in the skin and yet cause major disaster, or even death for the individual. The indicators serve as a connecting link between the individual life and the external actor.

For analytic clarity, the indicators can be separated from the rest of the individual's attributes to produce a subset of factors accessible from outside the person:

$$[[VI_1 \; VI_2 \ldots \ldots VI_n] \qquad [V_1 \; V_2 \; V_3 \; V_4 \ldots \ldots V_n]]$$

The structure must now be complicated further. The effect of action is a change in one of the indicator variables. How much that change will affect the total life of the person depends on the individual's other attributes. In effect, certain aspects of the person mediate between the individual life and the effects of the action. Individual wealth, for example, can almost completely mitigate or negate the effects of a loss of cash through theft. These mediating factors will be called *buffers* and are symbolized as (*VB*). The buffers mediate between individual and environment. The impact of change is a function of the indicator variables acting in combination with the buffers. Structurally, they can be separated from the other variables used to describe the individual or class to produce a second subset:

$$[[VI_1 \; VI_2 \ldots \ldots VI_n] \quad [VB_1 \; VB_2 \ldots \ldots VB_n] \quad [V_1 \; V_2 \; V_3 \; V_4 \ldots \ldots V_n]]$$

The full set of buffer variables (*VB*) can be used to identify all of the individuals who will be affected in the same way (normatively and with respect to the life of the person) by a particular change in the indicators. A combination of indicators and buffers is needed to identify the class of persons that is affected the same way by a common action in the environment. For reasoned policymaking, both indicators and buffers must be matched, or the effects of action will not be the same for everyone in the class. The effect of a fixed sum payment each week to the unemployed, for example, can be determined for any class sharing the same buffer variables. The effect of payments equal to a fixed percentage of prior income could not be found until the effect of such payments on the indicator variables was stabilized.

The normative variables are taken as a measure of the dimensions of life that have intrinsic importance—for example, state of health, psychic satisfaction, and freedom of action. The value of those variables is a complex function of the amount of change in the indicator variables and the values of the buffer variables. The heart of the normative variable is the *set of rules* that is used to determine those values. To take a simple example, if a driver is fined $10 for parking illegally, that produces a negative change in the value of at least one indicator variable (the "cash in hand" variable). One effect of that change might be a reduction of the individual's "freedom to move about" variable, which can be taken as intrinsic. How much reduction in that value would actually occur depends on such other factors as wealth, income, and access to credit. Rules are needed to combine the amount of the fine and, say, level of income to produce a measure of the effect of the fine on that dimension of the individual's life. The rule could be quite loose but incorporate cutoff points and other restrictions to increase accuracy in application. All that is needed is a rough basis for asserting that one situation is preferable to the other, that the life situation described prior to the change could be preferred on reasoned grounds to the life situation that followed the change. There is no need to produce an absolute or external measure of the effect of the change.

The completed structure, including indicators, buffers, and rules for calculating the value of the normative variable, is forbiddingly large and complex. Yet, it is employed habitually in everyday affairs, as a matter of course and with little thought, although usage has not led to clear articulation of structure and process. The reader need only consider the impact on his own life of a large and unexpected expenditure (say for medical care) to see how readily and efficiently such problems are handled in practice, and how well the analytic structure accounts for that activity.

The Normative Variables

$$[([VI_1 VI_2 \ldots VI_n] \ [VB_1 VB_2 \ldots VN_n] \ [R_1 R_2 \ldots R_n]) \ [V_1 V_2 V_3 \ldots V_n]]$$

The substance of the normative variables, the actual dimensions of human life that are needed for comparing outcomes, can neither be identified nor argued in abstract or general terms. A useful distinction can be made between dimensions of life such as wealth that are valued instrumentally, for the contribution they can make to the quality of life, and things that are valued intrinsically, as parts of life that count. But that does not take the discussion very far. Everything depends on the situation, the conceptual apparatus available, and the kind of reasons that can be offered for preferring one condition to another.

Happily, the normative variables need not be identified by generalized reasoning. Nor is identification of specifics prerequisite to determining procedures. As in theorizing, normative discussion begins with the concrete case seeking a solution. Any set of normative variables provides a point of departure. Application and use will lead to retention, modification, rejection, and replacement over time. Solution of a particular case provides a solution for the class of cases for which it is exemplar. If the class proves significant, the solution is thereby also made important. And since the discussion is ongoing, it does not begin at bedrock. There are normative variables available, however faulty, in language and practice. Thus, there is always some point of departure, however inadequate. Each choice provides an opportunity to improve the normative variables as well as the rest of the apparatus of choice. Choices do not, however, allow for total reconstruction of the machinery employed; internal contingencies do not permit it. Each choice is approached with an already-developed normative system; use is partly habitual and partly self-conscious. The solution to a new choice problem is always a combination of established assumptions, suitably modified, and new assumptions appropriate to the situation. How the process operates is uncertain and very difficult to discuss in abstract terms. There is no reference point save experience, and in such generalized terms, the meaning of "experience" is unavoidably ambiguous.

THE INSTRUMENTS OF CHOICE

For controlling the environment, an instrument is needed that will project the effects of action or change in the environment. The solution is a structure, rooted in experience, comprising two or more variables linked causally and according to rule, within prescribed limitations. For reasoned choice, the problem is to develop instruments out of experience that will select one outcome from a structured set generated by appropriate theories and supply an argument or justification for accepting the apparatus. Since the apparatus must be corrigible, defensible, and within human competence, the procedure followed is the same as for any other intellectual tool: the instrument is assumed, the results of using the instrument serve to correct and refine it.

The generalized procedure calls attention to one very important characteristic of the choice apparatus: *it must be able to deal with specific, concrete cases.* The results obtained by applying the structure to concrete cases provide the evidence needed to support, modify, and justify accepting it. That feature of the approach to reasoned choice developed here sets it apart from most current approaches to ethics or moral philosophy. The normative enterprise is forced to begin with the particular case and not the search for general principles. The substance of the ethic, the actual instrument of choice, must provide forced solutions to particular choice problems, otherwise it cannot be tested. The justification for the instrument is found in a comparison of the results obtained through use with the results that could be obtained by using the available alternatives.

Those requirements contrast very sharply with such recent efforts in ethics as John Rawls' widely heralded and discussed *A Theory of Justice.*[3] The general principles adduced by Rawls cannot be applied and therefore cannot be defended by reference to consequences. The "First Principle," for example, asserts that "Each person is to have an equal right to the most extensive total system of equal basic liberties compatible with a similar system of liberty for all."The principle cannot be applied because, to put it bluntly, the principle is vacuous, mere rhetoric without specific implications. An equivalent principle would be a game law that enjoined removal of any fish from a lake if that action would disturb the ecological balance of the region. The consequences of accepting the principle cannot be determined for the particular case, therefore for action purposes it is without meaning. How to justify such principles? Rawls' justification is based on the contention that "rational persons," placed in a vaguely described "original position," would choose his principles. For the sake of clarifying the situation, grant that persons with appropriate properties could be found and placed in the "original position," which is most unlikely. Why should that be accepted as supporting evidence for principles intended to govern action in the world? Rawls does not say. Further, the question how a principle that has no implications for action could serve as a guide to action would have to be answered somehow. Philosophy has produced yet another structure standing wholly outside human experience, yet purporting to guide those who live out the experience. Unfortunately, most philosophic approaches to normative inquiry begin with a search for general or universal principles rather than limited solutions to concrete cases. The enterprise is directed to goals that lie beyond human capacity. Meanwhile, the normative apparatus actually employed in society remains primitive and largely unexamined. Even the structures needed to make reasoned choices remain unarticulated and without labels.

Focusing on the instruments needed to make concrete choices allows for justification out of human experience. That sets the normative enterprise on a track where progress is possible at least in principle, although the obstacles remain formidable. Some easing of requirements is achieved by concentrating on a comparison of the outcomes from which choice is made. Criticism can begin with the available apparatus, concentrating on modification and improvement rather than development of entirely new structures. The criteria applied to outcomes can be relative rather than absolute. The instruments need only have limited and specific applications. Inquiry can be confined to real problems. Evidence can be limited to observation and experience, ignoring imaginary instantiation or logically possible results. And finally, the working apparatus need not be required to deal with every case without exception, and that sets a useful limit to ambition. The Caligula syndrome, the search for instruments that can handle the moral monster as well as the actions of ordinary persons, is simply mistaken. For most humans, most of the time, instruments that will handle most human problems are perfectly adequate.

Priorities and Policies. In forecasting, two or more variables are assumed to covary, and for controlling the environment, covariant factors are assumed to be causally linked. Both assumptions can be justified out of experience over time. For reasoned and corrigible choices, it must be assumed that one option in a set of two or more is preferable to each of the others, and a justification for that assumption must in due course be found in experience. The instrument in which that assumption is incorporated is called a *priority* system or preference system. The rules of action or choice that apply the priorities to a particular situation will be called *policies*. Policies are rules of choice that produce the preferred outcome in a priority system when applied. Both instruments are essential for reasoned choice.

A more precise meaning for both priorities and policies can be found in the process by which reasoned choices are made. Choice begins, necessarily, with a set of two or more outcomes open to some known actor at a specific time and place. Those outcomes will be projected upon the future by theories using some selection of normative variables. The first step in reasoned choice is to find reasons for preferring one of the outcomes to the others. Those reasons, to be examined more fully below, will refer to the conditions of life of the human population appearing in each of the options. Once a selection is made and a solution to the particular choice is identified, it is generalized to produce a preference ordering or priority system. The action is to be taken in that situation in order to produce the preferred outcome must be forced, required as a consequence of accepting the priority. That connection is made through the policy or rule of action. Any rule that will produce the preferred outcome can serve as policy, but rules vary in effectiveness and must be tested in use, and perhaps improved or replaced. The need for a separate rule of choice is a function of the generalized character of the priority system. It can be applied to situations variously conceptualized or described. Policies are not theories, and they do not project outcomes. Instead, policies extract the implications of a generalized priority system for a particular case. The test of the policy is its ability to enforce the preferred outcome in those situations where the priority system applies, that is, any situation in which the outcomes ordered by the priority system actually appear. The relation between priority system and policy is well illustrated in game preserves. Top priority may be assigned to maintaining lakes that are well stocked with fish of eatable size, distributed among a number of different species, for example. The policies followed to produce that preferred outcome will relate to such things as the limits imposed on the number, size, and species of fish taken from the lakes, and the length of the fishing season. The policies or rules of action, taken in combination, are expected to produce the preferred outcome. Again, the priority system may assign top preference to living without a headache. The policy or action rule could in that case involve taking two aspirins at regulated intervals. The justification for the policy is found in its ability to produce the preferred outcome in the priority system. The source of the policy is always a valid theory.

To illustrate the complexities of the structure, assume that a child is offered a choice from among a number of coins of different sizes, shapes, materials, colors, age, and so on, all of which have little value so that the effects of the choice on other persons can be ignored. The child must choose from among a number of film clips of the future in which the only difference is the coin that belongs to the child and the use made of it. The choice can be conceptualized in endless different ways, depending on the focus selected. Mercifully, the normative structure established in the society helps to simplify the task, for it would otherwise be unending. It can be assumed that the society already accepts a priority system in which more monetary value is preferred to less, other things equal. The reasoning is elementary: one choice is actually contained in the other, in terms of the conceptualization employed. Hence, the added monetary value is a bonus pure and simple. Not many priorities are so readily justified. If that priority system is accepted for the choice among the coins, the search can be ended and no new priorities need be created.

The process has thus far proceeded through three distinct steps: the outcomes were structured, reasons were found for preferring one outcome to the others, and the preference was generalized in a priority structure, conceptualized in terms of monetary value. Structurally, the priority system takes the form $A > B$, meaning Prefer A (higher monetary value) to B (lower monetary value). A rule of choice is now required to produce that preferred outcome in the situation at hand. In this case, an obvious derivative (Choose the coin with the highest monetary value) will serve as a policy or rule of action. More often, however, the policy is a transforming device linking priorities to specific choices by conceptual conversions. In the illustration, the rule "Choose the coin with the highest monetary value" will function if all of the coins have been described in those terms. Otherwise, additional policies will be needed to make the connection, and that is sometimes very difficult. For example, the rule "Choose the largest coin," applied to the set of coins offered the child, might produce the preferred outcome (specified in terms of monetary value) once, or even several times, and yet might break down eventually if a set of coins included small and valuable items.

When action fails to produce the preferred outcome, changes may be required in the priority system, the policies used to apply it, or both. Consider the game warden who is seeking to maintain an ample stock of edible fish of appropriate size distributed among several species. A particular set of policies is adopted which seriously reduce the available stock, leading to poor fishing and increased complaints from the public. Having tried both, the warden could conceivably prefer reduced fishing and increased complaints to prior conditions. Thus, he would alter the basic priority structure but retain the policies. If the original priorities retained their attractiveness, policy changes could be introduced that would restore the stock of fish. In some circumstances, say a major change in the state's recreational priorities, both local priorities and local policies might have to be altered dramatically to produce a lake suitable for powerboats or sailing.

Some of the characteristics of priority systems are of peculiar importance to the critic. The elements in the structure are always complete outcomes, and if some may consist of a single variable others are very large and complex combinations of factors. The priority system is built from below, beginning with the particular case. As the structure grows, it can be consolidated and integrated, as in theory, but the overall structure remains incomplete. Moreover, it is not a single integrated whole. Within each integrated substructure, the priorities must be ordered transitively: if A is preferred to B and B is preferred to C, then A must be preferred to C. The need for transitive ordering is particularly important as priority systems grow larger and more complex for maintenance of internal consistency becomes increasingly difficult. In everyday affairs, inconsistencies tend to remain unnoticed, an indication of the inadequacy of current sociology of values. One of the major functions of systematic criticism is to articulate such inconsistencies, whether in the priorities in use or in the justifications that are offered for accepting them. Total integration of the structure is a logical impossibility. Elimination of inconsistency, however, is both feasible and essential for long-range improvement of social performance.

Finally, each priority system, however narrow and weak it may be, is a generalized structure that is not limited with respect to time and place of application. As is the case with other intellectual tools, the power of the instrument is a function of its generalized character; some of its limits and weaknesses stem from the same source. The reason lies in the generalization process. Faced with a set of options that have been structured to show the values of some common set of normative variables, the actor seeks reasons for choosing one option over the others. The solution to the particular case is also a solution to some class of cases for which the particular case is exemplar. Identifying that class of cases is the central problem in generalizing, for each case can be construed as an example of any number of different classes. Perhaps the simplest approach to generalizing is to incorporate all of the variables used to structure outcomes in the definition of the class and to allow them a very narrow range of values. But that produces a very weak tool, with limited usefulness. More commonly, generalization proceeds by selecting key variables and eliminating others. The quality and usefulness of the priority system actually created will depend on the way in which the class is identified. Each time a member of the class of cases is encountered, the priority system can be applied to it. If the class is defined too narrowly, it may fit only the case in hand and find no further applications; both the need and the possibility of improvement are eliminated. On the other hand, if the class of cases is defined too broadly, the priority system will be applied to a wide variety of situations and produce erratic and unacceptable results. A major function of the testing process is to develop an effective definition for the class of cases to which a priority system applies and to set limits to application in ways that optimize reliability and usefulness. That is always a matter for judgment and experience to determine; the process cannot be formalized.

ARGUMENT ABOUT CHOICE

Methodological discussion of the kinds of arguments that can be adduced for justifying or criticizing choices focuses on the general features of the choice process, seeking reasoned improvement, and not on the solution to any specific choice problem. Technically, the quality of an argument is wholly independent of current practices. Nevertheless, the discussion tends to be severely complicated by the "state of the art" in society. The way in which normative matters are conceptualized and handled in current practice is a serious handicap for anyone concerned with reasoned improvement in performance. Normative inquiry tends to be construed in terms of overarching principles, identification of "good" and "bad," or finding the "right" thing to do rather than in terms of systematic comparison of achievable outcomes. Where comparisons are made, they tend to be selective and incomplete. The bias is toward debating intended to gain support rather than careful articulation of the costs and benefits of action. Moreover, in the absence of an adequate sociology of values, little is known of the relative desirability of different conditions of life under a variety of circumstances, or the efficacy of different sets of priorities in different societies. The amount of work that remains to be done simply to assess the present state of normative practice is staggering.[4] It follows that good examples of reasoned choice are virtually nonexistent and that illustrations are more likely to confuse than to clarify. For those reasons, among others, the discussion that follows will for the most part remain abstract, focusing on structural and procedural aspects of choice rather than its substance.

Another complication in the discussion of argument about choices flows from the integrated character of the various intellectual tools available for dealing with the environment in reasoned terms. Choices require fairly complex processes and involve the use of a number of intellectual instruments. Criticism of those instruments is cumulative because the instruments are contingent on one another. Concepts are criticized by referring to observations and measurements. Theories are criticized in terms of concepts, measurements, observations, logical properties, and assumptions. Choices are criticized with respect to the concepts and theories they employ as well as the priority systems and policies they incorporate. The quality of a reasoned choice is no better than the quality of the weakest link in the instrumental chain used to make it.

The cumulative character of systematic criticism raises yet another difficulty. Agreement on a course of action does not necessarily imply agreement on choice. For a choice to be agreed, each step of the process by which the choice is made, and each instrument employed in the process, must be agreed. That requirement, though strong, is essential for reasoned improvement of choices. It is common practice in various fields to attack disagreements about conclusions by working backward through the various stages by which the conclusion is developed, seeking the point of divergence. An illustration is found in mathematics teaching. In systematic criticism of intellectual activity, that practice is extended to both agreements and disagreements about conclusions. Until the chain of reasoning on which the conclusion depends has been exposed, it is technically uncertain whether or not agreement has been reached. To agree with a conclusion but not with the reasoning that produced it is to disagree.

A brief summary of the choice process will suggest the major points at which argument is required, and disagreement may appear. In some cases, the reference is to empirical rather than normative matters; since they have already been treated above, the discussion will be brief. So far as possible, the more narrowly normative dimensions of choice will be treated most fully. Reasoned choice involves five basic stages or processes: (1) projection of a set of two or more outcomes on the future, using some selection of normative variables; (2) comparison of those outcomes, seeking reasons for preferring one to the others; (3) generalizing the preferred solution in that case to create a priority system; (4) application of the priority system to specific cases through appropriate policies; and (5) refining the structure in the light of experience with use. Each stage offers a potential site for disagreement. The projection of outcomes, which is an empirical or theoretical matter, may be disputed with respect to accuracy, adequacy, or reliability. The selection of normative variables may be considered inadequate or inappropriate for the situation. A different set of priorities may be suggested. The reasons offered as justification for the priority system may be contested, or other reasons offered. And finally, the consequences of living with the priority system may be differently evaluated. Argument over the empirical dimensions of inquiry has already been considered in some detail and will be left aside. Analytically, the selection of normative variables can be subsumed in the assignment of priorities, therefore only the latter will be examined extensively. The kinds of refinements that the results of use justify cannot be discussed in general terms, for they refer to specific situations. The principal focus in strictly normative argument is therefore the priority system, the order of preference imposed on the available alternatives and the reasons offered for accepting that ordering.

THE EMPIRICAL DIMENSION OF CHOICE

Reasoned choice begins with a condition in the environment that requires change on normative grounds or with an actor who must choose between alternative outcomes that lie within his competence. Assuming that choices are justified in terms of future consequences, present actions must be linked to future conditions by appropriate theories. Forecasts do not provide a basis for reasoned actions. A forecast can produce expectations of wet weather; it takes a theory to suggest than an umbrella will keep the person dry. Theories are needed both to generate the selection of outcomes from which choices are made and to suggest the intervention strategies used to achieve the preferred outcome. Systematic criticism of theoretical projections will focus on their accuracy, reliability or margin of error, and adequacy for normative purposes. If outcomes cannot be agreed and the probability of occurrence attached to each is disputed, there can be no agreement on choice. If Jones believes that a choice lies between vanilla and strawberry ice cream, and Smith believes the choice lies between vanilla and chocolate ice cream, there is no agreement even if both select vanilla. Two different choices have been made.

The need to agree on the objects of choice before arguing the proper choice to make may seem too obvious to require emphasis. Yet, even a cursory examination of discussions of current events in the media suggests that in most cases of "normative disagreement," the objects of choice are not actually agreed. Moreover, the range of outcomes available for choice is seldom, if ever, completely articulated or explored systematically. The "position papers" developed by such public agencies as the U.S. State

Department or the British Foreign Office are perhaps the best examples available of careful discussion of fully developed major options, and even those are at times severely limited by constraints of time and space. In the press, or on radio and television, selectivity to the point of one-sidedness is the rule: outcomes are most commonly asserted in prophetic form and not developed by theory; aggregate concepts that defy systematization are common; and partiality intended to predispose choice is normal. In sum, when major issues are discussed, whether locally or nationally, the quality of the argument and evidence is almost invariably poor or even grossly inadequate. A careful examination of public discussion in St. Louis of such major issues as the need for a new airport or convention center, racial integration in the schools, welfare, abortion clinics, and hospitals showed the same results in every case.[5] Assertion of either favorable results or undesirable consequences without evidence or justification appeared on every side. Incompatibilities in reasoning and inconsistencies in argument were ignored. No complete and balanced statement of benefits and costs was provided in any case. Expert testimony adduced for both sides was qualitatively little better than the opinions expressed by the man in the street. In not one case did the evidence justify belief that a choice could have been made on reasoned and adequate grounds. Indeed, it is unlikely that the range of options actually available was ever seriously examined.

The propensity of those involved in the disposition of public affairs to bias the evidence in their own favor is understandable. Unfortunately, that tendency is strongly reinforced, or at least not opposed, by trends in the social sciences—the current vogue for "policy studies" and "evaluation" notwithstanding. Social scientists are not usually concerned with the practical implications of their inquiries. The reward system in the social sciences is fairly strongly skewed toward scholastic or "bookish" enterprises—most recently, the development of "models" whose academic worth seems to rise as they become further removed from everyday affairs and increasingly arcane.[6] Since "theories" tend to be established by proclamation rather than by capacity to fulfill purpose, their quality remains low and very often nil. Without a solid theoretical base, academic "experts" can argue both sides of any question without being overly concerned about contradictions. But if the experts disagree, what are those who must rely upon them—legislators, administrators, and citizens—to believe? If medicine was as much disputed as economics, there would be little need for hospitals and a much greater need for mortuaries. Although some academic advisors are probably more reliable than others, the criteria needed to distinguish them tend not to be known. The user has little option but to treat everyone as another voice in a Tower of Babel. In the circumstances, the approach to reasoned choice advocated here may be impossible to achieve, though it lies within human capacity. Even the first step, developing the theoretical capacity needed to structure the outcomes from which choices are made, has yet to be taken.

What seems most tragic about the absence of theoretical capacity is the contribution it could make to normative development. It is usually assumed as a matter of course that deep differences over fundamental values divide the peoples of the world as surely and as clearly as their cultural or physical differences. If that were true, the absence of human capacity to generate reliable theories would make little difference; the primary problem would be normative and not empirical. My own studies suggest that is not actually the case.[7] With due regard for the differences that situational variation enforces—what is appropriate for one set of conditions may be a disaster elsewhere—the primary aspirations, preferences, and priorities of members of the human species are remarkably similar at the roots. The belief common in international development circles in the 1950s and 1960s, that social development was held up in some areas by a perverse and inappropriate set of values, has by now been discredited.[8] It seems more likely that if the outcomes from which choices are made could be agreed upon, there could be agreement on the priority assigned to the outcomes, especially at the level of basic social conditions. Of course, given the complexity of the choices that must be made, both individually and socially, and the extent to which individuals differ biologically, culturally, physically, and psychically, elimination of normative disputes is most unlikely. Indeed, that would be very undesirable. A continuing tension with respect to priorities forces the kind of systematic reexamination and defense of current practice that is needed to keep the normative structure alive and improving. What society must have are the institutions and machinery that can provide a full and dependable statement of the alternatives from which choices are made and a set of procedures for resolving disagreements and for making decisions without destroying either the individual or the society.

PRIORITIES

What may be considered purely normative disagreements refer to three basic issues: the set of normative variables used to structure outcomes; the order of priorities attached to those outcomes; and the reasons offered for preferring one outcome over the others. For example, the use of a concept such as "anguish" to structure outcomes may be challenged, or its omission queried; the relative importance attached to anguish and physical pain or disfigurement could be disputed; and the reasons offered for preferring free movement in a body joint to the absence of pain may be questioned or denied. The first two issues can be merged. That is, the question which variables should be used to structure any particular set of outcomes can be settled merely by agreeing that *any* variable can be used to criticize a choice as long as it refers directly or indirectly to some aspect of human life. Once that much is agreed, the priority attached to each of the variables will actually determine the selection. Put another way, when the solution to a particular choice problem is generalized, the variables incorporated into the priority system will be selected to reflect the relative importance attached to them in the initial choice.

Priorities are the most sophisticated instruments to be found in the corpus of human knowledge, the last link in the chain that connects past experience to future needs. Science makes reasoned choice possible and necessary; reasoned choice aims at improvements in the human condition; priorities reflect current judgments of what constitutes an improvement. Ultimately, the normative variables and priorities refer to the conditions of life of the human population. The need to generalize preferences in order to create a base for reasoned action effectively rules out solipsism as a justification for priorities. Otherwise, each action or choice would have to be treated as a unique and nonrecurrent event, which would make reasoned choice impossible. The central problem in reasoned choice is to organize experience into priority systems that can be used as a basis for action and corrected by reference to the results of action. The structures and processes required are complex and difficult and probably cannot be simplified. However, such structures and processes are found in every society and culture for the problems are universal and they have been solved, however poorly, by all populations. The practical problem is to improve the quality of the available instruments, to convert them into "life optimizing" systems. Given the variety of human existence, and the manner in which the normative tradition has developed, that is an extraordinarily difficult assignment.

Human life is truly a many splendored thing and therefore hard to capture, encapsulate, and compare. It has breadth and duration, richness and intensity, potential and fulfillment, a past and a future. Life is lived subjectively and viewed objectively. Metaphorically, life is a journey through time that begins and ends at the same point for everyone. What matters with respect to life, speaking normatively, is the quality of the journey taken as a whole. The relative importance of specific changes in specific lives depends on a host of factors, many only dimly understood. Life can be extended and shortened, enriched and impoverished, strengthened and weakened. The meaning depends on the context. A change that influences individual capacity to act for the rest of the natural life might appear more momentous than a transient or reversible change. Yet, the overall effect of the former could be trivial, while the latter produced years of agonizing effort for the individual. Impact depends on initial states, on degree of helplessness, for example, as well as on action. Actions that influence the fulfillment of individual potential are particularly important and difficult because they can frustrate without raising the frustration to a level of consciousness that might lead to satisfaction.

The physical necessities of life, though obvious, cannot be ignored. For large parts of the world's population, the normative variables that matter most are those that identify the necessary conditions for living. But the danger of excessive concentration on food, clothing, and shelter is much remarked. A person condemned to live in isolation or to forego the pains and pleasures of close and enduring relations with other members of the species has been deprived of a priceless dimension of living, just as the person forced to proceed through life with a grievous physical handicap must forego a number of highly pleasurable experiences. When necessity has been satisfied, action continues, consequences are produced, and differences in priorities remain. Clearly, the need for ethics is not confined to wealthy societies. The kinds of decisions that must be made by those who control great wealth and power are different, and they may affect more persons in more ways, but at the level of the individual they are not necessarily more important. What is needed for reasoned and improvable choices depends on the scope of possibility. An ethic adequate for a poor and severely constrained individual or society is unlikely to be adequate for a powerful and wealthy individual or society. That is the reason why the procedures and practices necessary to develop and sustain an ethic are more important than its specific content when the education of the young is at issue.

Priority systems are produced by weighing and comparing outcomes that consist of different life situations for the same group of lives. The priority assigned to an outcome reflects the assessment or judgment of the actor or critic of the costs and benefits to human populations to be generated by specific actions. Choices or actions add to or subtract from the sum of specific human lives. Some actions affect enormous populations, generating changes that are literally incalculable; major wars or even "minor" military skirmishes have such effects. One of the more useful structures available for surveying systematically the effects of action, or structuring outcomes to facilitate judgment of priorities, is to consider action as a device for increasing or reducing the differences that separate discrete human individuals or populations.

The Differences That Make a Difference. Intellectual tools perform their functions because they are produced by organizing human experience for specific purposes in appropriate ways. The reasons that will be offered for preferring one outcome in choice to another will refer necessarily to human experience with the available options. That body of evidence will include both subjective reactions, including affectivity, reported in sets of descriptive propositions by the individuals concerned and objective data relating to observable dimensions of human life. Although ethics has traditionally attached great importance to subjective reactions as a wellspring for ethical behavior, even to the point of postulating an "ethical sense" of some kind, objective evidence plays a far greater role in most choices, especially those made collectively. Indeed, the class of decisions that can reasonably be left solely to subjective reaction or affectivity is extremely small. Even something as innocuous as the choice of a flavor of ice cream may be conditioned by knowledge of the physical effects of the ingredients on the body of the consumer. A subjective preference for the taste of chocolate is usually overridden if the substance produces a painful or irritating skin rash. Where it is not, that is often taken as a sign of immaturity or poor judgment. Ultimately, judgments about priorities will depend on human willingness to live with one set of conditions rather than another in full knowledge of the alternatives, and of the historical and other evidence pertaining to human experience with those options. Human experience can be extrapolated from person to person using quite modest assumptions about the degree of human similarity without engendering any serious problems for the critic. Where human experience provides no evidence whatever, whether directly or indirectly (by analogy or metaphor), no reason can be given for a preference. In such cases, action is of necessity regarded as an experiment; the results of action may provide grounds for preference that can be applied to future actions.

Present choices are linked to the accumulated body of human experience through the normative variables. That is, the normative variables in use in society or culture identify the dimensions of life that experience has judged significant. That linkage has its dangers, for it serves to tie present choices to past choices in ways that are not always desirable. On the other hand, the connection serves to underscore the close relation between present and past that reasoned improvement in normative performance enjoins. Radical transformations, whether in ethics or institutions, usually involve consequences that far exceed the human capacity to anticipate; they are literally unreasoned leaps into the unknown. That need not imply that all reasoned changes are minor or trivial in impact. A sustained effort to implement the assumed equality of life that reasoned choice requires, for example, would produce consequences as great as those flowing from any revolution and, hopefully, with a more desirable balance of positive effects.

For any individual, the value of one of the normative variables used to define the conditions of life is set by observation at a point in time. Those values can be mapped on an appropriate continuum. The overall condition of life of any individual or population can, for purposes of choosing, be mapped on an appropriate set of continua. In principle, every living human could be mapped in this way, stratified to identify geographic location, society, or even family. In this conceptualization, what is chosen is a mapped position for some individual or group (all those affected by the action) that is different from their former position. The effect of action is a change in the position of some individual or group on that set of continua. In that sense, action or choice either increases or decreases the differences among persons in specified ways.

When choices are stated in these terms, as positions mapped on a set of continua defined by normative variables, they can be related directly to observed and historical conditions. Those conditions, whether observed or historical, become a prime source of evidence for or against the priorities used to justify and direct the change. That is, the conditions of life of populations affected by action can be matched to appropriate segments of history, thereby providing access to information about the desirability of living under those conditions. Both history and literature can serve as *sources* of normative variables, but only history can provide evidence for use in arguing choices. Imaginative instantiation does not count as evidence. Of course, much of history provides little information about the relative desirability of specific changes in conditions of life and cannot be related to choice in a cogent way. But to the extent that history can provide information about the individual and social effects of adopting one set of priorities rather than another in particular circumstances, it needs to be mined. There is no alternative source of evidence.

Construing the effects of choice as a matter of increasing or decreasing the differences among individuals or groups calls attention in a very useful way to the need for baseline information that can be used to measure the effects of action. Reasoned social action requires an adequate inventory of the human population affected by that action, an inventory that incorporates the significant normative variables. The kind of information collected in the United States Decennial Census is grossly inadequate for criticizing, or even ascertaining, the effects of social action. Unfortunately, most of the recent efforts to develop "social indicators" in the United States and in Europe, though an improvement on the Census, remain inadequate for social criticism or reasoned social action. Social policymaking is very usefully construed as a special kind of inventory management, where the inventory refers to a human population. Systematic improvement through such management is literally impossible without some account of initial conditions. There would be no basis for asserting that an improvement had been made. The content of the inventory required is determined, in one sense at least, by the normative variables currently used by the society for regulating its communal affairs, subject to the limits that society imposes on collection of human data. Curiously, the imposition of such limitations is not always treated as a decision whose implications must be weighed systematically in terms of consequences. The Privacy Act of 1974, for example, would, if strictly enforced, have forced every local housing authority and welfare agency in the United States to cease operations. They continued to function only by violating the letter of the law.

Modes of Action. Focusing on increases or decreases in the similarities and differences among populations also serves to call attention to the modes of action used to bring them about. Analytically, three basic modes of action are available for use and each has different implications for the populations involved. They are most readily demonstrated by assuming two groups of persons and examining the effects of the mode of action employed using money income as an indicator. Strictly speaking, money is not a "normative" variable because it is valued instrumentally rather than intrinsically but it will serve nicely for purposes of illustration.

In the initial mode of action, the income level of the lower group on the income continuum is held constant and the income level of the upper group is increased. A typical policy employing that mode is an increase in income tax rates from which the low-income population is exempted. Since the desired or preferred value of the income variable is the highest possible, this mode of action reduces the relative advantage of the upper group but has no affect on the absolute position of the low-income group. In the second mode, the income of the upper-level group is maintained and the income of the lower-level group is increased. Again, the relative advantage of the upper-income group has been reduced but the absolute position of the lower group has been improved while the absolute position of the upper group has been maintained. Positive income supports, or a "negative" income tax, would have this kind of effect. Of course, there are overall costs associated with each mode of action (total revenue available to government, for example) that are ignored in this account. In the third mode, changes are made in the income levels of both groups. The direction of change may be the same or different for the two groups; the rate of change may also be the same or different in the two cases. The overall effect will depend on both direction and rate of change. For example, if the tax rates on the upper-income group are doubled annually while the tax rate for the lower-income group is increased by 10 percent, the gap between the two groups will decrease very rapidly and disposable income will tend to converge. If tax levels for both groups increase by a fixed percentage, the gap between them will increase. If the difference in rate of change is small, the difference between the two groups may change only a little even though the overall rate of change is very high, as in periods when taxes are increasing rapidly. Not all normative variables are most desirable at the highest measured level, of course, but the principles involved are the same for all such actions. The discussion serves to underline the importance of attending to both mode of change and rate of change in policy discussions. It does persons of low income little good to know that the gap between their current income and a decent living standard is being decreased if the amount of the decrease is only a tiny fraction of the difference and years or even decades may be required to eliminate the gap.

There are some definite advantages and limitations associated with the use of particular modes of difference reduction, depending on purposes and circumstances. In some cases, such as education, family background, or culturation, differences cannot be reduced by taking away what is already there. Under some circumstances, there may be serious psychological reactions associated with the use of particular modes of action that act as a significant barrier to use. Strong union supporters are likely to regard a pay cut as less acceptable, other things equal, than wage stabilization even in those cases where the relative and absolute position of the union member would be improved more by cutting pay. In most cultures, some aspects of society are regarded as part of nature, or even God-given, and therefore considered to be closed to the actions of either governments or individuals. In the United States, private property and the distribution of resources tend to be regarded in that light; in other societies, special status is accorded a particular religious organization, family, or even occupational group. Such considerations tend to limit public authorities and private citizens to token gestures or even outright avoidance of actions that might alter those aspects of society.

Disagreements. A normative disagreement occurs when there is full agreement on the content of a set of options but a different priority is assigned to each option. In many cases, disagreements that appear to be normative actually refer to the empirical dimensions of choice for it is often difficult or even impossible to be sure that "the same" choice has been made on two occasions. The uncertainty is particularly marked when choices are made at different times or within different cultures. For example, a patient who goes to the hospital with precisely the same objective conditions on two occasions some ten years apart may in fact give the surgeon two quite different choices. Advances in medicine during the interim during changes in the patient's physical condition may alter the options very significantly. The sheer complexity of social choices makes identification especially difficult and warns against too readily assuming that an action that resolved a problem at an earlier time will resolve "the problem" in the present.

Genuine normative disagreements, even those relating to quite simple matters, may be quite difficult to pinpoint exactly. For example, assume two prospective automobile purchasers who are agreed on the relevant performance characteristics of two machines but disagree on their desirability. Ordinarily, the locus of disagreement is clarified by requiring each person to produce reasons for preferring one outcome to the others. If no reasons are forthcoming, there is an impasse. If the only reason offered to support a preference is an appeal to overall subjective reaction, such as "I simply like that one better than the other," there is also no reasoning to contest and no basis for reconciliation. Only the preference has been stated, not the reasoning. If both have already agreed that durability is more important than appearance, that price weighs more heavily than trade-in value, and that safety is more important than style, either the criteria of choice have been applied improperly in one or both cases or some other aspect of the choice is the basis of difference. Suppose, for illustration, that further questioning reveals that one person prefers an automobile with rapid acceleration and high top speed while the other most values economy of performance. The source of the disagreement has been located.

What now? The disagreement centers on the different priority assigned to economy and performance by the two persons. To find the source of the disagreement, each person can again be asked to provide reasons for preference. Again, if no reason is forthcoming, the result is an impasse. However, one of the persons, a dull and stodgy professor of methodology, argues as follows. "An automobile is simply a way of getting back and forth to work, to the shopping center, and occasionally to a vacation site. I regard it as a necessary evil, costly and smelly but unavoidable. I wish I could do without one, but that is impossible given the location of home and university. I therefore prefer an automobile which opitimizes safety and reliability and operating costs." The second person, a gay blade, argues differently. "I enjoy driving as a form of recreation and frequently take part in road races. For my purposes, acceleration, high speed, and good handling characteristics are essential. I am prepared to accept higher operating costs, within the limits of my income, to obtain those features." The point of disagreement has been clarified still more.

The process can be carried further along the same lines, assuming the participants are willing to tolerate such prodding. Asked to justify or give reasons for regarding an automobile as an instrument for recreation rather than a simple means of transportation, the gay blade proceeded to cite first his subjective reaction to driving, to give a factual account of the pleasure felt during a race. In the cost-benefit analysis that produced the gay blade's choice, that affective reaction appears as the major benefit of the decision. While some costs were mentioned, others could be added: community resource costs reflected in higher gasoline consumption, or even the remote likelihood that the enticement to steal had been increased for local youth. The list actually incorporated into the priority structure indicates the costs that the gay blade is prepared to accept in order to obtain the subjective reactions associated with racing. On the other hand, some benefits may be overlooked in the initial statement, such as the additional safety factor built into the vehicle. Confronted with the fullest possible statement of costs and benefits associated with the choice between automobiles, the gay blade may recant and change priorities, and he may not. The only procedure available in reasoned argument for inducing such change is to press the analysis as far as knowledge will permit, point out the implications of carrying the same reasoning into other areas of choice—it would justify drug addiction, for example—and await a response from the chooser. Note that the professor, who does not obtain the same subjective reaction to driving, does not actually face the same choice as the gay blade. At the level of choosing between automobiles, there is a clear disagreement; the analysis dissolved the normative disagreement, replacing it with two different choices.

Justifying priorities. Faced with a choice between two outcomes, A and B, the actor must examine his priority system to see if that choice is somewhere covered. If a preference for X over Y has already been established, for example, and it can be demonstrated that the choice between A and B is covered by that preference, the initial justification for the choice is provided by the established priority system. The procedure is precisely analogous to the justification of expectations by reference to an established classification. Providing a justification for the priority structure is a more difficult matter. The primary assumptions in the theory of knowledge require the justification to refer to the conditions of life of those persons affected by the choice and to treat each life as the equal of any other, at least *qua* life. The underlying theory also requires that priority systems, like the other instruments needed to achieve human purposes in the environment, be forged out of organized human experience. The justification for the priorities may be found in past experience or the priorities may be applied in order to generate experience that can be used to test them. The characteristics of an adequate justification for a priority system cannot be stated in wholly general terms any more than the characteristics that justify accepting a theory or classification can be determined without reference to particulars.

The problem of justification is further complicated by the fact that Western society usually approaches normative affairs from a perspective that differs radically from the one employed here. Generally, they emphasize principles of action rather than comparison of the consequences achievable in action and abstract precepts rather than concrete human affairs. It is very unusual to find a real world issue argued in terms of the effects of action on the lives of those affected. Even the abortion issue, which focuses ostensibly on the foreshortening of human life involved, is rarely discussed in that context alone. Moreover, there is a marked unwillingness in most cultures to recommend a course of action involving significant effects on human life. Even free and open discussion of such issues sometimes appears tabooed. Instead, the manner in which such decisions should be made is debated and if possible those who are affected by the action are left to decide in their own way. Medicine provides the best illustrations available. If there is time, a physician will usually allow the patient to make very serious or deadly decisions, such as the use of radical mastectomy for breast cancer. From one perspective, the procedure is both humane and rational. It is much easier for the physician to supply the patient with relevant medical information than to obtain from the patient the information relating to subjective reactions, family features, and other conditions needed for reasoned decision. But the practice adds nothing to the patient's ability to make the decision nor does it further the decisionmaking capacity of the society. The basis for decision remains unknown, and untested. For critical purposes, the problem is not how decisions should be made but what decision to make and how to justify it.

Perhaps the simplest way to clarify the justification of priorities is to examine the case in which a priority is tried experimentally, to generate experience, using the simplest choice possible—adding one element to an ongoing life. Life with the added element can then be compared to life prior to adding the element to provide reasons for making the choice one way or the other. How did the addition change the life? If it made no change worth mentioning, the choice is normatively benign. What sorts of change should be looked for? Clearly, that depends on the specifics of the case, the nature of the addition made and the initial condition of the individual. Answers are supplied by living with the conditions produced by the choice. Those reactions can then be generalized and used to prepare a justification for the priority that directed the choice. The principal evidence available for justification is the willingness of informed and aware individuals to live with a preference system in full knowledge of the available alternatives. Behavior counts more heavily than rhetoric in these circumstances: adopting the priority given an opportunity, or rejecting it as quickly as permitted, are good indicators of preference in such cases. The importance of an adequate sociology of preferences, or history/anthropology of priorities and preferences, is manifest. They are the major sources of evidence for justifiying priorities. Unfortunately, such studies are almost wholly lacking, particularly with respect to modern industrial society.

Some very useful insights can be gained from a careful analysis of the factors involved in experiments with priority systems. It seems clear, for example, that the role of affective reactions in human action is commonly and perhaps universally exaggerated. As a measure of the effects of action, affective response suffers from an unavoidable ambiguity simply because it can be modified through deliberate conditioning. Moreover, the readjustment capacity of the human system serves to diminish the value of self-reporting when the effects of action are being examined empirically. Incapacities that are highly visible to an external observer tend to vanish from consciousness as the system adjusts to new circumstances and capacities. Finally, there may be good reasons to believe that an affective response is grossly inappropriate to both present circumstances and the future. The thrill and elation that may be associated with the feeling of soaring obtained by skiing off the top of an enormous cliff hardly justifies urging others to emulate the action.

The search for ways of evaluating the effects of action on human life leads almost unavoidably to an estimate of future potential as well as present state. Actions differ with respect to the extent, duration, reversibility, and intensity of their impact, among other things; they may continue to influence human life long after physical activity has ceased, or terminate immediately. The student who presented me with my first birdwatching handbook continues to this day to influence my daily life; the effect of some years learning to fly aircraft under the tutelage of the United States Air Force has nearly vanished. What is most encouraging about the effort to clarify such matters is how well the complexities are handled. Systematic criticism of real world decisions is likely to require prolonged and exacting efforts to untangle the empirical and normative aspects of choice, correct faulty projections, and estimate probabilities of occurrence. Even more time will be needed to produce evidence bearing on the relative desirability of the options from which choices are made. What makes the enterprise feasible is the amount of knowledge and experience already incorporated into the culture and socialization process. The person who approached a real world choice without *any* normative variables and priorities would have to invent them, and that would be almost impossible. Criticism of choice always begins with some basic assumptions, else it cannot begin. They may not be fully articulated, or even part of awareness, but they must be present analytically. The reasons why one option has been chosen rather than another may be as indeterminate as the reasons for the local weather prophet's forecasts. But choices, when they are based on a conscious effort to weigh the available alternatives and therefore "reasoned," however badly, must flow from organized experience. Every reasoned argument depends on such fundamentals. Often, and perhaps usually, they are partially obscured. The ongoing human situation makes it possible to articulate, or at least illustrate, those assumptions. The total human person can, in a sense at least, be used as a normative measuring instrument, if only cautiously. Seeking deliberately to surface the reasoning on which choice depends is sound strategy in the circumstances. It may not resolve differences but it can contribute to the clarification of the structures in use, and thus provide an opportunity to link those strategies to their individual and social consequences. The strategy can generate evidence.

The ultimate criteria for justifying normative actions are the actions or choices that individuals take knowingly and intentionally. In some circumstances, that could be expected to legitimate the most drastic forms of radicalism—revolution in a slave society, for example. On the other hand, so long as actions are based on reasoned argument, efforts to amend or modify existing practices are more likely than efforts to produce radical change. The approach to choice can be either revolutionary or reactionary depending on the situation. In fact, such labels are inappropriate here. A commitment to pragmatic justification and testing in use is unavoidable if the normative process is to be placed on a defensible base. And if the purpose of inquiry is to produce knowledge that can be used to improve the human condition, there is no good alternative available. Focusing on specific cases allows for the introduction of new concepts and priorities when they are needed, and as they are made possible. Dependence on reasoned argument does inhibit flights of sheer fancy but only as evidence in argument and not as a stimulus to creativity. Those who wish to "fly" may resent and resist such restrictions, but that is irrelevant to the quality and value of the approach.

NOTES

1. Good summaries of the philosophic approach to ethics can be found in John Hospers, *Human Conduct: An Introduction to the Problems of Ethics* (Harcourt, Brace, and World, 1961); Wilfred Sellars and John Hospers, eds., *Readings in Ethical Theory* (Appleton-Century-Crofts, 1952); William K. Frankena, *Ethics* (Prentice-Hall, 1963); Mary Warnock, *Ethics Since 1900* (Oxford University Press, 1966); Luther J. Binkley, *Contemporary Ethical Theories* (Citadel Press, 1961); and P. H. Nowell-Smith, *Ethics* (Penguin Books, 1961). See also Henry D. Aiken, *Reason and Conduct: New Bearings in Moral Philosophy* (Alfred A. Knopf, 1962); A. J. Ayer, *Language, Truth, and Logic* (Dover Books, n.d.); Abraham Edel, *Method in Ethical Theory* (Bobbs-Merrill, 1963); Charles L. Stevenson, *Ethics and Language* (Yale University Press, 1944); and Stephen Toulmin, *The Place of Reason in Ethics* (Cambridge University Press, 1960).
2. For materials on "public choice," see Dennis C. Mueller, *Public Choice* (Cambridge University Press, 1979); James M. Buchanan and Robert D. Tollison, eds., *Theory of Public Choice: Political Applications of Economics* (University of Michigan Press, 1972); Thomas R. DeGregori, "Caveat Emptor: A Critique of the Emerging Paradigm of Public

Choice," *Administration and Society*, August 1974; Richard B. McKenzie and Gordon Tullock, *The New World of Economics: Explorations into the Human Experience* (Richard D. Irwin, 1975): Mancur Olson, *The Logic of Collective Action: Public Goods and the Theory of Groups* (Harvard University Press, 1965); and Gordon Tullock, *Private Wants, Public Means: An Economic Analysis of the Desirable Scope of Government* (Basic Books, 1970). For the procedures and techniques of formal decision-making, see Howard Raiffa, *Decision Analysis* (Addison-Wesley, 1968); Victor A. Thompson, *Decision Theory; Pure and Applied* (General Learning Press, 1971); Christopher K. McKenna, *Quantitative Methods for Public Decision Making* (McGraw-Hill, 1980); Nicholas Henry, *Public Administration and Public Affairs* (Prentice-Hall, 1975); or E. J. Mishan, *Economics for Social Decisions: Elements of Cost-Benefit Analysis* (Praeger, 1973).

3. John Rawls, *A Theory of Justice* (Belknap Press, 1971). As a corollary, Brian Barry, *The Liberal Theory of Justice: A Critical Examination of the Principal Doctrines of a Theory of Justice by John Rawls* (Oxford University Press, 1973).

4. For a study of quite specific values and principles, largely from a legal perspective, see Charles Fried, *An Anatomy of Values: Problems of Personal and Social Choice* (Harvard University Press, 1970).

5. *The St. Louis Seminar*, mimeo., various dates, Center for Metropolitan Studies, University of Missouri-St. Louis.

6. For exceptions, see Duncan MacRae, Jr., and James A. Wilde, *Policy Analysis for Public Decisions* (Duxbury Press, 1979); Eugene Bardach, *The Implementation Game: What Happens After a Bill Becomes Law* (MIT Press, 1977); and Jeffrey L. Pressman and Aaron B. Wildavsky, *Implementation* (University of California Press, 1973) or Guido Calabresi and Philip Bobbitt, *Tragic Choices* (W. W. Norton and Co., 1978), among others.

7. Eugene J. Meehan and Roy C. Macridis, *Value Systems of Youth in Developing Countries: A Report Submitted to the Agency for International Development*, November 1969, or Eugene J. Meehan, *Report to UNESCO on Cognitive Testing in Costa Rica*, Center for Innovation in Human Development, Indiana University, 1972.

8. See Howard Newby, ed., *International Perspectives in Rural Sociology* (John Wiley, 1978), or Wisconsin Seminar Proceedings, *Natural Resources Policies in Economic Development and International Cooperation* (University of Wisconsin, Madison), 3 volumes, 1978-1979, or Denis Goulet, *The Uncertain Promise* (IDOC/North America, 1977); and P. T. Bauer, *Dissent on Development Studies and Debates in Development Economics* (Harvard University Press, 1972).

Policymaking

One of the more striking and far-reaching developments in the twentieth century has been the enormous expansion of the role of society in the life of the ordinary individual. Although the importance of the quality of collective action has greatly increased, the technology of public policymaking has failed to keep pace. There have been major improvements in the techniques used to store and process information, but the quality and usefulness of the information stored have improved little and its application to human affairs has been inept. Either the capacity is missing, or the capacity to use capacity has not been developed, or both. Much more is involved here than the need to add a few more scientists, social or physical, to the policymaker's staff or to finance additional "policy analysis" by academics. The type of analysis currently in vogue shows little promise of generating the kinds of information and theory needed by modern government. There is little reliable knowledge available, particularly in social science, and even less capacity to apply it systematically, with an eye to improvement. Policymakers are severely handicapped by these conditions, however good-intentioned they may be.

What is required, almost desperately, is a radical change in the kinds of purposes accepted in "scientific" or academic inquiry and the use made of the results of inquiry by those who make public policy. The constitutional foundations of the intellectual enterprise need refurbishing in the light of current needs and capacities. An improved concept of "knowledge" that can be linked to the fulfillment of human purposes seems essential. Such intellectual constitutionalism requires a major shift in the frame of reference of both academic inquirer and policymaker. The importance of securing that change is literally beyond exaggeration. In the long run, the constitutional principles adopted for making policies, the "policies" adopted to guide the policymaker, will have a greater impact on human affairs than any particular policy that could be adopted.

Present conditions in both government and academia render the needed reconstitution of the intellectual enterprise problematic. Among those who govern, suspicion of academic intellectuals is strong, and is firmly grounded in past experience. Policymakers tend to regard members of the academic community as self-serving, hypercritical if not hypocritical, and "abstract" or impractical to the point of uselessness—unwilling to take account of the real constraints that limit those who make decisions about real-world problems. The massive volume of completed inquiries that have led to further proposals for even lengthier inquiries with little or no suggestion of applicability is taken as solid evidence of the uselessness of the breed.

Among academics, policymakers tend to be regarded as birds of passage who are anxious to promote short-run spectaculars with low budgets, but impatient of subtleties and complications and unwilling or unable to deal with in-depth analysis or long-run concerns. The academic points to the same volume of completed research and asks plaintively why no effort has been made to implement suggestions or to follow advice, which is often dearly bought.

There is some evidence for both positions, but on balance the field belongs to the policymaker. The academic case fails badly when it is asked whether a willing and competent policymaker, seriously concerned to maximize the quality of his own performance, could find needed assistance within the intellectual community as presently constituted—excluding "hard science" technology, obviously. In general, the needed help simply is not available, and until it is being produced regularly and reliably, the complaint that recommendations tend to be ignored is mere cant, even if true. Most of the recommendations *deserve* to be ignored.

Social science research, from which economics cannot be excluded, strongly reinforces the anti-academic stereotype common in governing circles. There is little agreement on the goals of inquiry; disorganized individuals and groups pursue disparate ends by divergent means for incompatible reasons. Understandably, there has been little cumulation, little solid improvement in use, indeed, little use. The survival capacity of pretentious nonsense within a purportedly intellectual environment strains credulity. Physical science, social science, and the humanities proceed along separate paths, each maintaining its own (incompatible and nonintersecting) criteria of significance and acceptability. Academic support can be found or purchased for every side of every social issue; no accepted criteria are available for resolving such differences and disputes. What has emerged in the universities is a monk's culture, grounded in the methods used to educate the medieval clergy and nobility, fearful and protective of its privileged social position, unwilling or unable to assist in the improvement of human affairs, manning the rungs on a ladder leading nowhere beyond the schools. Styles change, fads come and go. The dominant trend in political science at the end of the 1970s, for example, was labeled "policy analysis" but often bore little relation to policy, as the newly emerging "public choice" movement was little concerned with the choosing actually being done in the society.[1]

In the circumstances, the academic community is ill prepared to supply the stimulus or the substance needed to redirect the intellectual enterprise. Yet, knowledge remains crucial, for knowledge, properly constituted, *is* power and includes the power to use power with humanity and intelligence. By demanding the kind of knowledge required to perform his assigned tasks, the policymaker can help to channel and direct the quest for knowledge and modify the criteria by which knowledge claims are assessed. By trying to supply the policymaker's needs, the social scientist or other academic can help to establish or restore the kind of relation between systematic inquiry and social purposes that has characterized the academic-community relationship at its best—in the work of the extension agent or the medical clinic (or the football clinic), for example. The catalyst to that relation is a theory of knowledge able to supply the required connection. One of the major virtues of the approach to reasoned argument outlined above is that it can provide that bridge. It can link systematic inquiry and reasoned criticism that is appropriate to the academic tradition to the satisfaction of human purposes through individual and social action. In the context of the analytic framework, policies are identified with the rules of choice that apply priority systems to specific situations. Such policies are defensible, corrigible, and useful; they are clearly related to real-world human concerns. That conception of policy accords well with much of current usage, though it is much more precise than is usually the case.[2] Adopted and used, the structure would do much to bring academic inquiry and social policymaking into a mutually supportive relationship with enormously beneficial side-effects for the community at large. Some of the major implications of approaching research and policymaking from that perspective, for both academics and policymakers, are examined in the remainder of this chapter.

In order to place policymaking on reasoned grounds and to link it firmly to the academic enterprise, some fundamental changes would have to be made in the ground rules that control policymaking, evaluation of policies, and academic research and publication. Indeed, some of the institutional arrangements used to deal with collective affairs might have to be changed. Constitutionalism is quite usefully construed as a problem in epistemology. Some of the changes would be modest, little more than shifts in emphasis. Others would go to the heart of traditional methods of making and justifying policy and of current procedures for studying and evaluating policy. The price of improvement is dedication to purpose, precision in usage, acceptance of stringent rules of evidence and methods of argument, and changes in the machinery used to make policy, monitor consequences, and adjust performance to improve results. The costs would be modest; the gains very substantial; and the principal beneficiaries the members of society generally.

The scope of the required change can be demonstrated very effectively by reference to medical practice. The modes of treatment that have been developed for dealing with specific diseases are perhaps the best examples of "policy" currently available anywhere in the sense the term is used here. A comparison with the "policies" the federal government has created to deal with low-income housing will suggest rather dramatically the kinds of change required. In medicine, policies are developed out of successful treatment of particular cases, suitably generalized. The generalized solution or policy is subjected to more or less continuous testing by application to real, singular cases. Evaluation is based on the consequences for the patient. If subclasses of patients are found who do not respond favorably to the treatment, it is suitably limited or modified. All known or even strongly suspected relations and side-effects are taken into account in policy evaluation. If the procedures used to develop and apply low-income housing policy were transferred to the field of medicine, some really startling changes would appear. The physician would aggregate all of the symptoms and vital signs of all of his patients, average the results, and prescribe treatment on the basis of the averages. The treatment would be applied dogmatically, disregarding differences among patients. The consequences of treatment would be ignored, but policy would change periodically for other reasons. If public pressures forced an evaluation of the consequences of acting on the policy, only results favorable to the physician would be reported; undesirable side-effects would be suppressed or ignored. Finally, the mode of treatment would in due course be abandoned and replaced, even though evidence in the files of physicians who had used the treatment suggested that in some cases it was effective—and no alternative treatment was available. I cannot stress too strongly that the foregoing is an actual summation and not a parody or gross distortion![3]

To develop useful and corrigible policies, and to apply them in ways that will produce improvement over time, changes are needed in four major areas of current practice, academic and governmental: (1) conceptualization—how policies are construed and thought about; (2) construction—the conception of an adequate policy accepted by policymaker and critic; (3) criticism—the criteria by which policies are evaluated and argued or justified; and (4) institutional arrangements—the way in which policies are made and applied. The discussion is illustrated mainly from the actions of the federal government, but the suggestions and criticism apply to most state and local agencies equally well and to many private firms.

CONCEPTUALIZATION OF POLICY

Corrigible and defensible policies or choice rules are necessarily part of an overall structure adequate for reasoned solution to particular choice problems. That structure must include an actor, a set of outcomes within the competence of the actor, and a priority system. A policy links the priority system to the choice of outcome and selects the action to be taken in the situation. Correction and improvement are carried out within the overall context and not in isolation. These features of the process have some important implications for the overall approach to policy analysis and criticism.

Since a policy provides a solution for a specific choice problem, the problem is analytically prior to the policy or the priority system. Problems are specific and particular, and the policy must provide a decision for the specific case. Detailed study of particular problems provides the only possible route to development and improvements in policy. The case study is fundamental for all forms of policy analysis, though that is perhaps most easily seen in medicine. Given current trends in social science, that condition suggests a major reorientation of academic inquiries, particularly in policy-related research. First, the common textbook assertion that governments somehow "formulate their objectives" and *then* generate the policies needed to achieve them is wrong and misleading. The order of development is reversed. If policymakers try to make policy in general terms rather than respond to particular problems, the result is an instrument whose implications in action are unknown—a contradiction in terms. While the practice is unfortunately common at all levels of government, it simply cannot succeed except accidentally, and no justification can be provided for such policies in advance of application. The source of error lies in a failure to distinguish between (1) creating a principle and deriving particular policies from it, and (2) generalizing already established sets of policies into more efficient form. The latter is legitimate and essential for integrating the knowledge stock; the former is mere oracularity.

The options available to any actor, whether individual or collective, are determined by real empirical capacity and not by legal stipulation. The implications of that requirement are most readily visible in foreign affairs, although they affect other areas equally. In foreign relations, the claim to national sovereignty implies a capacity to control all events within some geographic boundaries. No state could enforce that claim in practice, and it cannot be used to estimate the range of choice available to a government. The sovereign claim is an asymptote, a limit that governments approach in different degree but do not reach. The formal or constitutional "powers of the President" are subject to the same limitations. In practice, they may be exceeded or not reached, depending on personalities, circumstances, and related factors. National sovereignty does draw attention to one of the more significant choices available to public authority and not to private citizens, the choice of the scope of its own authority or jurisdiction. The importance of that choice increases steadily as the scope of acceptable and legitimate public intervention in human affairs widens. Where and how the right to create public jurisdictions should be bounded may well be the most important constitutional question of the next few decades, especially in the large, industrialized nations. Pressure to expand public authority into new areas will surely increase as the scope of the unintended outcomes flowing from large-scale human activities widens. The long-run implications of a trend already clearly visible are likely to foster concern and suspicion among radicals and conservatives alike.

In reasoned policymaking, the common practice of bounding the impact of policy either geographically or by reference to the citizenship of those affected by it is also unacceptable. The presumption that governmental policies have human consequences only within the territorial boundaries of the state is patently false when stated openly, but frequently honored in practice. Discussions of tariff legislation or import quotas illustrate the practice most accurately, but so do calculations of the costs of conflict that ignore the price to the enemy. The need to include all of the foreseeable effects of action in the calculation of benefits and costs may be more highly visible in foreign economic relations than in domestic affairs, but at every level of government there is usually some discrimination between members of the society and "outsiders." When local police allow known local residents to violate traffic laws that are inexorably enforced on those who are merely transient, the effect is the same. Recent litigation relating to discrimination in educational and other institutions on racial, sexual, or ethnics grounds suggests the pervasiveness of the practice.

Finally, what are usually considered the major "policies" of government ("foreign" policy, "housing" policy, and so on) are in fact complex bundles of individual policies, often quite disparate in subject matter or significance and affecting a range of different populations. In some cases, such labels are only a technical convenience, a useful symbol for designating a complex entity. Rarely if ever are such "policies" an adequate base for systematic efforts at improvement; there is no way to improve "housing policy" in the United States except by improving its constituent elements. Such overall policy packages must be analyzed or "unpacked" into substructures that allow governmental actions to be linked causally to effects of specific populations. "Housing policy," for example, includes such diverse functions as banking, construction, design, land use, mortgage rates, and management. Each of these areas is already a composite of factors, requiring further analysis before effective criticism or reasoned improvement can be carried out. Policies are usefully construed as maps. Maps that cover large areas are created out of maps that deal with smaller areas; if the smaller maps are heterogeneous, the large map may be useless, taken as a whole. The quality of the large map is contingent on the quality of the smaller maps. Those whose lives are affected by the use made of the map are obviously concerned with its quality. Unfortunately, map quality alone cannot guarantee usage; the outcomes produced by using the map also depend on the ability of those who patronize the map-makers to use them systematically. Indeed potential victims are obviously well advised to sponsor an institutional arrangement that can improve the quality of both activities if their effects are sufficiently important, as is suggested here.

CONSTRUCTION: ADEQUATE POLICY STATEMENTS

Reasoned choices are made by applying a priority system to a particular set of options using an appropriate policy or choice rule. The rule must actually *force* the selection of one of the options. For the rule to be compatible with the option is insufficient. For example, if the game laws specify that pike cannot be taken unless they measure at least twelve inches in length, the angler who wishes to obey the law (who accepts the policy and tries to apply it) and catches a pike that measures eleven inches, has a clear obligation to return the fish to water. The action is forced. But if a fish measuring thirteen inches in length is caught, the policy is silent and is compatible with either returning the fish to the water or keeping it. The individual is left with sovereign control over the decision; it can be made out of his own priority structure. Presumably, the priorities incorporated into the game laws are satisfied as long as the removal of pike less than twelve inches in length is enjoined. That is an empirical question in any case. For larger fish, the angler's priorities are decisive. If the angler's spouse threatens physical violence or legal action should he return to the domicile with fish in his possession, whatever their length, and the angler's priority structure gives precedence to peaceful households over fish dinners, all fish will be returned to water, regardless of size or species or legal regulations, unless he has some alternative destination in mind when the fishing has ended.

The development of rules of action or policies that can actually force selection of the outcome required by a priority system in a variety of contexts is likely to be a difficult task. Policies are tested, evaluated, and improved by comparing the consequences of use to the content of the priority system. Unless the action is logically entailed by the policy, it does not serve as a valid test. Therefore, if the implications of the policy for the case cannot be calculated, the structure is only a pseudo-policy, taking the proper form but not the substance of policy. Vague general statements, such as Kant's categorical imperative (Act as if the maxim of your action were to become through your will a general natural law), provide no guidance for the actor in real situations. They are merely compatible with some actions and not others. As Bertrand Russell points out, such maxims may be necessary criteria of virtue, but to obtain a sufficient criterion, which is required to enforce action, the effects of action have to be taken into account. This was something, incidentally, that Kant was not willing to do.[4] Kant's formulation is only a very elaborate form of question-begging.

A related problem arises from the common practice of stating policies in the form of simple injunctions (seek peace, eliminate war, provide everyone in the sociey with a decent home, and so on) or equally simple ideals or goals. The injunctive form ignores costs or suppresses them. When policies are merged with priority structures, as is usually the case in everyday discourse or even technical discussions of policymaking, the need to compare outcomes and find reasons for selecting one of them is removed. That eliminates the basis for reasoned improvable choice. In human affairs the form is too strong to be useful. No simple injunction has survived the test of time and use in real society, even the injunction against incest. Moreover, if specific injunctions did prove viable, no society could sustain more than a handful without contradiction, and the handful would not suffice for operating the society. Injunctions would therefore have to be supplemented by other bases for choice, and they would have to be justified on wholly different grounds. The same criticism applies to statements of ideals and aspirations, whatever their popular appeal. Technically, neither can serve as a guide to action. If an ideal is beyond human capacity, there is no way to determine whether or not a particular choice will move society or the individual closer to the ideal than before. If it can be known that a particular action actually is a step in the "right" direction, then the goal can in principle be achieved; therefore, it cannot qualify as an ideal. That is, there is no way to know that a step moves toward a goal until the entire journey has been mapped, just as there is no way to know that a curve is asymptotic to a line from a position on either the line or the curve. An observation point independent of both is required. The use of simple ideals tends in any case to a static perfectionism in ethics that equates change with deterioration. The pragmatic-instrumentalist conception of policies as tools open to human improvement accords far better with both human capacity and the historical record of human development.

CRITICISM: CRITERIA FOR POLICYMAKING

Policies are corrected or improved over time by applying them to specific cases, and comparing the consequences produced established priorities. In effect, the action forced by the policy is subjected to reasoned criticism. Criticism of action transfers automatically to *any* policy that requires that action, though not to the actor. Of course, such criticism is also likely to affect the priority system on which action depends. In the real world, they are always examined together, but for analytic purposes the two can be separated, thereby reducing potential confusion. Some of the major points of emphasis in systematic criticism or evaluation of policies are worth underscoring, even at the risk of redundancy. For example, systematic inquiry intended for use in policymaking, whether or not undertaken in an academic context, must have a purpose that fulfills some of the essential prerequisites to reasoned policymaking, an identifiable target population, and so on.

Radical Individualism. Rigorous enforcement of radical individualism in policymaking, evaluation of policies solely in terms of their human consequences, would revolutionize current practice both rapidly and beneficially. There is a pronounced tendency for discussions of the effects and effectiveness of policies to concentrate on changes induced in social practices and institutions. The arguments are virtually devoid of people. The effect of action on specific populations is simply taken for granted. Indeed, it is a rare occasion when an identifiable population appears as the beneficiary of action, and it is rarer still for the bearer of costs to be specified. The greater the stakes, the more abstract the costs and benefits tend to become. Those who govern speak freely and often of protecting vital interests, maintaining stability and order, achieving peace with honor, or providing for the common defense. More rhetorically, there is a commitment to protecting the poor and oppressed, securing equity and justice, or maintaining established institutions. Although the general public is believed to regard such pronouncements with favor, the relation between policy statements of this kind and the actual conditions of life of a specific population are almost never articulated. In fact, the effects of collective action on any real population are extremely hard to determine, mainly because the information needed to stratify the population in ways that will show the differential effects of action are not available and may be impossible to produce.

Conceptualizing the effects of action in abstract or institutional terms literally rules out improvement of performance on the basis of experience. The necessary conditions for improvement can no longer be satisfied. When the practice is common, it is not surprising to find that policies are treated like paper cups rather than fine china. They are used and discarded rather than cherished and maintained. There is a strong tendency for each new effort to make policy to return to ground zero, ignoring what has gone before. In the circumstances, much of what passes for criticism or evaluation is aimed primarily at short-run political advantage obtained by public relations techniques rather than long-run improvement in governmental performance. In the forty-year history of public housing in the United States, for example, no systematic effort was made to determine the nature and extent of need, the size of the eligible population, or the cost of inaction. Nor is there any evidence to suggest that major changes in policy were made on the basis of experience with the program in the past and directed to improvement in the quality of service provided. The result, predictably, was a sham and a shambles.[5]

Until public agents are required to specify both objectives and accomplishments in terms of the conditions of life of specified populations, linking proposed actions to particular improvements, there is little or no possibility of significant improvement in their performance. There is no way to test performance claims. That requirement extends even to matters of foreign policy. For example, most discussions of foreign relations assume implicitly that the population of a national state is homogeneous with respect to the effects of changes external to the society. Once stated, it is clear that assumption is both false and pernicious. Granting that most of the people who live in a large national state would be affected in very similar ways by nuclear warfare (death is genuinely egalitarian in its effects), few events affect large populations in such a homogeneous fashion. The effects of past military drafts have been quite different for the black and white populations of the United States, for example. Differential impact is likely with respect to most important government actions, whether they relate to subsidies, taxes, definition of legal rights and privileges, or their enforcement. But typologies of national populations that can show the differential effects of action, whether at home or abroad, are not available. Moreover, no single way of ordering large populations will show the effects of different kinds of actions with equal accuracy. A stratification that will show the effects of a military draft will not work well for examining the effects of changes in the tax laws, for example. Until social science and government develop the information and theory needed to order populations in ways that show the effects of action for most important classes of cases, policy improvement is unlikely, and policymaking will continue as a special case of driving a vehicle while blindfolded.

In effect, a commitment to the development of reasoned and corrigible policies entails a commitment to radical individualism. That in turn requires the society to develop adequate inventories of its population and the capacity to stratify the population in ways that will demonstrate the effect of public and private actions. Policymaking, as noted earlier, is quite usefully construed as a special kind of inventory management. The effects of action must be specified in terms of differences in the defining characteristics of some known population at two points in time and without some statement of initial conditions, the effects of action are indeterminate.[6]

An inventory can serve a number of purposes for an organization seeking to improve the quality of its performance. For public agencies, inventories are required to locate the subpopulations whose present conditions of life differ so grossly from the rest of society that they must be changed as quickly as possible. An adequate inventory must provide a baseline for structuring the jurisdiction of social agencies as well as a scoreboard for assessing the effectiveness of policies and perhaps administrations as well. For those purposes, the aggregates in current use are much too gross to be helpful. Loose aggregations of very heterogeneous populations can mask widely divergent reactions to a common external change. Moreover, they tend to encourage wasteful and inefficient "shotgun" tactics rather than careful targeting of resources. When costs are low and side-effects are trivial, procedures such as mass vaccination may be an acceptable price to pay for ignorance. If action is costly and side-effects can be lethal, inability to specify target populations accurately may render efforts at improvement very costly by requiring elaborate safeguards, or they may nullify them entirely.

Beyond the use to be made of the resulting inventory, the close study of human populations required to produce them should have a salutary effect on policymaking. By providing concrete exemplification for the meaning of "fortunate" and "unfortunate," detailed information about the conditions of life in which human populations actually live, the inventorying process can help the policymaker acquire a stronger sense of the urgency and signficance of social action. Human history and observation of the human present are the only available sources of information about the full implications and relative desirability of living under a range of circumstances as well as about the value of attacking those circumstances through different policies. The development of genuine social potential for mass improvement is relatively recent in time; experimentation with that potential has been minimal. The sociology of values has made little progress. More often than not, technological advance has been used to better the lot of the fortunate. At most, the less fortunate have been allowed to share in benefits heretofore prized by the well off rather than develop improvements better suited to their current conditions. In consequence, qualitative increases along certain dimensions of life, especially such material conditions as wealth, have been identified implicitly, and even explicitly, with qualitative improvements in the human condition. In the process, neither the long-run effects of massive increases in the scale of consumption generated by such practices nor the quality of life a society so oriented can produce was examined very adequately. There is at least some justification for asserting that since the end of World War II, the United States has provided mankind with an appalling example of the bankruptcy of human imagination in the presence of great material prosperity and with some of the strongest evidence available in history for assuming human inability to handle wealth with foresight, intelligence, and humaneness.

Policy Statements. Construed as rules of action to be tested against the results of action, policies can be criticized directly in terms of their consequences without examining the motivations, intentions, or psychic states of the actor. Once the potential for action is identified, reasoned criticism is independent of both actor and intentions. Criticism of a choice applies to any policy or priority system that leads to that choice, regardless of the actor. If it does not, an error in specification has occurred somewhere in the process. By focusing on the consequences of action, reasoned criticism brings out both sins of omission and the effects of inaction. Finally, condemning a choice on reasoned grounds *necessarily* entails a justified preference for another choice in the same situation, thus providing the base from which reasoned argument can proceed.

Within the conceptual apparatus that has been developed here, policy statements are treated as actions. A great deal of needless confusion is thereby avoided. In current practice, "policy statements" are usually identified as such by authors rather than observers. They are notoriously vague, inaccurate, ambiguous, evasive, deceptive, distorted, and unreliable. Treated as genuine policies, such assertions generate serious problems for the would-be critic. Treated as simple actions, however, "policy statements" can be subjected to the same kind of analysis of consequences afforded any other action. The value of the practice is particularly apparent in foreign relations. In principle, each national government is free to interpret the actions of other national states as it sees fit and to respond accordingly. For obvious reasons, accurate interpretations are preferable to mistakes. For the actions of governments, like the actions of private persons, are predicated upon very complex sets of assumptions about the results likely to follow from different actions in certain situations. In large measure, those projections depend on expectations developed out of past experience with analogous situations. Policy statements by governments have great potential value for stabilizing the information supply and thereby generating predictable expectations about future behavior from the government that generates the policy statement. If accepted definitions of the situation and common expectations with respect to the consequences of action can be created among nations, the risk of miscalculation and tragedy based on ignorance is thereby reduced. Of course, policy statements also contain threats, lies, bluffs, and deliberate efforts to misinform. Thus, they cannot be accepted at face value. Treating them as deliberate actions forces calculation of the consequences expected to flow from the action by those responsible, thereby identifying the major potential source of error and uncertainty in the process. Obviously, such considerations are not new, but the fact that the recommended approach to policymaking generates them more or less automatically is yet another reason for taking it seriously, other things equal.

Unfortunately, efforts to infer the policy actually being followed from the actions that are taken raise the induction problem in yet another form—even disregarding the possibility that the policy was incorrectly applied. Any action can be derived from a theoretically infinite set of policies. The fact that an action is consonant with a policy statement does not guarantee that one led to the other. Policy statements may coincide with both intention and action, and often do, but the degree of correspondence cannot be established by observation or even by the actor's testimony. Observation serves to *rule out* certain policies, assuming competent application. A child given a choice between a quarter and a dime has not followed the rule "Choose the smallest coin" if it chooses the quarter.

There are a great many occasions in which the best interests of everyone concerned are most fully served by requiring the actor to state the rules of action being followed as fully and accurately as possible—medical operations, bomb dismantling, and most public actions, for example. In intellectual affairs, absolute integrity and honesty with respect to such underlying assumptions is indispensable. The requirement is hard to enforce, particularly in public affairs. Nevertheless, it remains essential both for improving performance and for carrying out needed evaluations of public officials. If an actor specifies in advance the policies to be followed and the reasons for accepting them, a comparison of intentions and outcomes provides a sound if partial base for judging performance. When the actor refuses to divulge policy, criticism is nearly impossible. Worse, the policies actually employed cannot be improved out of experience, for when the rule of action is unknown, the action tests nothing and there is no learning. Learning by doing requires that what has been done is known, together with the situation in which the doing takes place. The common practice of attributing outcomes to policies without reference to evidence or argument lays the foundation for ritual as it eliminates the potential for reasoned improvement.

Disagreements. Because of the complex structures and processes required for reasoned choice, policy disagreements are often difficult to unravel and reconcile. The source of the disagreement may lie in either the structured alternatives from which a choice is made or in the priorities attached to them, in the empirical or normative dimension of choice. Many, and perhaps most, policy disagreements in the real world turn out to be empirical rather than normative. Analytically, such differences must be settled first, for normative agreement is contingent upon an agreed structuring of alternatives. If the process of structuring the choice is followed step by step, points of dispute can be identified, and perhaps resolved. If no reasons can be offered for supporting a policy, or the dispute ends in impasse, the disagreement is not reasoned and must be treated as a matter of taste. Extremely important social questions, such as racial prejudice, are often reduced to that position because those involved are unwilling or unable to support preference by argument. Even affective reactions constitute some reason for preference, and in a limited class of cases, they are decisive. Social preferences usually involve extensive and complex sets of implications that are not appropriate objects of affective reaction. The individual who speaks of "loving" the whole of humanity is only misusing the language. Such complex outcomes are argued in terms of intellectualized criteria of evaluation rather than affective reactions. Unfortunately, those criteria are very poorly developed at present and cannot be illustrated, nor is the sociological and historical evidence on which they depend available. But in principle, adequate reasons for preference based on comparison could be developed and strengthened over time out of human experience, and the human reaction to that experience.

At a minimum, systematic study of current practice can identify the choices in society for which no policy has been developed, the normative variables and priorities in use. It can also locate the social policies that are not dealing with the problems for which they were designed, and isolate the major differences in priorities among society's members. That alone would be more than adequate recompense for the effort required. However, there are fairly good reasons to believe that normative inquiry and argument over policies can extend beyond identification of points of agreement and difference. In real cases, it is almost always possible to find some reason for preferring one outcome to another. Sustained effort should improve that capacity substantially. The principal handicap to the enterprise seems to be the failure to realize that the process begins with the case and not the principle. Most of the deadly arguments over priorities arise out of resource conflicts, especially scarcity and the necessities of continued existence. Most social conflicts of any magnitude relate to efforts to modify the historically determined allocation of social and economic benefits in the society. At the level of particulars, a choice between well-fed children who develop normally and starving children who do not is made in exactly the same way for the same reasons everywhere in the world. Conflicts emerge when the time comes to select the children who starve and the children who eat well. Similarly, some priorities are so obvious they hardly generate discussion: children must be fed before they can be educated, at least to a point where development proceeds unimpaired. At some level of nutrition, priorities shift, and education will be granted an increasing share of the available surplus as long as nutrition remains adequate. Such sequencing operations frequently suffice for dealing with complex problems. The way physicians order the treatment of patients in an emergency ward illustrates the process well.

If policy disagreements cannot be settled and the issue is major, the end result is likely to be social disruption. The source will lie in disagreements over priorities. That probability is itself a force encouraging settlement, at least in reasoned discussion of such issues. The primary technique available for handling such issues is compromise. Unfortunately, if improperly used, it can be a primitive and inefficient technique with significant hidden costs. Although compromise avoids the disruption produced by open hostilities, it is always less efficient or more costly than a reasoned solution to a disagreement and the costs are not always distributed equitably. Most important of all, compromise cannot solve differences in priorities or the policies that apply them. Compromises evade such differences by changing the content of choice. For example, if Jones prefers tea to coffee and Smith prefers coffee to tea and neither one will alter preferences, there is an impasse. The impasse can be circumvented by altering the choice, say, by adding cream and sugar to both drinks. If both Smith and Jones prefer coffee with cream and sugar to tea with cream and sugar, a question that can be determined beforehand, the issue has been evaded. *It has not been resolved.* Since the preference has changed, neither side will lose face by agreeing on the new choice. But there is added cost, represented by the sugar and cream added to the drinks, and the poorer fit between end result and preference. In effect, such arrangements readily become a form of bribery. Not infrequently, the bribe is paid from the communal treasury, particularly in legislative compromises. By changing the substance of choice, compromises avoid change in the priority system. When continued disagreement is likely to produce serious social disruption and extensive social costs, the procedure is useful and even essential. But if every disagreement in society or legislature or family is compromised, the process eliminates all possibility of normative improvement. And the long-run effect of maintaining a static priority system in society can be just as disastrous as the effects of open conflict.

INSTITUTIONAL ARRANGEMENTS

No serious effort to place policymaking on a reasoned basis can omit reference to social institutions. Two points are particularly important in contemporary democratic society: first, the lack of an institutional setting in which the whole gamut of social activities can be brought together and rationalized; second, the tendency to rely upon collective bodies both to structure the substance of choices and then to decide them authoritatively. In the representative democracies, the institutional arrangements available for reviewing the choices among choices that society must make collectively tend to be inadequate. The effect of that inadequacy is most dramatically illustrated in such matters as budgetary practice. The major segments of the United States budget, for example, are treated as independent entities with unique histories. Resources are ordinarily allocated to the major departments by reference to prior allocations and not out of an appraisal of relative needs in society. That is, funds are not taken from the defense budget and placed in another category *because* they are needed more elsewhere. The amount of resources allocated to, say, housing or welfare, is not a function of some systematically determined assessment of need. At most, budgetary trimming is carried out in terms of global limits. Transfers based on priorities and needs are minimal.[7]

In effect, incremental budgetary procedures suppress what is perhaps the most important of all social choices—the choices of areas in which to make subsequent choices. For any actor, public or private, the set of actions available at any point in time is a function of capacity and resources. Ideally, that capacity is matched efficiently to needs and priorities. But there is always scarcity, if only of time and knowledge. Analytically, a choice of choices must be made, however resources are spent. When incrementalism is practiced in social affairs, habits, customs, and precedents suppress some alternatives and highlight others. Such practices have value, of course, because they solve the practical problem of focusing attention and resources on a few issues. But the potential hazard can be serious. Carried to extremes, incrementalism will inhibit or even prevent the introduction of new options into the resource allocation system, or the elimination of obsolescence. In every large-scale organization, public or private, some institution is needed where suppressed options can be examined, compared in significance to those currently followed, and if need be added to the current account. Otherwise, a very important class of choices (choosing not to include one or more sets of choices in the options from which choices are made) is excluded from open consideration.

The use of collectivities to legislate, make policy, or define the choices from which selections are made raises a different kind of problem for the critic. An identifiable human actor is a necessary precondition to reasoned and corrigible action. Acts of nature involve no human agent and no options, therefore they cannot be criticized in terms of available alternatives. When decisions are made by such collectives as the British Parliament or the United States Congress, the range of options can be determined only by referring to legal authority. There is no human actor actually able to produce the collective action. The meaning of the action is unavoidably ambiguous therefore there is no parallel to the kind of learning that can be produced from individual performance. With respect to collective actors, critics may agree that a collective decision was a disaster yet agree at the same time that the choices made by the individuals who contributed to the disaster were appropriate to their circumstances. Collective decisioning bodies must be regarded as agents capable of producing "acts of nature" of a rather curious sort. There is no way to assign responsibility for such actions to a human actor, therefore no way of designing a program that will improve performance. The problem has long been recognized, and a variety of solutions has been proposed, among them reliance upon tradition, reference to a "general will" or the development of highly disciplined political parties. None of these proposals has proved workable. For all practical purposes, the results of governmental action in the representative democracies can be lumped together with the effects of earthquakes and hurricanes.

The conceptual confusion involved in the use of collective actors tends to be obscured by the common practice of personalizing the collectivities—"General Motors today announced that . . ." Corporations, congresses, and courts are not human actors; Karl Marx and the Supreme Court of the United States notwithstanding. Organizations are legal fictions. Although they are useful tools able to serve a variety of purposes, they are not acting entities but entities dependent on human actors. Construing them as actors tends to forestall close scrutiny of what is perhaps the most important form of uncontrolled consequentiality at work in the modern world. A legislature is merely a formal device for aggregating a set of individual actions in ways that legally produce collective "actions." In the absence of an adequate theory of representation there need be no congruence between society's needs, the responsibilities assigned to the legislator by constituents, and the responsibilities actually exercised by the legislator. When representative bodies are populated by persons whose status is contingent on continued approval from a relatively small, geographically bounded portion of the whole society, then there is bound to be flagrant disregard for the social consequences of collective action so long as the status is highly desired and sought after. The system is best characterized as organized irresponsibility.

The problem could be resolved if the factors weighed by the individual legislator in official decisions could be bounded and the boundaries were understood and accepted by the constituents. The legislator's behavior cannot be judged in terms of collective actions because no single member of the collectivity can choose *for* the collectivity, barring collusion. But if the agent's status is determined by a subpopulation alone on the basis of subpopulation concerns

198 Reasoned Argument in Social Science

and collective actions, the legislator will be rejected by the constituents. For the representative who wishes to remain in office, the only safe course of action is to accept the limits maintained by the constituents. Those limits will tend to be parochial on all but the most earthshaking issues because the constituents have no available alternative channel for attending to local affairs. Unless the position of legislator is regarded as a one-time, short-term activity, there is no workable solution to the dilemma.

THE OUTLOOK FOR POLICYMAKING

Given the conditions that must be met to develop reasoned and defensible policies, the institutional arrangements available for doing so, and the normative structure currently in use, the outlook for policymaking is rather discouraging. If past history is any guide, efforts to improve the quality of policymaking, public or private, are likely to be prolonged, unrewarding, tedious, and only partially successful at best. Some part of the dreariness of the judgment may be a function of the methodological orientation of the analysis. Methodology serves mainly to locate error. Its chief positive contribution to human intellectual affairs is to formulate an adequate conception of the kinds of instruments required to achieve specific goals and the kinds of limits under which they operate. If the analysis is accurate, the results must be honored. Policies that claim to be reasoned must satisfy the limits that status enjoins.

The intellectual preconditions to reasoned policymaking are formidable, tendentious and difficult to achieve even under ideal conditions. Four preconditions are crucial in the context of public affairs: the conceptual apparatus needed to identify the central dimensions of human life must be available; the conditions of life of the population must be known in sufficient detail to determine areas of greatest need and to assess the effects of action; theories of sufficient precision and reliability to generate the options from which choices are made and the intervention strategies needed to bring about the selected option must already be available; and appropriate priority systems, generally agreed on and sufficiently articulated to handle the major choice problems facing the society, must be in place. Without information relating to population, need cannot be assessed or performance evaluated. Without theories, the substance of choice would remain unknown—there would be no choice. Without priorities, there could be no policies, no grounds for action. Beyond such general considerations, reasoned policymaking depends on a range of special knowledge about the conditions of effective social intervention in a variety of different circumstances. It is pointless to build maternity clinics to provide midwife services no one will use, as happened in Guatemala, because the policymakers did not know the factors that determined willingness to use the facilities. In the Guatemalan case, the status of midwife was inherited and not acquired.

If all of the concepts, theories, priorities, and germane information needed for reasoned social action were available, organizing those elements into programs amenable to legislative action would be a formidable task and would perhaps be beyond the capacity of the available institutions. The fact is, those essentials are *not* available, with minor exceptions, and are unlikely to become available in the near future, in the United States or elsewhere. The inadequacy of the present knowledge supply tends to be masked by an unfortunate, if understandable, propensity for humans to stress the positive dimensions of performance, reinforced by the equally common practice of confusing data with evidence or knowledge. As long as no one inquires what human purposes can be served reliably and efficiently, it is relatively easy to maintain that the world is well supplied with information. Statements about what is the case can, of course, be produced almost endlessly from available accumulations. But the capacity to link that information to significant human concerns and to defend those concerns as humanly significant—which is what converting data to evidence entails—is very limited. If every volume of written matter on earth could be submitted to the judgment of a competent arbiter who was instructed to burn everything that could not contribute to improvement in the human condition, only a very tiny fraction of the total would survive. And if most of the surviving material would relate to physical science, a vast number of "scientific" volumes would certainly end in flames. Much of the scientific information published each year is of little use to anyone but the author and the publisher. On the other hand, a great many important things remain undone for lack of scientific knowledge. Coal cannot be desulphurized cheaply and efficiently, oil cannot be separated from the surrounding shale, the common cold prospers, pollution runs rampant, and economies vacillate like the tides with incalculable effects for immense human populations. That is not meant to denigrate scientific achievement but to put it in perspective. A mere bucket of knowledge is available in physical science. The social sciences can produce barely a drop. Few if any of the structures that pass for theories permit reliable achievement of foreseeable outcomes by specifiable actions. Some of political science is useful for those seeking election; a few social or psychological theories are useful in limited areas of human behavior. For the most part, social science, including economics, is barren.

The peculiar status of economics might suggest it is an exception. In fact, the generation of economists who learned their trade in the tradition of Adam Smith, Keynes, or the Chicago School are virtually people from another planet. A physicist whose rocketry program was based on the gravitational forces found on an unspecified planet would be in precisely the position taken by the market-oriented economist. Neither has an intellectual apparatus that can usefully be applied to problems on earth. By concentrating largely on macrostructures and providing economic "advice" that is Delphic in character and heavily laced with arcane mathematics, economists have acquired much prestige but little capacity for reasoned and corrigible action. Of necessity, events on earth are largely ignored or considered selectively. Although economists maintain that their discipline is "relevant" and use their conceptual structure in ways that lend plausibility to the claim, the special definitions attached to the conceptual structure vitiate its use for human purposes. Terms such as "price," "market," "competition," or "demand," to take casual examples, cannot be linked to observations without marring the strict meaning that makes the overall structure calculable. Moreover, economists have accepted with little argument the very unfortunate assumption that false axioms may be used in tools that are needed for policymaking.[8] That is simply untrue. At best, structures concocted from false premises can be used to make forecasts. Such predictions can only suggest areas where policies are needed; they have no uses in policymaking. And empirically, there is no way to reconcile the recent history of the industrialized societies with the claimed competence of economists. The floundering of the United States economy between 1970 and 1980 should alone have been sufficient to destroy pretensions to theoretical competence. Unhappily, as events unfolded, that has not happened.

With rare exceptions, the policymaker will receive little assistance from the social sciences. The academic community is unlikely to provide the raw materials for reasoned action. Indeed, there are good reasons to believe that the universities no longer are, and perhaps never were, the appropriate location for such inquiries. Policymakers are well advised to rely mainly on their own resources, generating information and knowledge and the institutions to produce and apply them as they become aware of need. The best working assumption, in most cases at least, is that virtually nothing reliable can be found in social science. Moreover, the need for knowledge must be determined by those responsible for making policy and not by academics. If those needs can be specified clearly and accurately, some assistance may be forthcoming from the universities. But those in government who take a vague shopping list to the academic marketplace, and especially those who wander the marketplace with full purse and open mind seeking the imprimatur from the establishment, will merely enrich the charlatan and the demagogue, emptying the purse without filling the mind or improving the society. The gross failure of most American research foundations, public and private, to further a useful social science is mainly if not entirely attributable to their unwillingness or inability to shop for specifics of their own determination.

A "be your own research director" approach to public policymaking or administration may seem a staggering burden to impose on an already overburdened and inadequately supported institution. The imposition is less onerous than appears at first sight. Policymakers normally operate an ongoing enterprise. Their organizations have experience, history, folklore, mores and customs, and a positive momentum, however slight. In some cases, they have purposes. Past history can provide a launching site for future experiments which are the only feasible source of the raw materials needed for reasoned action when the current knowledge supply is very poor. In general, academics have not exploited these natural learning sites in the past for knowledge useful to the organization, and are unlikely to do so in the future. The time required to learn enough about operations to be useful to the organization conflicts seriously with the time demands and reward systems that operate in academic life. The organizations themselves have not exploited those experimental possibilities. The tradition does not suggest it, resources are not provided for the purpose, and there are no institutional arrangements available to facilitate the effort. In consequence, there are a great many organizations in society, public and private, but very few experimental stations. Somehow, that situation must be altered. A marriage is needed between intellectual competence and governmental or social need that can maintain the integrity of both parties. No other change would produce as much improvement in policymaking capacity as quickly or as cheaply. The problem is locating the domicile. Both the university and the governmental agency are inappropriate as presently constituted. The university is likely to remain an inappropriate site for the effort into the foreseeable future. Within government, special arrangements could be created that would provide an acceptable working solution to the problem. For example, a new type of agency could be created that combines access to information with awareness of needs and limitations (conditions that only government can satisfy) with the competence and integrity associated with the best part of the academic tradition.

For those in academic life, particularly social science, such institutions could be an intellectual stimulus of incalculable benefit. The principal reason for the paucity of present knowledge is found in the absence of clearly defined purposes for inquiry. An agency combining governmental needs with academic capacities would be admirably suited to supplying them. Purposes established, systematic efforts to achieve them will lead inexorably to the sets of questions examined in this volume and, I believe, to the same conclusions. Policymakers and academics alike need the intellectual equivalent to the coach's football team or the agronomist's corn patch, an external testing ground for beliefs and assumptions. Without it, there can be no desire to do, no way of improving the doing in the doing, no basis for identifying improvements as improvements. Purposes, and human consumption of efforts to achieve them, are the key to increased knowledge. Purposes serve to identify what is known, what needs to be learned, what is currently possible, and what should be chosen. Man can serve as both unit of measurement and instrument for measuring. The procedure may not seem impressive, but it can work satisfactorily.

NOTES

1. See Eugene J. Meehan, "Science and Policymaking: Achieving Mutual Reinforcement," in *Proceedings*, Wisconsin Seminar on Natural Resources Policy, Volume 1, 1978, and Eugene J. Meehan, "Philosophy and Policy Studies," in Stuart S. Nagel, ed., *Policy Studies and the Social Sciences* (Lexington Books, 1975). For typical examples of the materials being produced under the "policy analysis" rubric, see the *Policy Studies Journal, Public Policy, Policy Analysis*, and *Policy Sciences*. For the public choice society, see Thomas R. DeGregori, "Caveat Emptor: A Critique of the Emerging Paradigm of Public Choice," *Administration and Society*, August 1974. For examples of theory and practice, see James M. Buchanan and Robert D. Tollison, eds., *Theory of Public Choice: Political Applications of Economics* (University of Michigan Press, 1972); Robert L. Bish, *The Public Economy of Metropolitan Areas* (Markham, 1971); Dennis C. Mueller, *Public Choice* (Cambridge University Press, 1979); Vincent Ostrom, *The Intellectual Crisis in American Public Administration* (University of Alabama Press, 1973), or Gordon Tullock, *Private Wants, Public Means: An Economic Analysis of the Desirable Scope of Government* (Basic Books, 1970); and the journal *Public Choice*.

2. See Eugene J. Meehan, "The Concept 'Foreign Policy,' " in Wolfram F. Hanrieder, ed., *Comparative Foreign Policy: Theoretical Essays* (David McKay, 1971).

3. Eugene J. Meehan, "The Rise and Fall of Public Housing: Condemnation Without Trial," in Donald Phares, ed., *A Decent Home and Environment: Housing Urban America* (Ballinger Publishing Company, 1977).

4. Bertrand Russell, *History of Western Philosophy* (George Allen and Unwin, 1946), pp. 737-738.

5. Eugene J. Meehan, *The Quality of Federal Policymaking: Programmed Disaster in Public Housing* (University of Missouri Press, 1979).

6. See Bertram Gross, ed., "Social Goals and Indicators for American Society," *The Annals* (May-September 1967), or Mancur Olson, Jr., "An Analytic Framework for Social Reporting and Policy Analysis," *The An-*

nals, March 1970, pp. 112-126. But compare *The Quality of Life Concept: A Potential Tool for Decision Makers* (Washington, D.C., Environmental Protection Agency, 1973) for an example of the kind of confusion engendered by the effort. See also Helmut Klages, "Assessment of an Attempt at a System of Social Indicators, *Policy Sciences*, 4 (973), pp. 249-261.

7. See Lance T. LeLoup, *Budgetary Politics* (King's Court Communications, 1977), or Aaron Wildavsky, *The Politics of the Budgetary Process* (Little-Brown, 1974).

8. Most clearly stated in Milton Friedman, *Essays on Positive Economics* (University of Chicago Press, 1953), and F. A. Hayek, *Theory and History* (Yale University Press, 1957), esp. pp. 31-38.

Select Bibliography

Aiken, Henry D. *Reason and Conduct: New Bearings in Moral Philosophy.* Alfred A. Knopf, 1962.

Arrow, Kenneth J. *Social Choice and Individual Values.* 2d ed. Yale University Press, 1963.

_____. *Essays in the Theory of Risk-Bearing.* Markham, 1971.

Ascher, William. *Forecasting: An Appraisal for Policy-Makers and Planners.* Johns Hopkins University Press, 1978.

Ashby, W. Ross. *An Introduction to Cybernetics.* Science Editions, 1963.

Bailey, Norman A., and Stuart M. Feder. *Operational Conflict Analysis.* Public Affairs Press, 1973.

Baker, Keith. "Public Choice Theory: Some Important Assumptions and Public Policy Implications." In Robert T. Golembiewski, et al., *Public Administration.* Rand, McNally, 1976.

Bardach, Eugene. *The Implementation Game: What Happens After a Bill Becomes Law.* MIT Press, 1977.

Barry, Brian. *The Liberal Theory of Justice: A Critical Examination of the Principal Doctrines of a Theory of Justice by John Rawls.* Oxford University Press, 1973.

Bauer, Raymond A., ed. *Social Indicators.* MIT Press, 1966.

_____, Eleanor Sheldon, and Wilbert E. Moore, eds. *Indicators of Social Change.* Russell Sage Foundation, 1968.

Berlinski, David. *On Systems Analysis.* MIT Press, 1976.

Bilsky, Manuel. *Patterns of Argument.* Holt, Rinehart, and Winston, 1963.

Binkley, Luther J. *Contemporary Ethical Theories.* Citadel Press, 1961.

Bish, Robert L. *The Public Economy of Metropolitan Areas.* Markham, 1971.

Blalock, Hubert M., Jr. *Social Statistics.* McGraw-Hill, 1960.

_____. *Theory Construction: From Verbal to Mathematical Formulation.* Prentice-Hall, 1969.

_____. and Ann B. Blaclock. *Methodology in Social Science.* McGraw-Hill, 1968.

Bohm, David. *Causality and Chance in Modern Physics.* Van Nostrand, 1957.

Braithwaite, Richard B. *Scientific Explanation: A Study of the Function of Theory Probability, and Law in Science.* Harper, 1953.

Braybrooke, David, ed. *Philosophical Problems of the Social Sciences.* Macmillan, 1965.

Broad, C. D. *Five Types of Ethical Theory.* Littlefield, Adams, 1959.

Brodbeck, May. *Readings in the Philosophy of Social Science.* Macmillan, 1968.

Buchanan, James M., and Gordon Tullock. *The Calculus of Consent: Logical Foundations of Constitutional Democracy.* University of Michigan Press, 1962.

———, and Robert D. Tollison, eds. *Theory of Public Choice: Political Applications of Economics.* University of Michigan Press, 1972.

Calabresi, Guido, and Philip Bobbitt. *Tragic Choices.* W. W. Norton, 1978.

Campbell, Angus, and Philip E. Converse. *The Human Meaning of Social Change.* Russell Sage Foundation, 1972.

Cicourel, Aaron. *Method and Measurement in Sociology.* Free Press, 1964.

Colodny, Robert G., ed. *Frontiers of Science and Philosophy.* University of Pittsburgh Press, 1962.

DeGregori, Thomas R. "Caveat Emptor: A Critique of the Emerging Paradigm of Public Choice." *Administration and Society,* August 1974.

Dewey, John. *The Public and Its Problems* Henry Holt, 1927.

———. *Theory of the Moral Life.* Holt, Rinehart, and Winston, 1960.

Direnzo, Gordon J., ed. *Concepts, Theory, and Explanation in the Behavioral Sciences.* Random House, 1966.

Dror, Yehezkel. *Public Policymaking Reexamined.* Chandler, 1968.

Dubin, Robert. *Theory Building.* Rev. ed. Free Press, 1978.

Edel, Abraham. *Method in Ethical Theory.* Bobbs-Merrill, 1963.

Feigl, Herbert, and May Brodbeck, eds. *Readings in the Philosophy of Science.* Appleton-Century-Crofts, 1953.

———, and Wilfred Sellars, eds. *Readings in Philosophical Analysis.* Appleton-Century-Crofts, 1949.

Festinger, Leon, and David Katz, eds. *Research Methods in Behavioral Sciences.* Holt, Rinehart, and Winston, 1953.

Feyerabend, Paul K. "Philosophy of Science: A Subject with a Great Past." In Roger H. Stuewer, ed., *Historical and Philosophical Perspectives of Science,* Minnesota Studies in the Philosophy of Science, Vol. 5 (University of Minnesota Press, 1970).

Fishburn, Peter C. *The Theory of Social Choice.* Princeton University Press, 1973.

Flax, Michael J. *A Study in Comparative Urban Indicators: Conditions in 18 Large Metropolitan Areas*. Urban Institute, 1972.

Flew, A. G. N. *Logic and Language*. Vol. 1. Basil Blackwell, 1960.

_____. *Logic and Language*. Vol. 2. Basil Blackwell, 1962.

Fox, Karl A. *Social Indicators and Social Theory*. John Wiley, 1974.

Frankel, Charles, ed. *Controversies and Decisions: The Social Sciences and Public Policy*. Russell Sage Foundation, 1976.

Frankena, William K. *Ethics*. Prentice-Hall, 1963.

Fried, Charles. *An Anatomy of Values: Problems of Personal and Social Choice*. Harvard University Press, 1970.

Gale, George. *Theory of Science: An Introduction to the History, Logic, and Philosophy of Science*. McGraw-Hill, 1979.

Garn, Harvey A., et al. *Social Indicator Models for Urban Policy: Five Specific Applications*. Urban Institute, 1973.

Geach, P. T. *Reason and Argument*. University of California Press, 1976.

Gibson, Quentin. *The Logic of Social Enquiry*. Routledge and Kegan Paul, 1960.

Goodman, Nelson. *Fact, Fiction, and Forecast*. Bobbs-Merrill, 1965.

Goulet, Denis. *The Uncertain Promise*. IDOC/North America, 1977.

Graham, George J., Jr. *Methodological Foundations for Political Analysis* John Wiley, 1971.

Gross, Bertram, ed. "Social Goals and Indicators for American Society," *The Annals* (May-September 1967).

Hanson, Norwood R. *Patterns of Discovery*. Cambridge University Press, 1961.

_____. *Perception and Discovery: An Introduction to Scientific Inquiry*. Freeman, Cooper and Co., 1969.

Hayek, Friedrich A. *The Counterrevolution of Science*. Free Press, 1952.

Hempel, Carl G. *Aspects of Scientific Explanation and Other Essays in the Philosophy of Science*. Free Press, 1965.

_____. *Philosophy of Natural Science*. Prentice-Hall, 1966.

Hesse, Mary B. *Models and Analogies in Science*. University of Notre Dame Press, 1966.

Hindless, Barry. *Philosophy and Methodology in the Social Sciences*. Humanities Press, 1977.

Holton, Gerald, and Robert S. Morison, eds. *The Limits of Scientific Inquiry*. W. W. Norton, 1979.

Hospers, John. *Human Conduct: An Introduction to the Problems of Ethics*. Harcourt, Brace, and World, 1961.

Jones, Martin V., and Michael J. Flax. *The Quality of Life in Metropolitan Washington, D.C.: Some Statistical Benchmarks*. Urban Institute, 1970.

Kaplan, Abraham. *The Conduct of Inquiry: Methodology for Behavioral Science*. Chandler, 1964.

Kemeney, John G., and J. Laurie Snell. *Mathematical Models in the Social Sciences*. Ginn and Co., 1962.

Kerlinger, Fred N. *Foundations of Behavioral Research*. Macmillan, 1966.

Krimerman, Leonard I. *The Nature and Scope of Social Science*. Appleton-Century-Crofts, 1969.

Kuhn, Thomas S. *The Structure of Scientific Revolution*. University of Chicago Press, 1962.

_____. *The Essential Tension*. University of Chicago Press, 1977.

Kyberg, Henry E., Jr. *Philosophy of Science: A Formal Approach*. Macmillan, 1968.

_____, and Ernest Nagel, eds. *Induction: Some Current Issues*. Wesleyan University Press, 1963.

Lakatos, Imre, and Alan Musgrave, eds. *Criticism and the Growth of Knowledge*. Cambridge University Press, 1970.

Leatherdale, W. H. *The Role of Analogy, Models, and Metaphors in Science*. North Holland Publishing Co., 1974.

LeLoup, Lance T. *Budgetary Politics: Dollars, Deficits, Decisions*. King's Court Communications, 1977.

Long, Norton E. *The Unwalled City: Reconstituting the Urban Community*. Basic Books, 1972.

Louch, A. R. *Explanation and Human Action*. University of California Press, 1966.

Machlup, Fritz. *Methodology for Economics and Other Social Sciences*. Academic Press, 1978.

Mackinnon, D. M. *A Study in Ethical Theory*. Collier Books, 1962.

MacRae, Duncan, Jr., and James A. Wilde. *Policy Analysis for Public Decisions*. Duxbury Press, 1979.

McGaw, Dickinson, and George Watson. *Political and Social Inquiry*. John Wiley, 1976.

McKenna, Christopher K. *Quantitative Methods for Public Decision Making*. McGraw-Hill, 1980.

McKenzie, Richard B., and Gordon Tullock. *The New World of Economics: Explorations into the Human Experience*. Richard B. Irwin, 1975.

Meehan, Eugene J. *Contemporary Political Thought: A Critical Study*. Dorsey Press, 1967.

_____. *The Foundations of Political Analysis, Empirical and Normative*. Dorsey Press, 1971.

_____. "The Social Indicator Movement," *Frontiers of Economics*, 1975.

_____. "Cross-Disciplinary Transfers: The Case of Public Choice." Forthcoming.

_____. "Science and Policymaking: Achieving Mutual Reinforcement." In *Proceedings*, Wisconsin Seminar on Natural Resources Policies, Madison, Wisconsin, vol. 1, 1978.

_____. *The Quality of Federal Policymaking: Programmed Disaster in Public Housing.* University of Missouri Press, 1979.

Mills, Glen E. *Reason in Controversy: On General Argumentation.* 2d ed. Allyn and Bacon, 1968.

Minsky, Marvin, and Seymour Papert. *Perceptrons: An Introduction to Computational Geometry.* MIT Press, 1969.

Mishan, E. J. *Economics for Social Decisions: Elements of Cost-Benefit Analysis.* Praeger, 1973.

Mitroff, Ian A., and Ralph H. Kilmann. *Methodological Approaches to Social Science.* Jossey-Bass, 1978.

Morris, Morris D. *Measuring the Condition of the World's Poor: The Physical Quality of Life Index.* Pergamon Press, 1979.

Mueller, Dennis C. *Public Choice.* Cambridge University Press, 1979.

Murphy, Jerome T. *Getting the Facts: A Fieldwork Guide for Evaluators and Policy Analysts.* Goodyear Publishing Co., 1980.

Nagel, Ernest. *The Structure of Science: Problems in the Logic of Scientific Explanation.* Harcourt, Brace, and World, 1961.

_____, et al., eds. *Logic, Methodology, and Philosophy of Science.* Stanford University Press, 1962.

_____, and Richard B. Brandt, eds. *Meaning and Knowledge: Systematic Readings in Epistemology.* Harcourt, Brace, and World, 1965.

_____, and James R. Newman. *Gödel's Proof.* New York University Press, 1958.

Nagel, Stuart S., ed. *Policy Studies and the Social Sciences.* Lexington Books, 1975.

Natanson, Maurice, ed. *Philosophy of the Social Sciences.* Random House, 1963.

Nettler, Gwynn. *Explanations.* McGraw-Hill, 1970.

Newell, Allen, and Herbert A. Simon. *Human Problem Solving.* Prentice-Hall, 1972.

Nowell-Smith, P. H. *Ethics* Penguin Books, 1961.

Olson, Mancur. *The Logic of Collective Action: Public Goods and the Theory of Groups.* Harvard University Press, 1965.

Ostrom, Vincent. *The Intellectual Crisis in American Public Administration.* University of Alabama Press, 1973.

Phares, Donald, ed. *A Decent Home and Environment: Housing Urban America.* Ballinger Publishing Company, 1977.

Polanyi, Michael. *Knowing and Being*. Ed. Marjorie Grene. University of Chicago Press, 1969.

Popper, Karl R. *The Logic of Scientific Discovery*. Science Editions, 1961.

_____. *Conjectures and Refutations: The Growth of Scientific Knowledge*. Harper and Row, 1968.

_____. *Objective Knowledge: An Evolutionary Approach*. Oxford University Press, 1972).

Pressman, Jeffrey L., and Aaron B. Wildavsky. *Implementation*. University of California Press, 1973.

Quine, Willard Van Orman. *Word and Object*. MIT Press, 1960.

_____. *The Ways of Paradox and Other Essays*. Harvard University Press, 1976.

_____, and J. S. Ullian. *The Web of Belief*. 2d ed. Random House, 1978.

Rawls, John. *A Theory of Justice*. Belknap Press, 1971.

Rescher, Nicholas. *Methodological Pragmatism*. New York University Press, 1971.

_____, ed. *The Logic of Decision and Action*. University of Pittsburgh Press, n.d.

Revlin, Russell, and Richard E. Mayer. *Human Reasoning*. V. H. Winston and Sons, 1978.

Rieke, D., and Malcom O. Sillars. *Argumentation and the Decision-Making Process*. John Wiley, 1975.

Riker, William H. *The Theory of Political Coalitions*. Yale University Press, 1962.

_____, and Peter C. Ordeshook. *An Introduction to Positive Political Theory*. Prentice-Hall, 1973.

Rokeach, Milton. *The Nature of Human Values*. Free Press, 1973.

Rudner, Richard S. *Philosophy of Social Science*. Prentice-Hall, 1966.

Runciman, W. G. *Social Science and Political Theory*. Cambridge University Press, 1963.

Russell, Bertrand. *History of Western Philosophy*. George Allen and and Unwin, 1946.

_____. *Human Knowledge: Its Scope and Limits*. Allen and Unwin, 1948.

Ryan, Alan, ed. *Philosophy of Social Explanation*. Oxford University Press, 1973.

Salmon, Wesley C. *The Foundations of Scientific Inference*. University of Pittsburgh Press, 1966.

Savage, C. Wade, ed. *Perception and Cognition Issues in the Foundations of Psychology*. Minnesota Studies in the Philosophy of Science, Vol. 9. University of Minnesota Press, 1978.

Scheffler, Israel. *The Anatomy of Inquiry*. Alfred A. Knopf, 1963.

Schelling, Thomas C. *Micromotives and Macrobehavior*. W. W. Norton, 1978.

Schultze, Charles L. *The Public Use of Private Interest*. Brookings Institution, 1977.

Scioli, Frank P., Jr., and Thomas J. Cook, eds., *Methodologies for Analyzing Public Policies*. Lexington Books, 1975.

Sharkansky, Ira, ed. *Policy Analysis in Political Science*. Markham, 1970.

_____. *Wither the State?*. Chatham House, 1979.

Sheldon, Eleanor B., and Wilbert E. Moore. *Indicators of Social Change*. Russell Sage Foundation, 1968.

Simon, Herbert. *Models of Man*. John Wiley, 1957.

Simon, Julian. *Basic Research Methods in Social Science*. Random House, 1969.

Sjoberg, Gideon, and Roger Nett. *A Methodology for Social Research*. Harper and Row, 1968.

Smith, John E. *Purpose and Thought: The Meaning of Pragmatism*. Yale University Press, 1978.

Spence, Larry D. *The Politics of Social Knowledge*. Pennsylvania State University Press, 1978.

Spragens, Thomas A., Jr. *The Dilemma of Contemporary Political Theory: Toward a Post-Behavioral Science of Politics*. Dunellen Press, 1973.

_____. *Understanding Political Theory*. St. Martin's Press, 1976.

Sproule-Jones, Mark H. *Public Choice and Federalism in Australia and Canada*. Canberra, The Australian National University, 1975.

Stinchcombe, Arthur L. *Constructing Social Theories*. Harcourt, Brace, and World, 1968.

Suppes, Patrick. *The Structure of Scientific Theories*. 2d ed. University of Illinois Press, 1977.

Toulmin, Stephen. *The Philosophy of Science: An Introduction*. Harper and Row, 1960.

_____. *The Place of Reason in Ethics*. Cambridge University Press, 1960.

_____. *Foresight and Understanding: An Enquiry into the Aims of Science*. Harper and Row, 1961.

_____. *The Uses of Argument*. Cambridge University Press, 1964.

_____. *Human Understanding*. Vol. I, *The Collective Use and Evolution of Concepts*. Princeton University Press, 1972.

Tullock, Gordon. *The Politics of Bureaucracy*. Public Affairs Press, 1965.

_____. *Toward a Mathematics of Politics*. University of Michigan Press, 1967.

_____. *Private Wants, Public Means: An Economic Analysis of the Desirable Scope of Government*. Basic Books, 1970.
Warnock, Mary. *Ethics Since 1900*. 2d ed. Oxford University Press, 1966.
Weingast, Barry R. "A Rational Choice Perspective on Congressional Norms," *The American Journal of Political Science*, May 1979.

GOVERNMENT DOCUMENTS

Behavioral Sciences and Medical Education: A Report of Four Conferences, DHEW Publication No. (NIH) 72-41, n.d.
Measurement and Predictors of Physician Performance, Philip B. Price et al., Aaron Press, 1971.
Measuring Social Well-Being: A Progress Report on the Development of Social Indicators, Organization for Economic Cooperation and Development, Paris, 1976.
Personal Privacy in an Information Society, The Report of the Privacy Protection Study Commission. U.S. Government Printing Office, 1977.
Perspective Canada. Ministry of Supply and Services, Canada, 1974.
Perspective Canada II. Ministry of Supply and Services, Canada, 1977.
Science Indicators, 1978. National Science Board, National Science Foundation, 1979.
Welfare Work Incentives. Michigan Department of Social Services, 1974.

Name Index

Subject Index

Action
  choice and, 20
  communication and, 134-35
  creating rights and obligations,
    137-38
  resource allocation, 135-37
  types of, 133-38, 167-69
Additive measures, 53-54
Affective reactions, 26-27
Ambiguity, conceptual, 40-44
Argument
  choices, 129, 156-75
  expectations, 75-79
  forecasts, 82-83
  quality of, xii-xiii
  reasoned, xi, xii, 27-29
  theories, 108-21

Causality
  need for assuming, 16
  Mill's methods and, 99-102
  role in theory, 86-87
Change, 13, 15, 68-69
Choice, 5, 19-27, 125-76
  action and, 20, 133-38
  argument about, 156-75
  context and, 129-33
  empirical dimensions of, 159-62
  instruments used in, 22-23,
    150-56
  normative variables, 142-50
  policies and, 152-56
  priorities, role in, 162-75
  procedures, 138-45

  reasoned, 22-25, 126-50
  structures and processes, 138-50
Classifications, 14-15
  application, 76-77
  development, 72-75
  expectations and, 69-79
  improving, 79
  relation to experience, 72-75
  structure, 70-72
Collective terms, 196-98
Composition fallacy, 42-44
Concepts, 12-13, 14-15, 38-44
  aggregates, problems with, 42-44
  ambiguity, 41
  development of, 39-40
  indicators for, 48-50
  policymaking and, 44
  standardization, 41-42
  theory and, 106-7
  vagueness in, 40-44
Conceptual frameworks, 13, 57-61
Controlling the environment, 5,
    85-123
Creativity in inquiry, 7, 19

Definitions, 44-48
Description, 12-14, 31-61
  accuracy, 34-55
  adequacy, 55-61
  evaluation, 32
  incompleteness, 56
  justification, 32-34
  subjectivity, 35-37
Diagnosis, 109-15

ABOUT THE AUTHOR

EUGENE J. MEEHAN is Professor of Political Science at the University of Missouri in St. Louis. He is the author of *Theory and Method in Political Analysis*, *Value Judgment and Social Science*, *Foundations of Political Analysis*, *The Quality of Federal Policy-making: Programmed Disaster in Public Housing*, and many other books.